T0383908

SIMPSON

IMPRINT IN HUMANITIES

The humanities endowment
by Sharon Hanley Simpson and
Barclay Simpson honors

MURIEL CARTER HANLEY

whose intellect and sensitivity
have enriched the many lives
that she has touched.

The publisher and the University of California Press Foundation gratefully acknowledge the generous support of the Simpson Imprint in Humanities.

The Center of the World

The Center of the World

A GLOBAL HISTORY OF THE PERSIAN GULF
FROM THE STONE AGE TO THE PRESENT

Allen James Fromherz

UNIVERSITY OF CALIFORNIA PRESS

University of California Press
Oakland, California

© 2024 by Allen James Fromherz

Library of Congress Cataloging-in-Publication Data

Names: Fromherz, Allen James, author.
Title: The center of the world : a global history of the Persian
    Gulf from the Stone Age to the present / Allen James Fromherz.
Other titles: Global history of the Persian Gulf from the Stone
    Age to the present
Description: Oakland, California : University of California Press,
    [2024] | Includes bibliographical references and index.
Identifiers: LCCN 2023051627 (print) | LCCN 2023051628 (ebook) |
    ISBN 9780520398559 (hardback) | ISBN 9780520398566 (ebook)
Subjects: LCSH: Persian Gulf—History. | Persian Gulf—Economic
    conditions.
Classification: LCC DS326 .F76 2024 (print) | LCC DS326 (ebook) |
    DDC 953.6—dc23/eng/20240109
LC record available at https://lccn.loc.gov/2023051627
LC ebook record available at https://lccn.loc.gov/2023051628

Manufactured in the United States of America

32   31   30   29   28   27   26   25   24
10   9   8   7   6   5   4   3   2   1

To Mary Elizabeth Tomlin-Fromherz, born October 13, 2023, into a world of wonder

Contents

Illustrations

Acknowledgments

The idea for *The Center of the World* emerged more than a decade ago, in 2013, while I was living in Oman on a fellowship provided by the Sultan Qaboos Cultural Center. Thank you to Kathleen Ridolfo and to the people of Oman, who have made their culture and heritage their most precious asset. Much of my research also occurred while I was a Senior Humanities Fellow at New York University Abu Dhabi (NYUAD) in 2016. This school's hands-off, flexible policy toward researchers allowed me to rent a Land Cruiser and see the hidden corners of the Gulf. The conversations I had at NYUAD were instrumental to the development of this book. Both of these fellowships required long periods away from home. I thank Mary Elizabeth, Mabel, and William Tomlin for putting up with my absences. My mother, Robin Wright-Fromherz, my father, Allen Fromherz Sr., and my sisters, Rebecca and Amy Fromherz, have always been rocks of support. A mother asking "Where is the next book?" keeps the writing front of mind, even if the work develops over decades. I dedicate this book to Mary Elizabeth Tomlin-Fromherz, born into a world filled with wonder.

I am a proud member of one of the best, if underestimated, history departments in the country. Georgia State University (GSU) was a founding member of the world history movement in the United

States, and my colleagues have encouraged me to look beyond area studies, to see the world in everything. I thank our chair, Jared Poley, and my fellow professors Ghulam Nadri, Rachel Ernst, and Ian Fletcher for our conversations about the world and Islam. An internal grant, the Scholarly Support Grant at GSU, was helpful, providing me with time and space for writing. I am grateful to Ahu Kostak-Bulat and Victoria Johnson for organizing the GSU conference on Sultan Qaboos. Dean Lindsey Cohen and Provost Nicolle Parsons-Pollard have funded the activities of the Middle East Studies Center, which brought many important voices in Gulf studies to campus. My friends in the Gulf have my gratitude, including Dr. Abdulrahman al-Salimi of Oman, Sheikh Abdullah Al-Salmi, and, among others at the NYUAD Humanities Center, Alex Sandu, Reindert Falkenburg, and Michael Cooperson. To friends at Qatar University, where I taught back in 2008: we will never forget Al-Zahoor. Marwa Maziad, Jinnyn Jacob, Steven Wright, and Amira Sonbol, it has been a pleasure following your careers. Mickie Mathes, we miss you. My love for the vast and beautiful landscapes of the Gulf started back in 2004, when I interned for the US Embassy in Muscat. Thank you, Ambassador Richard Baltimore, Tanya Anderson, Eddie Quiring, and Kent Luquette for the memories.

The journey I took from a tree farm in rural Oregon to Middle Eastern studies began with the encouragement of Professor Gene Garthwaite of Dartmouth College. Professor Dale Eickelman, also of Dartmouth, has also been a mentor. The clear and accessible writing of Professor Hugh Kennedy, my PhD supervisor at the University of St. Andrews, and of Professor Amira Bennison at the University of Cambridge showed me that it is possible to write books that both are about "big themes" and contribute to scholarship. Professors Diana Wylie, James Miller, Aomar Boum, and Gwyneth Talley have been references and sounding boards. Finally, I also dedicate this book to those graduate students I have had the honor of advising over the past fifteen years, many of whom are boldly pursuing careers in academia. Eman Abdullah, Samantha Harvel, Nico Pacetti, John Sullivan, Patricia Coates, Jeffrey Kinnier, Munazil Yusuf, Javier Guirado Alonso, and Xavier Barrow, thank you for your contributions to our seminars!

I am grateful to Eric Schmidt, my acquisitions editor at University of California Press, for his patience and persistence. Working with UC Press has been an exceptional experience, due to his leadership and support. Megan Pugh, thank you for being a developmental editor extraordinaire. Juliana Froggatt, thank you for improving the manuscript with your keen copy-editing eye. Jyoti Arvey, Cindy Fulton, and the entire production team, I appreciate your professionalism. Finally, thank you to the Press Committee and the review board of UC Press for your suggestions, and to the anonymous reviewers of this manuscript for your constructive feedback.

Note on Transliteration

Arabic, a phonetic language, has vowels and consonants that do not correspond exactly to English letters. There are also some Arabic sounds without equivalents in English. This is also true of Turkish and Persian, languages that have sometimes adopted Arabic letters, with a few additions. Scholars have devised a system of transliteration that allows the representation of Arabic sounds and letters in English. For example, to indicate a short vowel, *u* is used, to indicate a long vowel, *ū*. To avoid confusion, the English vowel *o*, which is like a short *u*, is omitted from "scientific" transliteration of Arabic. To add to confusion, however, *o* is used for Persian and Turkish. For the most part, I have avoided use of long vowel and consonant symbols except to indicate the difference between two Arabic sounds: the *'ayn* letter ('), which sounds a bit like the *i* in the word *rind*, and the *hamza* ('), which is more of a glottal stop. You will occasionally see transliterated words when I quote directly from a text in which the symbols are used by the original translator or text. This is done to respect the translator.

To understand the meaning of all the symbols and their corresponding Arabic letters, readers can consult the transliteration chart of the *International Journal of Middle East Studies* (*IJMES*), which also includes Persian and Turkish systems (https://www.cambridge.org/core/services/aop-file-manager/file/57d83390f6ea5a022234b400/TransChart.pdf; accessed April 30, 2024). Even where the *IJMES* transliteration scheme is not used, the internet has now made it possible for Arabic speakers to look up a name or phrase and verify the original Arabic, Turkish, or Persian script.

In my opinion, the use of long vowels and other symbols has become largely unnecessary, creating a barrier between the text and the non-Arabic reader. It can also lead to some very odd and even contentious situations where proper names are made to fit into the straitjacket of the "scientific" transliteration. I have spoken Arabic in many parts of the Middle East. Every region has its own version of Arabic, creating a rich diversity. The Gulf is full of words and place names that have Persian and Arabic equivalents, and the English spelling of names has become a part of a mixed/shared identity history. Changing an *o* to a *u* or an *e* to an *i* to fit a particular transliteration can take away either the Persian or Arabic character of a place and create needless "division," a type of linguistic border policing between language groups that have interacted and overlapped. More and more people of the Gulf are representing their own identity through English. Choosing Mohammed, for example, versus the "scientific" spelling of Muḥammad (which is almost never used with the *ḥ*) could mean that person is choosing a *khaliji* versus a "standard" identity. While devised as a means of respecting and accurately representing the languages of Arabic, Persian, and Turkish, charts can sometimes do the opposite: forcing words and names into an allegedly "scientific" straitjacket that does not exist in common usage, neutering the dynamism of language, and preventing its history and mutability from being freely expressed, especially as English becomes widespread. This blocks regional variation and "dialects," such as *Khaliji* Gulf dialect, that are marginalized as supposedly "nonstandard" Arabic. I have attempted to use the spellings of names and places as they are most seen in place, in texts or online. Any errors are my own. The use of one spelling over another does not indicate a judgment or an attempt to force a word or name into a cultural identity category.

Chronology

18,000 BCE	Last glacial maximum. Rivers and marshes exist where the Gulf is now.
6,500–4,000 BCE	After a warming period, the shoreline of the Gulf takes shape.
3,500–3,000 BCE	Writing emerges in Sumer, near the Gulf.
2279 BCE	Sargon, founder of the Akkadian Empire, dies. Sumerian cuneiform tablets from the era mention Magan, ancient kingdom in Oman.
c. 2000 BCE	Dilmun thrives on today's Island of Bahrain; Hili Tomb built. Trade between the Gulf and the Indus Valley (Harappan) civilization.
1750 BCE	Ea Nasir, the ancient merchant, does business in the Gulf.
530 BCE	Cyrus the Great, founder of the Achaemenid Persian Empire, dies.
323 BCE	Alexander the Great dies. His general, Seleucus I founds Seleucid Empire and the later-autonomous Charax Spasinu port near today's Basra.
2nd century BCE	Parthians replace Seleucids as Persia's rulers.

650 BCE–300 CE	Caravan/port cities of Gerrha, on the eastern coast of Arabia, and Tylos (Bahrain) are largely autonomous and dependent on trade.
115–118 CE	Roman Emperor Trajan reaches the coast of the Gulf, takes Charax. Hadrian abandons Trajan's Babylonian conquests.
224 CE	Ardashir I conquers Parthians, establishes Sassanid Persian Empire securing silk trade.
379 CE	Sassanid Shah Shapur II, "the great," raids Arabian Peninsula, defeats Romans.
579 CE	Kosrow I (Anushirvan), philosopher and shah, builds Gundeshapur, a university near the Gulf.
c. 570–632 CE	Prophet Muhammad spreads Islam in Madina and Mecca. Embassies are sent to Gulf Arab polities.
636 CE	Battle of Qadisiyyah. Muslims defeat Persian forces. Persian culture eventually incorporated into Islamic world.
637 CE	Omani sailors take the Arab conquest to the sea.
638 CE	Basra founded as base for Arab conquests into Persia and further east.
657 CE	Battle of Siffin, between 'Ali and Mu'awiya. Mu'awiya, founder of Umayyad caliphate, declared the winner. Capital moves from Madina to Damascus.
680 CE	Battle of Karbala. Hussein the grandson of the Prophet killed by forces of Yazid, (Sunni) Umayyad Caliph and successor to Mu'awiya.
728 CE	Death of Hasan of Basra, ascetic, founder of Sufism, and model for later Sufis.

750 CE	Abu al-'Abbas al-Saffah, "the blood shedder" founds 'Abbasid Caliphate. His successor, al-Mansur, moves capital to Baghdad.
796 CE	Sibawayh, a native Persian speaker who spent time in Basra, dies. He systematized Arabic grammar in his book *Al-Kitab*.
801 CE	Rabi'a of Basra, great female Sufi saint, dies.
9th–10th century	The *Ikhwan al-Safa'* (Brethren of Purity) secret society of merchants flourishes in Basra.
869–883 CE	Zanj slave revolt occurs near Basra.
930 CE	Qarmatians seize black stone from the Kaaba in Mecca, bringing it to the Gulf.
10th century	Siraf port flourishes. Earthquakes and competition from rivals, like Kish Island, lead to its gradual decline.
1226–1230 CE	Ibn al-Mujawir writes about women in charge of Kish Island port while men are away
Early 15th century	Kingdom of Hormuz, autonomous and rich, receives a visit by Chinese Admiral Zheng He.
1507 CE	Alfonso de Albuquerque defeats King of Hormuz, who becomes vassal of Portugal. Portuguese forts and factories built in the Gulf and along E. African coast.
1650 CE	Ibadi Muslim Omanis and Hindu Banians capture Muscat from Portugal. Omanis rebuild Portuguese forts along the African coast, creating a maritime empire.
1620s–1742 CE	Ya'rubi Ibadi Imams rule over Oman, expelling Portugal from its forts.
1737 CE	Saif bin Sultan II, the Ibadi Imam, joins with the Persians against his rival. Persians occupy parts of Oman.

1744 CE	Ahmad bin Sa'id defeats Persians in Oman, founding the Busaidi Dynasty.
1792 CE	Muhammad ibn al-Wahhab dies decades after forming a pact with Muhammad bin Saud. Although stemmed by the Ottomans and Egypt, Wahhabism spreads throughout the Arabian Peninsula, adopted by some, but not all, Gulf Sunni Arabs.
1804–1856 CE	Sayyid Sa'id bin Sultan reigns over a multiethnic maritime empire, from both Muscat and Zanzibar. He forges competitive alliance and agreements with the British and sends an embassy to the United States.
1820 CE	General Maritime Treaty between Britain and Sheikhs of the Gulf prohibits plunder and piracy.
1858 CE	British Raj established over India, replacing East India Company.
1850–1920 CE	Height of pearling in the Gulf. By 1919, Mikimoto cultured pearls begin to replace natural ones, causing a market crash.
1922 CE	End of the Ottoman Empire. Sultan deposed.
1931 CE	Oil spurts out of the Jabal al-Dukan well in Bahrain, followed by discoveries of oil throughout the Arabian side of the Gulf.
1932 CE	King 'Abd al-'Aziz, with support from Wahhabi reformers, establishes Saudi Arabia.
1939–1945 CE	WWII and high prices due to oil exploitation cause inflation and food scarcity in underdeveloped parts of the Gulf, "years of hunger."

1950–1971 CE	British Protectorate's last years. Development of modern urban infrastructure throughout the Gulf.
1961 CE	Kuwait independent from Britain.
1970 CE	Qaboos bin Sa'id becomes Sultan of Oman, instituting a "Renaissance" in development, education, health, and cultural preservation.
1971 CE	Sheikh Zayed bin Sultan becomes President of the newly founded United Arab Emirates.
1979 CE	Jebel Ali Port Dubai, now the biggest and busiest port in the Middle East, constructed through the efforts of Sheikh Rashid and inaugurated by Queen Elizabeth II.
1979 CE	Iranian Revolution overthrows the Pahlavi Shah. Ayatollah Khomeini emerges as Supreme Leader. Shi'a clerical rule established.
1980–1988 CE	Iran-Iraq War causes mass casualties, creating instability and uncertainty in the Gulf.
1980 CE	The Carter Doctrine commits the US to securing trade through the Gulf.
1981 CE	The GCC (Gulf Cooperation Council) founded.
1990–1991 CE	First Gulf War. Coalition of US and Arab allies drive Saddam Hussein from Kuwait. He remains in power until the second Gulf War (beginning 2003) and his death in 2006.
1991 CE	Collapse of Soviet Union. Era of US military dominance and triple containment in the Gulf.
1995 CE	Sheikh Hamad becomes ruler of Qatar. He funds successful Al-Jazeera satellite TV station.
1996 CE	Qatar finishes first phases of the then-secret Al-Udeid Air base, built for US and British forces.

2010 CE	Khalifa Tower, highest in world, opens in Dubai.
2011 CE	The US Pivot to Asia announced by President Barack Obama.
2017 CE	Qatar Crisis brings disputes between Qatar and UAE/Saudi Arabia into the open. Crisis largely resolved in 2021.
2019	Yemeni Houthis launch drone attack on Abqaiq oil facility in Saudi Arabia. Iran denies supporting the attack.
2020 CE	Qasem Soleimani, head of Iranian Revolutionary Guard Quds Force, killed in US airstrike.
2020 CE	Bahrain and the UAE sign the Abraham Accords.
2022 CE	World Cup in Doha.
2023 CE	Iran and Saudi Arabia restore diplomatic ties. Gaza crisis; Qatar mediates.

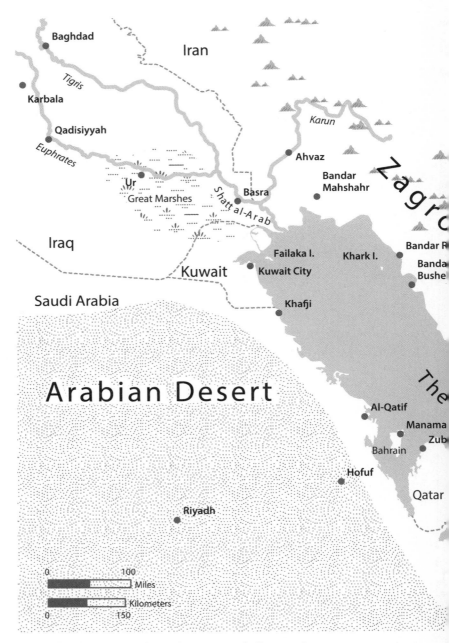

The Persian Gulf. Designed by Jeffrey Young and Allen Fromherz.

Introduction

The Global Gulf: Center of the World

The Persian Gulf is the center of world history. At the middle of the Middle East, it is the world's crossroads. Aligned on a northwest-southeast axis, it serves as the hypotenuse of Eurasia: the easiest (nonair) route linking the Mediterranean to India, via Babylon. On exiting the Gulf, ships come out of the Strait of Hormuz and find themselves on the doorstep of the Indian subcontinent and its vast riches. The Gulf is where trade first emerged, from Dilmun, on the Gulf island of Bahrain, and Ur, one of the world's first cities, built near the Gulf before its shoreline shifted, to the Indus Valley Civilization. At the port of Basra, where the Tigris and the Euphrates flow together, merchants prepared their goods for the journey upstream to Baghdad, Islam became a world religion, and freethinking humanists and Sufis challenged and expanded the foundations of their faith. In Oman and along the Swahili coast, a European empire, Portugal, was defeated and replaced by the Omanis, who created a Gulf maritime empire. Even the British, with their dominant navy, largely left the Gulf rulers to their own devices and avoided controlling the Gulf shores, intervening only when the crucial shipping route from Basra to Bombay was disturbed. Recognizing the area's strategic value, the United States has often inserted itself into conflicts between autonomous states, which include both allies and adversaries. Recently, the

US doctrine of triple containment, which aims to prevent any one power from emerging as a local hegemon, has stopped Saudi Arabia, Iran, and Iraq from singlehandedly dominating the Gulf region. Its deserts, mountains, and marshes, however, have been the main factors containing imperial power over the Gulf. This unique and extreme geography has both made commerce imperative to survival and allowed it to flourish outside the control of empires even while remaining close and often connected to them. The Gulf has seen the rise and fall of great emporia dedicated to free trade and dependent on long-distance maritime commerce among China, India, and the Middle East. Today, from Doha to Dubai, port cities on the Gulf are global economic powerhouses, autonomous centers of open trade and exchange, places where adversaries anywhere else might peacefully cross paths and do business, where hundreds of different tongues are spoken in the malls, airports, and markets. Although the Gulf of the twenty-first century may seem completely new, purchased by petroleum wealth, its history of free trade and autonomous port cities goes back millennia.

Over thousands of years of history, the Gulf has been surrounded and used by some of the world's greatest and most powerful empires, but none has ever fully dominated it, thanks to its natural barriers. Gulf geography includes three distinct hazardous realms, unsuitable for dominion by any premodern empire: great deserts on the Arabian side, high mountains on the Persian side, vast marshes on the way to Babylon.[1] While it might have been possible, with great effort—not only in establishing imperial defenses but also in supplying them with consistent water and food—for an empire to control one of these, it would have been foolhardy and indeed impossible to try for all three at once. Even if an empire managed to hold the marsh ports, it would still be vulnerable to raids from "pirates" hiding in the mountain and desert ports, and people in the Gulf's different extreme regions could play rival empires off one another, promising to ally with the most generous benefactor.[2] Persia and Portugal may have built forts in all three climes, but they did not dominate commerce and were easily overwhelmed, avoided through the use of unofficial ports and routes, and even overrun by Arab raids. Part of what kept the marshes, deserts, and mountains from being easily managed was that they were not impenetrable. In fact, they had plenty of holes for small groups, if not for imperial armies: there were too many alternate channels, alternate coves, alternate desert paths, and oases for any empire to fully monitor. This prioritized decentralized trade around imperial checkpoints, what empires liked to call "smuggling." Thus, while geography made it difficult for empires to harness commerce throughout the Gulf, it also stimulated the proliferation of multiple routes and multiple ports, both taxed and untaxed, that connected the region to imperial capitals, allowing a shifting of the chessboard in a way that favored merchants and nonimperial actors. The lack of fertile land for farming along much of the shore has also meant that many Gulf cities and other communities have had to rely on trade to survive.

As this suggests, the Gulf's relationship with empires is complicated. Its prosperity is connected to and sometimes dependent on imperial centers. The rise of particular empires has led to prosperity and stability. As we will see in chapter 2, on Basra, a close imperial city, such as Baghdad in Mesopotamia, could be highly beneficial to the Gulf economy, leading to a burst of cosmopolitan culture. The same was the case for Dilmun, which benefited from the prosperity of Babylon (see chapter 1). Modern Dubai, by contrast, has risen alongside a naval security guarantee from the faraway United States (see chapter 6). The Gulf, however, has also almost perpetually been a site of rebellion and a place where toleration of nonimperial belief systems was common. Emperors often gave autonomy to local Gulf port rulers in exchange for tribute. Local Gulf rulers acted not as typical kings, collecting taxes on land and harvests, but as merchant princes, who had to encourage trade and used tolerance as a tool to attract every type of business. Thus, instead of sharing a common imperial history, the people of the Gulf have always been heterogeneous, united instead by the trade that has flowed from their region into the vast Indian Ocean. The Indian Ocean is the Gulf's great magnet. Drawing people through the narrow Hormuz Strait, it beckons the different people of the Gulf's difficult deserts, marshes, and mountains.

The Gulf has served as a fluid space of transit, where people from different places—and different ethnic, linguistic, religious, and cultural backgrounds—have shared economic interests, ideas, experiences, and even homes. This coexistence has been marked by ample conflict, thanks to both internal rivalries and outside conquests, yet Gulf history also includes mixing, relative tolerance, and cosmopolitanism, especially in centers of trade. At times this ethic of tolerance was strategic, used only to maximize the number of goods and merchants coming to a port. However, there are also overt expressions of a cosmopolitan ethic in the literature of the Gulf. Tolerance was usually a necessity: merchants who were not accepted in one port could simply leave for another. Sulayman the Merchant, who wrote an account of his travels during the ninth-century heyday of the Gulf port of Siraf, reminded readers of the adaptability and cultural sensitivities needed for business in such an international marketplace: "There is, in India, a caste in which members do not eat at the same plate or at the same table; they find this a defilement and an abomination. When these Hindus come to Siraf and when one of our great merchants invites them to eat a meal with them, even if the meal is attended by one hundred persons . . . he makes certain that each of these has their own plate and table."[3]

Sometimes the merchants' ethos of tolerance went beyond pragmatism. It became rarified, turning into a literary expression of "humanistic" ideals that encapsulated universal human experience.[4] Cosmopolitanism as a moral concept emerges in the poetry of Saadi Shirazi (d. 1292), who traveled the region:

> All men and women are to each other
> the limbs of a single body, each of us drawn
> from life's shimmering essence, God's perfect pearl;
> and when this life we share wounds one of us,
> all share the hurt as if it were our own.
> You, who will not feel another's pain,
> you forfeit the right to be called human.[5]

Over centuries of mastering the art of trade and attracting merchants from far-flung places and cultures, Gulf port cities created this cosmopolitan ethos, one that put profit before the whims of dogma and despot. From desire or necessity, they were often free from the concerns of centralized powers and cultural conformity. This established fertile ground for literary and philosophical expressions of a form of medieval humanism based on experiences and encounters far more diverse than those of the Abrahamic cultures of the medieval Mediterranean.

Gulf literature often symbolizes the many religious, ethnic, and linguistic communities that have passed through as ships at sea (see figure 1). In one story from the Persian *Book of Kings,* a wise man imagines representatives of every faith setting out into the world. Seventy ships, representing seventy faiths, prepare for their global journey, starting in the Gulf:

> When [the] seventy ships were launched onto the Gulf,
> and all the sails were raised,
> [there was] a single broad ship in the shape of a bride,
> embellished like the eye of a rooster.
> The Prophet [Muhammad] was in it with ʿAli . . .[6]

FIGURE 1. Ships of faith: Firdausi's Parable of the Ships of Shi'ism. Folio 18v, *Shahnameh* (*Book of Kings*) of Shah Tahmasp, c. 1530–35 CE. Metropolitan Museum of Art, New York.

The Gulf was the world's first global sea, a place where many faiths and cultures set sail. Like a slingshot, it flings people into the vast world of Indian Ocean monsoon trade. Like a net, it captures them from as far away as India, the east coast of Africa, Indonesia, and China, bringing them through its narrow throat and belly into the heart of Mesopotamia, the rich agricultural land of empires and kings between the Tigris and the Euphrates Rivers.

The word *Khalij* reveals the region's multicultural character. *Khalij* is shared by Arabic and Persian as the term for the Gulf. Persian is in the Indo-European language family and Arabic is Semitic: the different systems and cultures of the peoples who speak them have led to rivalry over the centuries. Nonetheless, these languages share many words, due to millennia of interactions across the Gulf. *Khalij* can mean "a canal cut from a river, extending to a place where use is made of it." Sometimes, it simply means "a river." Unlike the English word *gulf,* which implies division, *khalij* "connects" to a port of call.[7]

It is little wonder that the Gulf has had many names. So many different peoples have traversed it and depicted it as part of their world view. In ancient Babylon, the Gulf was called the Bitter Sea, possibly due to its high salt content. An eighteenth-century European map labels it "Gulf of Basra and Qatif" as well as "Sinus Persicus" (Persian Gulf), showing the variability in names for the Gulf.[8] *Sinus,* the Latin word for "gulf" or "bay," suggests a space, a cavity, a place of free transfer or connection between organs. It is only recently that an artificial line, the international maritime boundary, like a surgeon's wound, has split the belly of the Gulf in two, between Iran to the east and the Arab states to the west. The line starts at the Gulf's navel, at the Shatt al-Arab—which is formed by the confluence of the Tigris and Euphrates Rivers and empties into the Gulf—and slices down through the Strait of Hormuz. On one side of the divide, Iran demands that it be called the Persian Gulf; on the other, the Arab states call it the Arabian Gulf. This divisiveness almost seems predetermined, but it was not always the case.

One of the reasons for the perception of the Gulf as a place of conflict is the experience of the United States in the region since the 1980s. For those born between 1980 and 2000 in Europe and the United States, their "first war" was the US-led Gulf War in Iraq, vividly streamed by CNN. For the Boomer generation, the Persian Gulf denoted the Iran hostage crisis, OPEC, long lines at the gas pump, and the importance of securing the region for the sake of our own oil-consuming economy. Iraq has been perceived as a threat not only to the oil fields of Kuwait and other Gulf states but also to world trade passing through the Gulf. It therefore posed a threat to the deeper status quo of the Gulf, in which no imperial power or nearby center could dominate or completely control this most strategic body of water. Iran and Saudi Arabia have likewise been viewed as dangerous, especially as they have made moves to manage or influence smaller neighbors. The 2019 attack on the Saudi oil refinery in Abqaiq and the US assassination of the Iranian Revolutionary Guard commander Qasem Soleimani in 2020 heightened a sense that this region is a powder keg, always ready to explode.

At the level of great powers, it is true that desire by certain elites to harness the Gulf has long been a source of turmoil. Shah Shapur II, for instance, built a "Great Wall of Persia" against the Arabs. Conflict, however, is only part of the picture. As Lawrence Potter writes, "Gulf history has become highly politicized, and the historic hybridity of its port cities has been obscured," especially as new nation-states make claims to its past.[9] There is another story of the Gulf, of not only cultural mixing among Persians and Arabs but a web of many groups, diasporas, and identities streaming into the region from the west along the Tigris and Euphrates or from the south and east through the Indian Ocean and Strait of Hormuz. A liquid launchpad for so much of history, the Gulf was never owned entirely by any one group or imperial power or fixed identity. Looking beyond the Persian-Arabian or Shi'a-Sunni divide, the history of the Gulf is global history par excellence. A starting point of the world's written story, the Gulf, as described some of the first cuneiform tablets, has remained one of the most well-connected regions by sea. At the same time, it is a place where multiple distinctive faiths and cultures have thrived and interacted, in its ports and on ships.[10] Their members have mixed in its markets and port cities, later returning home to communities deep in the mountains, in the marshes, or in desert oases, far from shore.

The Gulf attracted ships from as far away as China, Cochin, and Kenya. Landing on its shores, they gathered goods and prepared for the much more dangerous and profitable journey into the sea of opportunity: the Indian Ocean. Many factors influenced which harbor a ship's captain or its merchant owners chose. The safest, most welcoming, most cosmopolitan, and least costly ports, those with the lowest customs taxes, have often been the most successful. Their dependence on long-distance trade was a powerful incentive to sustain and increase commerce, so Gulf ports were built to entice and welcome a diverse range of merchants, sailors, and other people. Connecting the sea trade with the network of desert caravans in Arabia, mountain passes in Persia, and the Tigris and Euphrates Rivers in Mesopotamia, ports on all sides of the Gulf were most often autonomous, even openly rebellious, decentralized and lightly ruled by merchant princes who themselves engaged in profitable long-distance commerce, moved across vast distances by the monsoon.

Merchants were often in the Gulf only temporarily, on a seasonal basis, waiting for the next monsoon to carry them and their cargo to the east coast of Africa or to India. Populations thus increased and decreased wildly, according to the trading season. Most of the time, those in a port needed to at least appear to tolerate one another—and sometimes cultural influences went much deeper than that: groups of merchants often celebrated cosmopolitanism and the embrace of otherness, while philosophers, poets, writers, and rulers played on differences and contradictions instead of ignoring them. Of course, there were also times when this system was threatened, when a less tolerant ruler or group tried to take over and impose religious or cultural conformity—or excessive taxes. But merchants who felt unwelcome simply took their business elsewhere, leaving the port that was under the thumb of empire or dogmatism to decline and even disappear if conditions didn't improve. With most ports separated from the Gulf's main agricultural lands and sometimes from adequate supplies of freshwater, trade was an existential matter. The Gulf is dotted with silent archaeological remains of once great cities that failed to continue to attract trade. Sometimes, on the other hand, there were many cosmopolitan and welcoming ports competing with one another. This would lead to a race to the bottom in taxes and customs dues, forcing Gulf rulers and other elites to dedicate themselves to trade, to venture into distant markets to try to make up for lost revenue. At some Gulf ports, the merchant-ruler was just as likely to be absent on business in a far-off port as present and ready to decide an important local matter. He was often at sea, recovering from a storm in the Seychelles, or trading somewhere on the coast of India or Africa. Port operations, especially the all-important collection of the customs tax, could be managed by his delegate: a wife, a faithful slave or servant who could be relied on not to mount a rebellion, or someone from a completely different tribe or faith—so as to prevent a faction from his own family or tribe from taking over while he was away on business.

Today, many parts of the world exist in an economic system similar to the one the Gulf has known for millennia: diversified, service centered, and connected to global networks, not dependent on agriculture as the primary industry. This was far from true before industrialization began in the nineteenth century. Instead, agriculture was by far the one activity that dominated most of the economies world-wide. The Gulf, however, was an exception. Since the rise of civilization in Mesopotamia, it was almost always a center of world trade. At least as far back as the beginning of writing, the economy of Gulf ports was highly dependent on commerce, especially long-distance trade in both commodities and luxuries. By contrast, in imperial centers such as Babylon, Baghdad, Isfahan, and Beijing, agricultural production was the be-all and end-all. Surplus food was needed to feed armies and state officials. In such societies, canals had to be maintained, great public works required taxation (because sacred kings could not be polluted by commerce), and most people never went more than five miles from their birthplace. Fixation of identity and place—except for hajj or other pilgrimage—was common. Although the Gulf ports often had to import food and sometimes even water, they could avoid the high infrastructure taxes required for a successful alluvial, or riverbank, agricultural civilization. At the same time, they were always vulnerable to changes in trading patterns, unlike large landed polities, for which long-distance trade was a relatively small percentage of the preindustrial economy. Indeed, some major agrarian cultures, such China and Japan, have chosen to isolate themselves from world trade for centuries at a time. For a Gulf port city, of course, this was not possible: the disappearance of trade often meant devastation, and the merchant and the ruler were one and the same.

Merchant princes were usually more successful than large agricultural states at encouraging other merchants to use their harbors, pay their (minimal) customs fees, and bring yet more merchants. But so desperate were they for trade that in a few rare cases they forced merchants to visit their ports, as when a medieval ruler of the island of Kish kidnapped traders from the port of Siraf and took them to his port instead. This sort of tactic did not usually work in the long run. Merchants had to be let loose to sell their goods, sail into the Indian

Ocean, and then return with their ships laden with more merchandise, sometimes after years away. Unlike farmers and peasants, who were tied to the land, merchants and traders often had choice of space and place—if the winds were favorable. If they were mistreated or their culture or religion was disrespected in a certain port, they might never return there but instead choose another one nearby. Strategic Gulf cosmopolitanism, however, was not an unchanging idea or constant formula. Rather, different ports in different historical contexts used different means to attract commerce and trade. It is for this reason that this book is organized around particular ports and periods: to show not that some dream of cosmopolitanism always worked or was always the same but that adaptation to the harsh imperatives of Gulf geography reflected and was based on each community's complex of economic, religious, political, and social trends. This adaptation could be costly, even deadly if done improperly, but the payoff was potentially great for Khalijis: the people of the Gulf.

The Gulf's geography has exhausted armies and navies and favored small groups, traders, and merchants who wanted to avoid taxes imposed by empires. Persia's imperial centers were on the plateau of the Zagros Mountains. For Babylon, the metropolitan center was usually found in the land of reliable canals built between the Euphrates and the Tigris northwest of the Gulf's marshes. The centers of desert empires lay to the west, such as Mecca, Medina, and some of the oases of the Arabian Peninsula. The desire of each of these empires to reach the Gulf and potentially control the whole body of water and its shores was clear. The Gulf was the one reliable harbor for and liquid highway to the Indian Ocean, a resting place for anyone waiting for a change in the monsoon winds, which could take a sailing ship, free of charge, from Africa to Arabia to India and beyond. Getting to the Gulf, however, required paying an enormous price. Its main trading cities were not just ports but gates that opened, closed, and collected tolls, controlling the traffic going both ways through the difficult geographic gauntlet of the marshlands, the deserts, and the mountains.

For an empire, the mountains pose the problems of precipitous height, difficult passage, lack of water, and too many competing and easily defended natural coves. A stony backbone with the same curve as the one in the small of a person's lower back lies along the northeastern coast of the Gulf, where there is also a rift or valley of relatively deeper waters near the shore. Formed by high mountains, baked by the sun, and lacking freshwater, the coves and *bandars* (the Persian name for a natural mountain harbor) on this shore provide access to the uplands and plateaus of the Zagros Mountains—the location of the fabulously wealthy capital cities of the Persian empire, the world's first hyperpower, which were connected to the Silk Roads of central Asia. Although there is comparatively little room for a city before the mountains jut up into the sky, some empires were able to establish footholds on this beach, such as the British, who based their headquarters in the Gulf at Bushehr, in what is now Iran. Nearby, the Portuguese built a massive fort complex on the dry island of Hormuz, in the Strait of Hormuz, created by a valley between Iran and Oman. Lack of water was a serious hindrance to expansion, and there was very little in terms of agricultural subsistence or food security. While cisterns and *qanats*, incredible underground water channels built by ancient Arabian and Persian engineers all along these mountains, could provide some relief, most of the food and water was imported. When storms very occasionally made their way into the Arabian Peninsula and across the Gulf, they would cause sudden and destructive floods, especially since the incline of the land was so precipitous. Long-standing mountain port dwellers on all sides of the Gulf adapted to this by building permanent dry channels. In the Strait of Hormuz, one such people, the Kumzari, reliant on trade and fishing, have a unique culture and language, which combines the languages of all the empires that have tried to control the Gulf over the past millennium, including Portuguese, English, Persian, and Arabic. Theirs is the only native non-Semitic language spoken on the Arabian Peninsula for the past fourteen hundred years.[11] While such inhabitants of small ports could rely on fishing, ship building, and mastery of the environment to sustain their numbers, larger cities and ports controlled by empires needed trade and shipping not only for economic prosperity but for survival. As the story of the city of Siraf will reveal, this made them particularly vulnerable to sudden shifts in global trade. Even when empires could secure their Gulf ports, the rest of the shore outside those footholds was often completely ungovernable, full of "pirate" coves and steep, hazardous passes guarded by freedom-loving tribes who were quick to move between hidden fjords. The mountains of Oman and the Musandam Peninsula, for instance, were used as a natural fortress that has housed and protected the Ibadis, a distinct group of Arab Muslims who elected their own imams, or leaders, for centuries. Even before the rise of Islam in the seventh century, the Arabs of Oman long and successfully resisted outright rule by the Persians.

If the mountains were too precipitous and dry to control, the marshlands were too flat and wet. Fed by multiple major rivers systems—those of the Karun, the Euphrates, and the Tigris—the vast marshes near modern-day Basra were impossible to drain or manage for centuries. Far less predictable than the Nile, the rivers of Mesopotamia were in a constant state of flux: a canal built one year might be washed out in the next flood. While the carefully tended canals and irrigation ditches farther north and west, up the Tigris and Euphrates, helped to feed the world's first great civilizations, the marshes could trap and consume whole armies. Recently, however, they have been threatened. Agricultural development in the 1950s and 1960s dried up some, and in the 1980s and 1990s Saddam Hussein tried to drain them all to displace the rebellious Marsh Arabs, committing a type of ecological genocide as he prepared for his march into Kuwait.

Saddam, who saw himself in the mold of an ancient Babylonian emperor, knew the marshes were the main stumbling block between Iraq and its potential domination of the Middle East. For centuries, the marshes and the marsh people, who were specially adapted to their ecosystem, stymied the attempts of Babylonians, Persians, caliphs, Portuguese, and Turks to completely control access to the Gulf. Before Saddam, the Mesopotamian marshes covered an area of almost eight thousand square miles across a basically stagnant, almost completely flat plain. Indeed, the elevation of the Euphrates decreases only about thirty-nine feet across 190 miles, which allowed the river to meander and create fluid banks of land, mud, and water—an ecosystem of reeds where Marsh Arabs built and maintained grass houses and regularly constructed a kind of impressive but temporary meetinghouse called a *mudhif*. Marsh Arabs, called Attalae in ancient writings, organize their lives around the rhythms of the water and seasons of flooding and desiccation. During times of flooding, they knew how to avoid getting stuck dead in the silt of shifting banks, unlike ships unfamiliar with the marshes. At times of drought, particularly ambitious imperial forces might invade, hoping to capture parts of the temporarily more manageable marshlands. Fortresses and ports could attempt to control some of the routes between the Gulf and the rivers that fed into Babylon. For the most part, however, these outposts, including Ur during the ancient period, Charax during the Hellenistic period, and Basra during the Islamic period, were buffered from and often in a state of open revolt against the imperial center upstream. Moreover, the marshes were vast enough that routes around imperial tax collectors could be found along channels that changed with every wet season. Would-be rulers had to pay off or constantly surveil the Marsh Arabs to gain even grudging cooperation from them.

The Gulf's third realm, the desert coast—the land of scorched sand, rocks, and occasional oases that forms the "belly" in the Gulf's southwest—was perhaps the most perilous of all. It also contains precious treasures: underground freshwater, some of the richest petroleum deposits in the world, and pearls of great value—a land of high risk and high reward. In the Gospel of Matthew, Jesus compares the kingdom of heaven to "a merchant in search of fine pearls: on finding one pearl of great value, he went out and sold all that he had to buy it."[12] The pearl of Jesus's parable, one large enough and fine enough to justify risking everything, would likely have come from the Gulf.

One empire that briefly controlled this desert realm was started by Arab peoples already familiar with desert lands. Soon after the Arab conquests, however, the center of the Islamic empire shifted to Baghdad in old Babylon and the desert returned to its usual state of rebellion against central rule, becoming home to the Qarmatian sect of Islam, a group of Bedouin Arabs who took the sacred Black Stone from the Kaaba in Mecca and brought it to the Gulf. Even today, the political geography of the Gulf's desert side is divided among different emirs and emirates, reflecting this region's fundamentally autonomous nature. The main ports were historically on islands fortunate enough to have freshwater springs, such as Dilmun on Bahrain. It was only in the twentieth century that desalination plants, geoscaping, and other artificial means began to be used to build and maintain ports, overcoming and upsetting the geographic constraints of the past. For instance, because constantly shifting sandbanks and shallows made reaching the Gulf's desert side notoriously hazardous, Dubai used dredging to create a deep-water port and clear shipping routes to attract world trade. Earlier, in the first decades of the nineteenth century, the British with their large and bulky ships faced some embarrassing defeats in the Gulf. They sometimes refused to go onshore to meet the Arab sheikhs who would sign their treaties of maritime peace, instead dropping anchor far enough away from the shallows to ensure that they could leave and encouraging all the sheikhs to come aboard. Moreover, the desert route to the west, especially for those who did not know or control its watering holes and oases, was extremely perilous. Even the Arab Bedouin who have lived and adapted to this environment over centuries avoid vast stretches of the desert, such as the Rubʿ al-Khali, the Empty Quarter: a quarter-million square miles of hyper arid dunes and gypsum plains that see less than two inches of rain a year. These deserts and their winds, which sometimes flow constantly toward the Gulf, have formed a baking-hot barrier between it and powers rising to the west or coming from the north.

For the people who have adapted to its extremes to live on its shores, the Gulf's harsh geographies of deserts, mountains, and marshes have been natural fortifications requiring almost no cost to maintain. They have also let residents take advantage of trade routes through the geographic barriers they knew best. While frustrating empires, they have moreover encouraged interaction and coopera-tion across the waters of the Gulf, a space shared by the peoples of all three realms, as well as visitors from the heterogeneous world of the Indian Ocean and imperial centers to the north (Babylon), the west (Greece, Rome, Arabia), and the east (Persia). To the south was Oman, a power that at times rebelled against imperial rule and at times tried to control the Gulf. But even the Omanis, who knew the region's geographic extremes so well, met difficulties in securing all three realms of marsh, mountain, and desert. Even if it could not be controlled from the land, could the Gulf, as a natural harbor, be a good place from which to project imperial power? This was probably Alexander the Great's aim when he sent his admiral Nearchus to chart its shores. Nearchus's view, however, was obscured by both high cliffs and his own lack of interest in the local population. There were seemingly few places with freshwater, but he described groups of wild-fish eaters on shore and made a report that was not particu-larly promising for Alexander's plans. James Stavridis, a US admiral at the turn of the twenty-first century, faced a similar challenge. His mission was to clear mines from the Strait of Hormuz, one of the narrowest and most fraught sea lanes in the world. Like many would-be tamers of the Gulf, he was an outsider, one of a long line of people—Portuguese, British, American—reluctantly drawn there to secure external strategic interests. Little wonder that this veteran seaman, even with all the equipment of modern naval operations, found the Gulf too crowded, confined, and conflicted, not very amenable to the US mission of ensuring the independence of the Gulf States and, of course, the flow of oil into world markets.[13] A millennium ago, Sulayman the Merchant, like Admiral Stavridis, reported problems with the Strait of Hormuz. The only passage, between two particular mountainous islands, Kusayr and 'Uwayr, was so difficult as to be "impracticable for the Chinese ships."[14] The perils of the Strait of Hormuz are still the subject of sailors' tales—and news reports: in the 2020s, Iran used small motorboats with machine guns to capture hulking oil tankers as they passed slowly through.[15] However, it is the Gulf's very narrowness that creates a psychological sense of close encounters between ships, both friend and foe, making it such a rich caldron of interaction. Historically, merely building and establishing, let alone deploying, a Gulf navy presented many logistical challenges, helping to make imperial control a costly task. There are no real forests or other supplies of wood along the Gulf, except some short mangroves. Teak had to be imported from Africa or South Asia. The Persian Empire had hardwood forests in the Elburz Mountains, near the Caspian Sea—but while Rome captured Carthage and incorporated its naval prowess, dominating the Mediterranean and calling it Mare Nostrum, "Our sea," Persia did not have much experience turning its timber into large caravels or warships.[16] Without an effective navy, it could not really lay claim to the Gulf, despite being the empire perhaps best placed to do so. On the other hand, empires with successful navies of strong ships built with metal nails and pinewood, such as those of the Portuguese and the British, were frustrated by the Gulf. Although the Portuguese brought superior guns and fort technology—leaving a legacy in the strongholds that still dot the shoreline—their attempts at controlling trade were circumvented from the beginning, and the Omanis, a local power, defeated them. The British did not even try to establish power on land, instead signing treaties that allowed local sheikhs to maintain their autonomy.

For such an important piece of world history, the Gulf is fairly small, especially when compared to the earth's other great bodies of water. It is ninety-seven thousand square miles, almost exactly one-tenth the size of the Mediterranean, and about the size of the Great Lakes put together. Its winds and currents are usually somewhat predictable but also often violent. The shamal, a northwesterly wind, blows in the summer during the day and dies down at night. Sometimes it becomes intense, bringing massive dust storms that can cause major damage onshore and to ships. Sudden extreme shamal winds may have contributed to the fall of Babylon's Akkadian Empire, considered the world's first, in 2200 BCE.[17] Other unexpected dangers regularly arise on the open waters of the Gulf. Captains of small boats with shallow berths that carried goods between Gulf cities mentioned the risk of even simple voyages in the tenth century. The fear of shifting sandbanks is palpable in almost all sailors' tales. According to one medieval journal, "We were surprised by a gale of Ras al Kamila. We threw part of the cargo into the sea. The waves rose so high that they overshadowed the boat, and then broke under it. More than once I lost sight of the sky; it was hidden by waves between us and it and veiled from our sight."[18]

Although the Gulf is historically ancient, geographically it is very young. Twenty thousand years ago, during the Ice Age, where the Gulf is today there was a long, fertile river valley inhabited by prehistoric humans. This land of marshes and lakes surrounded the Shatt al-Arab, which now empties into the Gulf but then would have run all the way to the Indian Ocean. When the Ice Age ended and melting ice sheets raised sea levels, the primordial Gulf began to push away from the Indian Ocean into the river lowlands. This occurred between 12,000 and 4000 BCE, with many resulting cycles of rising and falling water levels, frequently displacing people along the shores.[19] A series of deluges occurred at different times and places, maybe creating the psychic-trauma origin of the many flood myths and stories found in ancient texts including the Bible, changed the landscape. However, the seawater in the Gulf reached close to its current level, with some fluctuations, only around 4000 BCE, and something like a gulf rather than a channel has been around only about ten thousand years.[20]

The Gulf's riparian character did not disappear with the global rising of sea levels.[21] It is still possible today to see freshwater springs off the island of Bahrain, bubbling up into the salty water. Over thousands of years, fisherfolk seeking out sweet water during long seasons of pearling have used them. When the Gulf's basin was exposed, these springs created great freshwater oases next to the prehistoric river. Perhaps those oases and the once verdant land inspired ancient tales of Eden. As the climate changed, however, this paradise was flooded, lost beneath the waves. But according to archaeologists, the inundation of the marshes and the river also led to "increased population densities and early group formation, community stability, enhanced maritime trade, and the emergence of social hierarchies in lower Mesopotamia."[22]

Even relatively recently, there may have been significantly more freshwater around the Gulf than is now available for agriculture and settlement on its shores—although it hasn't been tropical since its Miocene and Pliocene days (5.4-2.4 million years ago). As Arabia turned into savanna around one hundred thousand years ago, the first humans there would have experienced a very different climate than what exists today: the region as a whole may not have changed much from the homeland of the first hominids in Africa. Human remains dating to eighty-five thousand years ago have been found in Arabia, called "the other cradle of humanity." Archaeologists have also found evidence of lakes and large ponds in Hofuf in eastern Saudi Arabia that lasted until eight thousand years ago, as well as the bones of large animals, including elephants, that once roamed the Arabian Peninsula.[23] Great wadis, or riverbeds, show evidence of periods of higher precipitation as the monsoon, with predictable rainfalls determining life and death for the land, moved north and south with shifts in the earth's orbit and other major geological changes.

Around two thousand years ago, drying conditions allowed for the foundation of the famous "caravan cities" such as Tylos (Bahrain) and Gerrha on the east coast of Arabia. The Greek geographer Strabo hinted at Gerrha's dual aspect as a port for the desert and the sea: "The Gerrhaeans traffic by land, for the most part, in the Arabian merchandise and aromatics, though Aristobulus says, on the contrary, that the Gerrhaeans import most of their cargoes on rafts to Babylonia, and thence sail up the Euphrates with them, and then convey them by land to all parts of the country."[24] From Gerrha to Tylos to Tyre (in Lebanon), desert and maritime ports linked the Gulf to the Mediterranean. Scholars see the shift to desert trade out of Gerrha, in fact, as evidence of increasingly attractive alternatives—such as camel caravan—to maritime routes or shipping on the Tigris or Euphrates River. The rise of Petra, the distant Nabataean capital in what is now Jordan, was linked to Gerrha's success on the Gulf.[25]

Variability of climate, however, could easily cut off typical trading routes. In the marshlands, whole cities might be bypassed by annual Babylonian floods, which carved new channels to the Gulf. Al-Mas'udi, a Muslim historian of the tenth century, affirmed Aristotle's theory that seas and oceans, indeed all the world's water, had shifted from one place to another over the course of the ages: "All the seas are in constant movement; but, compared to the mass of the seas [that we can see with our own eyes], the extent of their surface and the profundity of their depths, this movement is imperceptible." Riverbeds and seabeds have a lifespan, a "period of youth and of decline, of life and of death; they develop and disappear like an animal or a plant."[26] The shifting of shores caused constant shifting of lives and fortunes on the Gulf, cutting off or opening up trade and ending or establishing geographic advantages for cities and villages.

Ultimately, human adaptation and adaptability have been the keys to long-term success in this region. From the time of ancient Ur to modern Dubai, the Gulf has had ports where merchants, traders, and seafarers broke away from competing centers of power, setting out into the unknown. As they interacted with and changed in the diverse world of the Gulf ports and the Indian Ocean, most also kept a strong sense of local identity or sense of origin. This allowed Gulf trading diasporas to scatter around the rim of the Indian Ocean. The Ibadi merchants of Oman, for instance, follow a distinct school of Islam. They see the mountainous city of Nizwa as their spiritual center, far from the ports. Many of their religious scholars, leaders, and interpreters of doctrine have lived in the hinterland. But there have also been merchant Ibadis in the ports and spread throughout the Indian Ocean and North Africa. Their ability to be global with a local home base created ready-made communities abroad. An Ibadi merchant originally from a tribe in the mountains of Oman could rely on support from other Ibadis from the same tribe in faraway Zanzibar, Bombay, or even Java. (This goes the other way too: The Banian Hindus, a caste of traders who were an essential part of almost every Muslim-controlled port on the Gulf, never lost their attachment to India. Much more recently, Catholic Filipinas who have gone to the Gulf in search of work have created informal social welfare organizations in the streets, malls, and markets there.)

Cosmopolitanism connected merchants and places of commerce to the hinterlands, areas of distinct identities protected by mountains, marshes, or deserts. One of these was the Liwa Oasis, now in

FIGURE 2. Fort, Liwa Oasis, Abu Dhabi, 2016. Photo by author.

the United Arab Emirates, deep in the desert, where forts were built to protect the date palms (see figure 2). For hundreds of years, while its men went to the coast to fish for pearls and sailed off to trade those pearls in distant lands as far away as India, the women, who stayed at home, would tend to the date crop and maintain the traditions of the family and tribe.[27] In similar ways across the millennia, Khalijis have been exposed to the outside world but also remained highly cohesive within their protected oases, mountains, and marshlands. Both this mixing and this separation have been parts of Gulf society since 5000 BCE. Studying the Gulf over the long term can help answer some of the most pressing questions of our own global age.

Are humans able, through cosmopolitanism, to grasp and feel part of a wider sense of humanity? Do we need a sense of tribe, clan, and identity? The Gulf has always contained these contradictions: in port cities from ancient Dilmun on Bahrain through medieval

Islamic Basra and Siraf to Muscat, Hormuz, and Dubai, distinctive communities have created a globally connected Gulf culture, dependent on the free flow of people, commerce, and ideas. For example, in the early Islamic period, the Nestorian Christian Monks of Bani Yas Island, off the coast of what is now Abu Dhabi, isolated themselves to contemplate God—but also sent glassware and other products around Asia. Basra's Brethren of Purity, traders who regularly traveled between the Gulf and India, used secrecy to maintain their merchant-religious-hermetic club but also produced some of the most profound philosophical literature of the tenth century. Bedouin tribes such as the 'Utub fled famine in the Arabian desert to settle on the coast, becoming rulers of ports.

The ability of Gulf residents to combine distinctive local identity with global cosmopolitanism seems alien to the assumptions of Western political philosophy, which describes human history as a natural progression from rural to urban. From Aristotle's notion of the polis, the city, to Hobbes' *Leviathan,* it has distinguished between the "sophistication" of urban power centers, embodiments of hierarchical rule, and the "simplicity" of nonurban areas, dependent on tribalism. More recently, books by Kwame Anthony Appiah and Francis Fukuyama have debated the merits of cosmopolitanism and identitarianism. Appiah called identity "the lies that bind," while Fukuyama termed it "the demand for dignity."[28]

The central question of this age-old debate is this: are humans really tribal at heart, wanting the best only for the communities with which we identify, or are we innately imperial social beings, always desiring to unite for a much larger polity or purpose? The Gulf, the place with the longest history of globalization and one of the most interconnected parts of the world, shows us different ways to understand the tension between group identity and interaction with a larger human community. While their distinctive and protective geographies encourage them to be tribal on land, at sea the different peoples of the Gulf interact with outsiders from both near and far. They have often lived and traveled on the same ships, zones of humanity on the sterile surface of the sea, which instills a forced unity against the elements and other perils of the journey. People who might fight each other on land must sleep, eat, and live together while on the sea. Although passengers from different religious groups, for instance, might try to separate, the hull of a ship is always small enough to keep them in contact. Moreover, ports, as transition zones between sea and land, by nature bring different types of people together. In those such as medieval Siraf and Portuguese Hormuz, separate communities were often packed closely side by side in the tight, protective confines of the city walls and battlements, built to keep out piracy from land or sea. This mixing promoted intermarriage, by which traders could build families in ports as far away as India or Indonesia, which gave them a more comfortable way to wait out the monsoon winds. Finally, because a port city would quickly shrivel and die without trade and comparatively advantageous taxation, different levels of society had a vested interest in openness and toleration of diverse groups from throughout the Indian Ocean.

While today a vast majority of Gulf citizens are Muslim, the Gulf's past is about more than the history of Islam. The Banian Hindus in Muscat, for instance, continue to make their multigenerational mark on Oman's landscape. While the majority of Hindus are not Omani, in 2012 around six hundred Banians held Omani citizenship. The leader of Oman's two hundred thousand Hindus, from the Khimji family, has been called "the only Hindu sheikh of the Arab world" and was selected as a *shaikh al-tamīma,* or overarching representative of their community, their confederation of families.[29] From 2008 to 2013, the Bahraini kingdom's Houda Nonoo, a descendant of Iraqi Jews who had fled to the Gulf two generations earlier, was the first Jewish and woman ambassador to the United States from a Middle Eastern Muslim country.[30]

Unlike the Gulf, imperial centers, while sometimes fostering cosmopolitanism, just as often tried to enforce conformity to the will of the king, shah, or caliph. *The Sea of Precious Virtues,* a medieval Persian "mirror for princes," warns rulers against dwelling in cities that are too diverse, too open, and too tolerant. One should not live in a place "where there are different sects and legal schools, and each calls the others unbelievers. . . . Nor in a city where God's sanctions are not enforced: for example, (where) bloodshed is not requited, thieves' hands not severed, drinkers of wine not beaten, and criminals not reproved. . . . One should not dwell in a city dominated [in number] by the infidel enemy." The most dangerous cities of all, according to this text, were those "ruled by women."[31] Arab writers also alerted readers to the decadent dangers of the cosmopolitan city. Ibn Khaldun (d. 1406 CE) in his *Muqaddimah,* a work of historical sociology written for elite ministers and rulers, cautions against giving in to the temptations of urban life. One could not enjoy this luxury without loosening the rules of God and leaving one's agricultural realms vulnerable to raids by more vigorous and moral Bedouin with stronger *'asabiyya* (tribal solidarity) and therefore distinctive identities. These Bedouin could always claim that they enforced "true" Islamic laws, legitimizing their potential establishment of a new dynasty. Involvement in trade and indulgence in its companion luxury could pollute and confuse religious values and call into question the nobility of one's birth. Merchants were best kept at a distance.[32]

For port city rulers there was a different ethic: the danger was not that people would rebel but that they would leave if homogeneity and religious rules were enforced too strictly. Kings of agriculture-based realms have an incentive to demand unity and laws to prevent revolt against taxation, in order to maintain the hierarchy and a fairly large bureaucracy, but ports work in largely the opposite way. Moreover, while relative immobility of the population is important for land-based rulers, mobility is the source of revenue for ports, whose rulers must lower customs taxes to a competitive level and welcome any-body willing to pay, willing to trade. For millennia, successions of sheikhs, emirs, and kings with marsh, mountain, or desert roots pre-sided as market managers in the Gulf's port cities while maintaining ties to their kin in the hinterlands, on whom they called for support when their power was threatened. The merchants in these ports were often pleased to leave the tasks of ruling and collecting customs fees to other parties, whom they were equally happy to assist and advise, regardless of their religion or tribe. This created a symbiotic relation-ship in which merchants were free to make money and the ruler was able to collect customs. It was obviously against the ruler's interests to destroy the town's wealth, so the customs couldn't be too onerous, or the merchants would disappear.[33] Gulf ports also rely on a network of retainers, guards, tax collectors, and sailors established through-out the Indian Ocean. The most successful ones have not concen-trated all their commerce in one place. Instead, they formed links with other ports in the Gulf, India, and Africa. After all, ships need multiple stopover points and transit hubs. A city like Siraf or Hormuz on the Persian shore would try to sign a treaty with or even take possession of a port on the Arabian side, such as Sohar or Manama. Alliances and other associations, including duopolies and triopolies, attached the Arabian and Persian shorelines to the Gulf of Oman and the Indian Ocean. This required diplomatic skill and the ability to change partners, often at the drop of an anchor.

Gulf rulers also had to be trusted as fair, acting as gift givers, not just tribute takers, and as arbitrators when disputes emerged be-tween merchants. Often deliberately humble in appearance, with their dress showing only a small sign of their authority, they did not wear a crown or use pomp and ceremony. Still to this day, the rulers of the Gulf, even if they recently adopted the title of *prince* or *king*, perhaps to raise their status in international circles, appear un-crowned in public photos and traditional settings, in the same dress as their fellow citizens. Modesty and accessibility have long been common among Gulf rulers, reflecting a moral obligation not just of Islam but of the values and economic system of the ports. The early nineteenth-century ruler of Muscat and Zanzibar Sayyid Saʻid bin Sultan, despite controlling a vast empire of ports across the Arabian Sea, exemplified this attitude. He maintained a reputation for fair treatment of different religions and nationalities, from American through British to Indian—anyone who was willing to come to his port, trade, and contribute to the customhouse. With the equity of its government a welcome alternative to the despotism of surrounding countries, Muscat attracted, among others, Arabian, Persian, Syrian, Christian Sabaean, Kurdish, Afghan, Banian Hindu, and Baluchi merchants. After fleeing persecution in Iraq and in other parts of the Arab world where they were required to wear identifying badges, many Jews arrived in Muscat, where there was no such rule and they were allowed to trade unmolested. The US diplomat Edmund Roberts observed that "all religions, within the sultan's dominions, are not merely tolerated, but they are protected by his highness; and there is no obstacle whatsoever to prevent the Christian, the Jew, or the Gentile, from preaching their peculiar doctrines, or erecting temples."[34] Although there have been plenty of dramatic exceptions, a certain pragmatism is a long-term characteristic of Gulf culture, fostered by the demands of trade, including the need to accommodate peoples of different faiths who have connected the Gulf to the rest of the world. Gulf rulers before and after Sayyid Saʻid bin Sultan have protected foreigners such as Babylonian Jews, Banian Hindus, and Parsi Zoroastrians and allowed polytheistic temples to be built—but also expected traders from these groups to serve them and to give them preference and access to markets in their homelands in India, Africa, and beyond.

There were many reasons for such intense commercial connections, but the main physical force that links the Gulf with the Indian subcontinent and with Africa is the monsoon. It could be argued that this periodic huge sea wind, which brings rain that turns deserts green in June and July, is the most important feature of the entire Indian Ocean system, of which the Gulf is the most important appendage. The monsoon changes direction approximately every six months, blowing from the northeast and then reversing to blow from the southwest. This is a happy circumstance for navigators: it allows for seasonal flows between ports such as Hormuz and Muscat in the Gulf and destinations far to the northeast, such as Goa in India, and to the southwest, such as Zanzibar in Africa. It also explains, to a large degree, the deep geographic diversity of Gulf society, which seems almost predetermined by the monsoon.

At the end of the sixteenth century, Richard Hakluyt, a promotor of English colonization and exploration, wrote a history of English seafaring. One of the most valuable parts of this work was on the monsoon, a word that comes from the Arabic *mawsim,* "season." England was then far behind both Spain and Portugal when it came to trade in the Indian Ocean. Hakluyt, however, helped crack open the door to a future era of British influence there. Unlike a highway or a road, which has to be maintained and doesn't change position once laid down, the monsoon offers a far more flexible system of travel, permitting voyages over vast distances in a matter of months and even weeks. As Hakluyt pointed out, it is far from a simple shift of winds. There are multiple monsoon seasons, each with particular risks and directions. The first monsoon from Goa to Hormuz, for instance, is in October, "passing with Easterly windes along the coast of Persia." But there are two more possible departures: a January monsoon follows a similar route and was called the *Entremonsoon,* while a monsoon between March 25 and April 6 requires sailing by the island of Socotra, south of Yemen. This last was the "most troublesome of all" passages, full of risky navigation to catch the correct wind up to Ra's al-Hadd and Hormuz. Leaving from Hormuz for

Goa, ships can set out in September, December, or April. Going to Africa, one can leave in April or October. The optimum time for Red Sea departures is "betwixt the first and last of Januarie"[35] Equivalent to the Dubai airport today, Hormuz and other nearby ports have welcomed captains, pilgrims, merchants, mystics, and mendicants biding their time before a monsoon. Simply wait for the right season, and ships will depart with remarkable regularity. Nature thus serves as the ultimate air traffic control of these voyages. The coming of the steamship and the airplane, which led to the closing of some ports, often enhanced preexisting routes and rhythms determined by the monsoon.

Despite the regularity of the monsoon, caused by differences in how the Eurasian landmass and the Indian Ocean absorb heat from the sun, no imperial interest was able to use it to control the whole Indian Ocean world-system, including the Gulf. While the Mongols captured, held, and developed the Silk Roads, land routes between East and West, the Indian Ocean remained a largely unconquerable space. The reason was probably practicality as much as size. Safavid Persians, in the seventeenth century, could sell their bureaucratic services to courts and kings as far away as Thailand, even if they could never control these places themselves.[36] The British relied on local agents and treaties with independent rulers.[37] Despite their bellicose arrival on the scene in the sixteenth century, the Portuguese also had to accommodate diverse traditions across the Indian Ocean.

Today, a dispute between Persians and Arabs over the name of the Gulf obscures the histories of the many other peoples, neither Persian nor Arab, who have made it their home. Africans and Asians from throughout the Indian Ocean have lived on the Gulf's shores. Far from only recent migrants following the oil boom, they have arrived over millennia as slaves, traders, important merchants, and even spouses: some of the marriages between Gulf sheikhs and Asian or African wives have resulted in future rulers. Even if the dispute between Arabs and Persians over political ownership of the Gulf could be resolved, Gulf culture could never be restricted to Arab and Persian. It was and is a place of global connections where the ability to adopt different identities and to speak different languages is an asset. The latter, in fact, was the "key to success" in trade and politics in nineteenth- and twentieth-century Bahrain,[38] whose cities had a transnational community of Persians. Other pearl and early oil towns had significant levels of Arab and Persian migration and integration, the continuation of a "hybrid Arab-Persian culture [that has] flourished in the Gulf for many centuries."[39] In pre-oil Kuwait, a "tolerant and open society emerged." There was no "mono-vocal" identity.[40]

Beyond what has been ahistorically claimed as an exclusively Persian or Arab Gulf, there was the ancient Dilmun Gulf, the Persian Sassanian and later Safavid Gulf, the Portuguese, Dutch, and Omani Gulfs, the Ottoman Gulf, the British colonial Gulf, an African Gulf connected through trade to the East African coast, the Cold War Gulf, and the South Asian Gulf, connected to India and even the Far East. All of these Gulfs have added depth and layers of human interaction to the history and culture of the region and its peoples. The Gulf is a window onto new possibilities for the Middle East in the twenty-first century, not only geographically and economically but also as a hybrid social, political, and cultural space.[41] In this dynamic milieu, where cosmopolitanism is the rule rather than the exception and open markets are often required for survival, cultural diversity and economic exchange have catalyzed not only change but also the creation of deeper layers of history. Yet despite its complexity, Gulf society has characteristics that have remained fairly constant over the long term. Shifts in political or religious realities and the confluence of so many who came from elsewhere have not shifted its unimagined maritime identity.

The Gulf is a largely autonomous, fluid space between empires. Throughout its more than ten-thousand-year history, the extremes of its geography have made it nearly impossible to control. No power—not the Portuguese with their impressive forts, not the Persians with their vast, multiethnic armies, not the British at the height of their influence—ever ruled the entire space in the way that the Roman Empire controlled the Mediterranean. Gulf communities have remained relatively adaptable, taking advantage of the fluidity of their environment and even the extremes of temperature and geography to encourage commerce and offer port services. The prominence of different places in the Gulf changed according to the health and economic power of the empires that surrounded it, as well as various other factors, even far-flung events in China, central Asia, and western Europe, such as the repression of foreign traders in Canton (Guangzhou), the coming of the Mongols, and the rise of Portugal as a maritime power in the sixteenth century. Ports are therefore the best portal for viewing the history of the Gulf, and this book is organized around particular entrepôts and cities that represent all three of its realms: the desert, the mountains, and the marshes. These ports also most embodied the crucial commercial, cultural, and political exchanges within the Gulf in particular eras. My aim is to show the Gulf's geographic and cultural diversity by focusing on places throughout the region, although one is not strictly on the Gulf: Muscat, which is very much a part of Gulf culture, is on the Gulf of Oman. Neither is each chapter about only a single port.

Chapter 1 focuses on the storied port of Dilmun, whose ruins are on the island of Bahrain and linked to Ur, the port that connected the Gulf through the marshlands to Babylon. Dilmun and Ur flourished as a joint trading center from the fourth millennium to 800 BCE. The Gulf was at the very heart of the first known "world-system" of trade, between Babylon and the Indus valley. Other ports, such as Charax Spasinu and Gerrha, emerged later, during the classical and Hellenistic periods, providing a link with the land-based caravan trade as well. The rise of Islam in the seventh century had a significant impact on Gulf history, including the appearance of a major imperial power in Arabia. The city that most embodied this for the Gulf was built entirely in the Islamic era by Arab and Muslim conquerors and those conquered by Arab armies: Basra, the subject of chapter 2. It benefited from the rise of the 'Abbasid world empire, based in nearby Baghdad, without being directly under the thumb of the ruler and his court. This allowed it to become a cauldron of Arabic and Islamic culture, the place where Arabic grammar was invented, and much early Islamic history and thought was first put into writing. Chapter 3 is about Siraf, Basra's sister port on the mountainous Persian shore, which embodied the challenges of the Gulf in the medieval period, during and after the decline and fall of the 'Abbasid Empire. Of all the Gulf's port cities, Siraf experienced the most dramatic fall, and there is little left other than ruins to testify to its former status as the Dubai of its era. As chapter 4 explains, after Siraf, Hormuz emerged as the preeminent trading center at the Strait of Hormuz, which forms the opening of the Gulf. The Portuguese "conquered" this kingdom in the early sixteenth century. Nonetheless, as will be explained, they were never able to impose their rule effectively or completely on this crucial linchpin of their Indian Ocean empire. The defeat of Portugal by the Omanis of Muscat in 1650, a highly symbolic victory over a European power, heralded the next era of Gulf history. High mountains protected Muscat, the focus of chapter 5, as it evolved into one center of a vast Omani empire that had major impacts on the Gulf even as it lost the fight for dominance in the Indian Ocean to the similarly emerging British Empire. Unlike in other parts of its domain, however, the British Protectorate did not end the autonomy of Gulf ports or rulers so long as they agreed not to disrupt British trade and access to India. In part because of this, the anticolonial revolutionary movements that arose across the British Empire were rarely successful in the Gulf, where British influence, traditions, and governmental and legal legacies instead left their marks in ways that were seen as largely positive. Finally, after the British formally withdrew in the 1970s, Dubai transformed itself, becoming the port city that most embodies the present Gulf era, as chapter 6 explains. Instead of simply appearing from out of nowhere, like a mirage in the desert, Dubai is a success precisely because it leveraged the Gulf's long history of cosmopolitanism, encouragement of trade, low-cost commerce, and comparatively relaxed attitudes toward cultural differences. Other cities trying to replicate its achievement have spread the "Dubai model" of economic development around the world.

The one risk that may upset the Gulf model of port cosmopolitanism is, ironically, too much success: enough power for Gulf rulers and states to make imperial claims, creating the very kind of system locally that the region has prevented outside empires from imposing, to its advantage. Because its ports link major markets and powers, its rulers have had to act as facilitators, not overlords. They have generally avoided interfering in the affairs of merchants, and each ruler has often acted as primus inter pares with fellow tribe members and the local population. Now, however, the Gulf states have become so centralized and their rulers so powerful—presiding over increasingly large bureaucratic and oil-industrial complexes—that the temptation to create more-exclusive national identities and to project commercial success into political dominion over other states might be too hard to resist, becoming the rule rather than the exception. This would be an anomaly in the Gulf's history as a global, nonimperial space—a resting place, even refuge, where distinctive cultures can thrive within a relatively tolerant cosmopolitan environment.

From the emergence of long-distance trade out of Mesopotamia to the pearl boom and bust of the early twentieth century, ports dedicated to commerce have risen and collapsed along the Gulf shore, leading to mass transfers of wealth and trade. One reason is the great effort needed to establish a successful port there. In the marshes, canals had to be constantly maintained to avoid flooding, and drought could lead to serious water shortages and salt in drinking water. On some mountainsides, there was often little to no potable water, so it had to be imported on ships. On the desert shores, sandbanks made it difficult to get ships of significant size into port, and temperatures and winds were not favorable to human habitation. Nonetheless, people have adapted and found ways of clinging to the Gulf's difficult geographies. Defying nature to pursue profit, Gulf residents have used incredible means to secure water, food, and life in a region that has seen the world's highest recorded temperatures, where, for part of the year at least, the main threat is not pirates but perspiration. Persia's ancient qanats, or underground canals, and Oman's *aflaj* (the plural of *falaj*), networked water channels, are still used by some Gulf communities. The island city of Hormuz had no sustainable water supply, so the Portuguese built vast cisterns there to maintain their fort and control over the city. Siraf had to import all of its grain and water. Even today, Dubai, Doha, and Abu Dhabi, like many other modern Gulf cities, rely on huge desalination plants. Similar to a defensive wall, the Gulf's climate has secured independence and kept people out, especially those who might want to overstay their welcome or impose imperial demands on trade. For those who belonged, existence was fairly free in the ports, as long as you could find food and water.

Clumped along the shores of the Gulf, the variety of small and large emirates, sultanates, republics, and kingdoms—Kuwait, the United Arab Emirates, Oman, Qatar, Bahrain, Saudi Arabia, and Iran—have undergone major economic and social shifts over the past half century, owing to the discovery and exploitation of oil. In fact, however, the Gulf's current political geography reflects the pre-oil past, when globalization, trade, commerce, and immigration were just as integral to the region's survival. Far from transcending history, the success of the modern Gulf is due to the continuation of past practices and cultural legacies, not only Persian or Arabian but also from a confluence of peoples from around the world. Cultural and social history helps us understand both the booms and busts of the short term and the underlying sinews of the Gulf's past. It is through such a long-term perspective—also taking into account geography and climate—that the Gulf as a whole can begin to be understood, even as an in-depth look at particular places reveals the impact of these long-term forces.

The Gulf is the world's first and oldest example of globalizing space—and nonimperial at that. Although the beginning of globalization is traditionally placed in the sixteenth century, with the rise of the modern European empires, its history in the Gulf encompasses not just the past five hundred years but instead the past five thousand.[42] The Gulf is therefore very useful for researchers in global history, which is "not [simply] an object of study, but . . . a particular perspective," one whose "distinct approach explores alternative spatialities, is fundamentally relational."[43] Rather than focus almost entirely on empires, global history can also explore the spaces in between, enriching our understanding of human interactions over time. What better place than the Gulf, which has defined its existence and its success as a space between civilizations from the earliest to those more recent, to understand a global past?

The history of the Gulf itself is a slippery subject. Although almost always surrounded by ambitious imperialists, "Gulf people" lack a single imperial history and have never had a common national category. Gulf identity is not defined by a particular state, a single culture, or one religion. It is an identity that is situational, similar to that of the passengers on a ship full of communities that are separate but still loyal to the ship and all wanting to come to their shared destination. In fact, only since the twentieth century and the delineation of oil concessions has the Gulf been divided and confined to defined notions of the nation-state, to borders. Even with these changes, the Gulf remains a crossroads of multiple identities and extraordinary global culture, with cities that seem to be nowhere and everywhere all at once.

The Gulf and its people have adapted to almost five thousand years of long-distance trade and commerce as the region's primary economic activity. Since history's first records were kept, attracting global merchants and merchandise has been the purpose of Gulf ports. Their viability has depended on global economic structures and trends, such as the prices of goods from pearls to petroleum, while these places have been largely independent of imperial authority. The peoples of the Gulf have survived and thrived by promoting and profiting from far-flung interconnections while maintaining their distinctive native communities. They were also among the first to face the tensions brought about by a culture and economy of global networks. The history of the Gulf can therefore show us how to be open to the world while keeping a sense of local meaning and identity.

1 *Dilmun*

From the Beginning of World Trade to the Rise of Islam
(2800 BCE–632 CE)

World trade began on the Gulf. The sailors and merchants who found
their way, some four thousand years ago, from Mesopotamia and the
Indus valley to the city of Dilmun, on what is now the island nation of
Bahrain, must have felt they were reaching paradise. Amazingly,
they would have seen freshwater bubbling up from springs below the
shallow salt water as they approached the harbor. Because these
springs were supremely useful, allowing pearling ships to get freshwater right out of the sea, they were worshipped: immortal underground waters seeming to defy the impossible, and the impotable.
Today they are encircled by stones, the freshwater forming a shim-
mering column as it rises through the heavier, salt-saturated Gulf,
distorting the view of the seabed. When those early merchants
landed in Dilmun, they would have found a green, cultivated island
with safe ports, harbors, and shipyards. Dozens of low, cylindrical
towers and ziggurats, dedicated to the city's early kings, could be
seen in clusters stretching across the island's west.[1] Toward the middle of the island was the temple of Barbar, dedicated to Enki, the
Sumerian god of wisdom and freshwater, and his wife, Ninhursag,
the goddess of fertility and the mountains, where freshwater begins.
In the temple's cella was a sacred well, with steps going down into the
ground to access Enki's "immortal" freshwater, the aquifers that

made their way into the Gulf. Although the entire Arabian Peninsula was wetter at that time than it is now, Dilmun was still fabled for its life-giving springs and underground channels. To sailors, it might have appeared as an emerald jewel on the horizon.

In ancient Sumerian myth, Dilmun was the home of Enki, responsible for the subterranean rivers and streams upon which so much life depended and for bringing freshwater to the land, at the request of the mother goddess Ninhursag. Ancient cuneiform tablets tell us that

> The land Dilmun is pure, the land Dilmun is clean;
> . . . .
> In Dilmun the raven utters no cries,
> . . . .
> The lion kills not,
> The wolf snatches not the lamb
> . . . .
> [From the 'mouth whence issues the water of the earth,' bring thee
>   sweet water from the earth];
> . . . .
> . . . .
> Let thy well of bitter water become a well of sweet water
> . . . .
> Let thy city become the *bank-quay* house of the land[2]

Dilmun was probably not actually a promised land of interspecies peace, but it did provide "sweet water" and respite for the world's first global merchants as they made the hazardous but likely lucrative journey from Mesopotamia to the Indian Ocean. And like other ancient religious sites on the Gulf, it was a vibrant commercial and transit center, a place where traders from different lands, speaking different languages and worshipping different gods, met to exchange goods and boost their fortunes.

After stopping on this island, merchants tended to head for other ports along the Gulf. Some Sumerian traders would journey to Magan, in what is now Oman, bringing great quantities of wheat in exchange for copper or diorite, a precious and durable dark stone.[3] Back in Mesopotamia, diorite was used to fashion sculptures of great Sumerian rulers, such as the pious King Gudea of the twenty-second century BCE, who—depicted seated on his throne, his large hands clasped before him—today peers at visitors inside the Louvre Museum from across the millennia.[4] Other Sumerian traders sailed farther east, through the Strait of Hormuz and past the Gulf of Oman to the rich and sophisticated lands of the Indus Valley Civilization, or went west, to ancient Egypt, a source of gold and silver. They imported copper and precious stones including carnelian beads from the Indus valley. Sometimes ships themselves were the most valuable import of all, dismantled at the quay after their stores were unloaded. Because timber has long been a scarce commodity in the Gulf, this wood was needed for building projects. Reed baskets, textiles, grains, and ceramics were exported from the Gulf. This system of trade was made possible by port cities like Dilmun. Even before the dawn of writing, the Gulf connected the "cradle of civilization," the fertile land of the rivers Tigris and Euphrates, to the Indian Ocean.[5]

The fortunes of ancient Gulf ports changed over the coming centuries: under the Hellenistic and Persian Empires, for example, Gerrha and Charax, which served both the land trade by caravan and the maritime trade by ship, rose in power, while Dilmun lost some of its splendor. But the relative autonomy of Gulf ports endured, as did the broader system of commerce. From the age of Sumeria, the first large-scale civilization on earth, around five thousand years ago, through the rise of the Persian Empire and the conquests of Alexander the Great in the fourth century BCE to the coming of Islam in the seventh century CE, the Gulf connected empires without being fully overtaken by them. Residents and visitors in these cities enjoyed a level of independence which resulted from their own strategic tolerance of cultural difference and mixture, as well as the flexibility and relative freedom of movement that living on the water and away from the centers of imperial power allowed.

The Ancient Gulf

We know about early Gulf cities like Dilmun in part because Mesopotamia, the land between the Tigris and the Euphrates Rivers, was home to the first system of writing. When American and European archaeologists and historians first investigated this region, in the nineteenth and early twentieth centuries, they focused primarily on its connections to biblical stories. While they made clear that the Bible's time line of human origins does not track with geological data, discoveries of lost cities and monuments, tablets, and reliefs have revealed striking similarities to episodes from Genesis and Exodus. This excited the largely Christian public of Europe and the United States, particularly those invested in proving of the accuracy of the Bible. The Gilgamesh myth, for instance, written in cuneiform, tells the story of Utnapishtim, a hero who, like Noah, survives a great inundation. Another story from a tablet includes the legend of a ruler named Sargon of Akkad, who, as a baby, was left in a reed basket by his mother—the inspiration, scholars believe, for the story of Moses:

> My lowly mother conceived me, in secret she brought me forth.
> She set me in a basket of rushes, with bitumen she closed my door;
> she cast me into the river, which (rose) not over me.[6]

As finds such as these were taken from Iraq and placed in collections in the British Museum, the Oriental Institute (now the Institute for the Study of Ancient Cultures, West Asia and North Africa) in Chicago, and other venues, few archaeologists focused on the Gulf or its ancient role in connecting Mesopotamia and the Indian Ocean.

Less mentioned in the Bible, the Gulf was presumed to be a backwater, somewhat empty of history. That attitude changed after the extensive exploitation of oil there brought in large numbers of expatriates—some engaged in industrial development and some familiar with new archaeological and historical methods. Geoffrey Bibby, for one, who had been employed by the Iraq Oil Company in Bahrain in the 1940s, in the 1950s assisted in excavating one of the region's most shattering discoveries: Dilmun. Some scholars argue that this legendary city of "paradise" in the Sumerian myth of Enki and Ninhursag was in lower Mesopotamia, its ruins now lost beneath marshes and palm groves.[7] Instead, Bibby and Bahraini locals showed that it was on what is now a relatively dry Gulf island hit by the harsh winds of the Arabian Desert.[8] Dilmun culture, which was dedicated to merchant trade and exchange, was so influential that it spread to other parts of the Gulf and beyond. Special seals used by merchants at Dilmun and impressed with animals and symbols were also found in excavations in Ur, near modern Basra, and even in the distant Indus River valley. Likewise, personal accounts of merchants from four thousand years ago describe trade among Ur, Dilmun, and a string of cities along the Gulf and into the Indian Ocean. World commerce began in the Gulf, which bridged the ancient desert route to the Mediterranean and the maritime route to the Indian Ocean. To the northwest was the promised land of Canaan and to the southeast the ancient island of paradise mentioned in the Epic of Gilgamesh and called Dilmun.

Soon, more astonishing discoveries were made in other parts of the Gulf. They included the ancient rock tombs of Hili, now in the United Arab Emirates oasis of al-Ain and scattered around the coast of Abu Dhabi. Along with several Bronze Age forts nearby, these testify to a thriving culture from four thousand years ago. Instead of being built for a single, high-ranking person, the large, perfectly cut tombs have shelves for multiple bodies and could reveal the

FIGURE 3. Tomb relief, Hili Archaeological Park, al-ʻAin, United Arab Emirates, 2016. Photo by author.

FIGURE 4. Communal tomb with relief and finely cut stones in Umm al-Nar style, Hili Archaeological Park, al-ʻAin, United Arab Emirates, 2016. Photo by author.

FIGURE 5. Ancient rock art from Musandam, Khor Qida, Oman, 2016. Photo by author.

possible existence of egalitarianism within this ancient society. One tomb has a relief of two human figures holding hands between two oryxes; its meaning has yet to be fully deciphered, but it evokes a group of people united across the great beyond (see figures 3 and 4). This culture is also marked by the use of agricultural infrastructure and a complicated series of channels, now called *aflaj,* to bring lush vegetation to the desert and extend the cultivated land around the oasis.[9] The riches of the Iron Age were widely distributed throughout the Gulf, suggesting that trade, especially in copper and iron, was thriving and benefiting communities on all sides of the region, including those deep in such oases. Wherever archaeologists have looked, such as the most remote mountains and coves of the Musandam Peninsula, the northeastern tip of the Arabian Peninsula, they have found evidence of human habitation and commerce from that period, such as petroglyphs from around four to five thousand years ago depicting trading ships, people on horses, and irrigation channels (see figure 5).

Farther north, many traders set off for the Gulf from Ur in search of copper and other goods. Although today its famed archaeological site is near the modern city of Basra in southern Iraq, Ur was once much closer to the Gulf. Silt carried by the Shatt al-Arab, the channel into which the Tigris and Euphrates Rivers flow, has moved the river delta farther south, but for Ur's residents the Gulf would have been just a few miles downstream. It was the city of the moon god Sin and the capital of a realm now referred to as Sealand, a place of earth and water. Above all, Ur was a city of trade.[10]

Abraham, the patriarch of Jews, Christians, and Muslims alike, is believed to have come from Ur around 2000 BCE.[11] He left not by water to the east but via caravan and nomadic routes overland to Canaan in the west. There, the story goes, he attained prosperity for his family, gained distinction as a prophet of the God of Israel, and founded true monotheism. Although Western tradition often depicts him as a simple Bedouin patriarch, some biblical scholars have speculated that if Abraham did exist, he was probably a merchant with wealth and status. Trading, especially overland, was considered an elite, almost ambassadorial activity, often reserved for princes and requiring special seals and permission from kings.[12] Abraham could have been a second or third prince, eager to establish a new kingdom, perhaps his own dynasty, and to forge lucrative trading links between Babylon and the Mediterranean. It is difficult to determine the exact date when his story emerged: the first written Abraham texts may have been embellished by later, Babylonian Jewish writers who wanted to claim a patriarch from Babylon, not from Egypt (Moses). But ample archaeological evidence about other Ur residents helps us understand the connections between this Sumerian city and points farther afield, including a remarkable four-thousand-year-old cuneiform text that describes the experiences of a Dilmun-based Ur merchant named Ea Nasir, who lived around the same time as the prophet Abraham.[13]

While Abraham went west, Ea Nasir set out to the east, into the Gulf, in search of copper, a metal in high demand. He journeyed first to Dilmun, which controlled the copper trade and had settlements and dependencies as far away as the island of Failaka, off the coast of what is now Kuwait. Ea Nasir went on to travel to India.[14] He was participating in what historians describe as a "world-system," in which distant cities and peoples are linked closely enough by economic exchange that a decline in one will reverberate through and impact the whole.[15] The relics of that world-system include small square and circular clay trading seals, which have been found scattered throughout the Gulf, from Bahrain and the east coast of Saudi Arabia to Failaka Island and Oman, and as far away as the Indus valley (see figure 6). They indicate, Peter Magee writes, "a massive expansion of economic activities centered on Dilmun."[16] Different seals bear scripts from various places, most likely as adaptations to facilitate trade in different markets. They seem to have originated as a Gulf and Indus valley currency, made of ivory, semiprecious stones, or, most commonly, a soapstone called steatite. Elam, a great civilization born on the Zagros Mountains and with access to the Iranian plateau, was part of this trade. The minting of seals caught on there. Clay seals with Elamite inscriptions were recovered from the port and religious site of Liyan, a major—possibly the largest—ancient sanctuary of the Gulf, on the coast of Iran near what is now the city of Bushehr (Bushire).[17] Many other seals include the script of the Harappan civilization, in the Indus valley, a society with major cities, advanced infrastructure including plumbing, and sophisticated forms of artistic expression.[18] Excavations have also discovered gray-green pottery in the intricate "intercultural style," which originated in the Gulf region of Iran and dates from the third millennium to the second millennium BCE, from Syria to the Indus.[19] One such vessel found on

FIGURE 6. Dilmun stamp seal with hunters and goats, early second millennium BCE. Metropolitan Museum of Art, New York. Gift of Martin and Sarah Cherkasky, 1987.

Tarout Island, off the Gulf coast of eastern Arabia, shows two zebus, a type of humped cattle that was a symbol typical of the indus valley culture (see figure 7).

Amazingly, archaeologists have uncovered Ea Nasir's townhouse in Ur, built with the wealth he generated from trade.[20] The structure would have been reached by traversing a warren of narrow alleys winding irregularly around many blind corners. Neighboring abodes were attached to shops or showrooms that probably displayed merchandise. Ea Nasir's walls were made of mud brick and covered in attractive plaster, likely designed to gain attention from passersby. There was a clear hierarchy of houses, reflecting differences of wealth. Some had more rooms or were closer to the temples. Schools were near Ea Nasir's home; perhaps he heard the chanting of children learning their lessons in textbooks found onsite. The temple of Nanna, also near his house and built atop the famous Ziggurat of Ur, which probably inspired the Tower of Babel, housed bureaucratic archives with relevant information about trade and traders. According to its surviving tablets, business was bustling for many. This is reflected in books from a temple accountant, but Ea Nasir seems

FIGURE 7. Vessel with two zebus, 2600–2350 BCE. Found on Tarout Island, Saudi Arabia. Metropolitan Museum of Art, New York. Gift of Mrs. Constantine Sidamon-Eristoff, 2014.

to have suffered some setbacks too. It appears he resorted to subletting—that part of his house had to be sold off and was incorporated into his neighbor's structure. What's more, tablets describing his copper trades include a letter to him from a perturbed customer who asks, "Who is there among the Dilmun traders who has acted against me in this way?"[21] Nevertheless, both Ea Nasir's tablets and temple tablets show that great quantities of goods were being imported to Ur from Dilmun in the 1790s BCE, not only copper but also coral, ivory, carnelian, pearls, and silver. In return, Dilmun received commodities such as cooking oil and especially wool. In the 1780s BCE, a decade after the last of Ea Nasir's known tablets, the Babylonian ruler and lawgiver Hammurabi captured Ur. He and his son, who succeeded him, seem to have cut off trade with Dilmun, whose efforts to maintain its monopoly on the Gulf copper trade came to naught. Generations later, in the middle of the sixth century BCE, the last of the neo-Babylonian kings, a man named Nabonidus, mounted what many consider the first major archaeological restoration. He rebuilt the Ziggurat of Ur and the temple of the moon goddess Nanna, putting his own daughter, the princess Bel Shalti Nannar, in charge as the high priestess.[22] The Ziggurat was as ancient to Nabonidus and his daughter as ancient Rome is to archaeologists working in the twenty-first century, and the king's rebuilding of the temple and reestablishment of the cult of the moon would have been an attempt at renaissance. Although these efforts were successful, they would come to naught against a rising power emerging in the highlands: Persia.

The Classical Gulf

Ur, which was part of the Dilmun Civilization, was an influential port city for thousands of years, but as its access to the Gulf gradually silted up, its residents left, abandoning much of the site by around

500 BCE, not long after the archaeologist king Nabonidus restored its Ziggurat and temple of Nanna. Meanwhile, monumental events in Persia and Greece were shaping the history of Eurasia, with the Gulf at the crossroads. Built on the model of the prosperous temple-port, new cities were founded: Charax, in the marshland, and Gerrha, on the eastern coast of Arabia. They joined the network linking the Gulf to India, first proved by Dilmun at its main site on Bahrain and at Ur.

The sixth century BCE was a turning point in the Gulf and in world history. The first true "king of kings," Cyrus the Great of Persia, established a new way of ruling his vast realm. He demanded tribute from the peoples he subjected but was strategically tolerant of religious and cultural differences, which helped him maintain and expand his heterogeneous empire. The Persians conquered Babylon and exiled the king Nabonidus without a fight. They did not, however, destroy the carefully restored temple of Nanna. Archaeologists have discovered bricks in the temple of Nanna with the mark of Cyrus, who ordered this shrine of his enemy, Nabonidus, to be rebuilt and restored after his conquest. Cyrus asked his workers to leave an inscription on the wall saying, "The great gods have delivered all the lands into my hands."[23] This was a major innovation—some would say the invention of empire as a polity with many peoples and many gods. In the past, the defeat of a king meant the defeat of his god and often the razing of his temple as well. Instead, Cyrus claimed to be the beneficiary of all the gods, no matter the culture or place from which they came. In this way, he made the first great step toward a true multiethnic, heterogeneous empire—an umbrella over cultural and religious differences.

Cyrus famously released the Jews from their Babylonian captivity and returned what had been stolen from their Jerusalem temple. For this he is recognized as a savior in the Hebrew Bible, which calls him the messiah, the deliverer. In the Old Testament, Artaxerxes, who came after Cyrus and continued many of his tolerant policies, sends his Jewish cup-bearer Nehemiah from Babylon with an armed guard and timbers from the royal forests to rebuild the walls of Jerusalem.[24] The Jews were not alone in receiving Persian largesse. Cyrus financed the building of new temples to many gods all along the Tigris River. Of course, not all Persian rulers were quite as enlightened: even Cyrus's son Cambyses II ridiculed the Egyptian gods and destroyed their temples. Overall, however, a policy of strategic tolerance, within limits, allowed the Persians to prosper. They controlled far more lands, known by archaeologists as the Achaemenid Empire, and were far more successful than previous powers, such as the Assyrians, who often tried to displace, exile, and outright extinguish their enemies. What's more, the Persians created institutions, such as an ancient postal service and a system of satrapies, or regions, that enabled them to maintain most of their laws and customs even far from the imperial center.[25]

Some fifty years after Cyrus, Xerxes I also created a great multiethnic army, including Arabs and other peoples from the Gulf, and invaded the Aegean to try to crush the Greeks.[26] Unfamiliar with the geography and unprepared for the organized defiance of a group of city-states, he was unexpectedly defeated. The Greeks, by stopping the Persian advance into the eastern Mediterranean, were gaining power. Alexander the Great of Macedon, who had been tutored by the philosopher Aristotle, sought to extend that power. He tried being a deity in many guises and a king of the world, wanting, like Cyrus and the other Persian monarchs, to universalize his rule. That meant pushing into Persian territory and exploring whether the Gulf might be conquered to control the lucrative trade to India. After defeating Darius III of Persia at Gaugamela in 331 BCE, Alexander ended the Achaemenid Empire and absorbed its vast, varied lands. Not satisfied with this victory, he kept moving toward India. There he finally stalled, but his victories left a Greek imprint on south and central Asian cultures and arts that remains to this day. In the literature of

Persia and in the Qur'an, for example, the righteous ruler Dhul-Qarnayn seems to be a version of Alexander, known for building legendary gates to control the frightful "Gog and Magog" steppe barbarians and prevent them from invading the "civilized" world.

After Alexander's death, in Babylon in 323 BCE, his empire, so large and varied that it proved unwieldy, was divided among his generals. Seleucus Nicator (the Victor) took the title of *basileus* (king) and founded the Seleucid Empire, which extended over much of the Asian territory that Alexander had conquered. Seleucus founded a new port on the Gulf, near ancient Ur and what is now Basra, called, of course, Alexandria. Later, this Alexandria on the Gulf was renamed as the "palisade" or "Charax" Spasinu, in the combination of Greek and ancient Aramaic spoken by the polyglot Arab and other merchants and traders who crowded into the city. As the Seleucid Empire fragmented in its turn, Charax became the capital of a semi-independent Gulf kingdom called Characene, which lasted from around 150 BCE to 200 CE and managed to wield authority over large parts of Mesopotamia. During its heyday, this city was a hybrid, loosely governed, cosmopolitan zone, open to trade and merchants.[27]

When the Parthian Iranians came to replace the Greek Seleucids as the local imperial rulers, the marshes stopped them from holding complete dominion over Charax for long periods. Nor were they able to harness the power of the Gulf writ large. In fact, the Persians' failure to fully harness Gulf ports may have prevented them from breaking out of their geographic constraints while battling Rome, whose empire expanded eastward in the first and second centuries CE as its navy gained mastery of the Mediterranean. Only Ardashir, one of the Persian rulers to accurately boast of some command over multiple parts of the Gulf, briefly ended Charax's independence, in the third century CE, and even then he faced revolts by the Attalae, the predecessors of the Marsh Arabs.[28] The Romans had no better luck at dominating the Gulf route. Although Trajan (d. 117) received the submission of Charax's ruler Athambelus, it was largely symbolic, and largely temporary. Hadrian, Trajan's successor, wisely moved the Roman Empire's eastern boundary back around Palestine and the Mediterranean. He foresaw the challenges of maintaining the Roman army in far-flung, rebellion-prone regions such as Mesopotamia.

Largely freed from imperial dominion, Charax was connected to the Mediterranean and all the way to the Palatine Hill in the heart of the city of Rome through Palmyra, now in Syria, a semi-independent kingdom ruled in the third century CE by Queen Zenobia. Trading representatives who also acted as diplomats went between Palmyra and Charax, negotiating transport and logistics. One of these was Isidore of Charax, who combined his experiences with knowledge gained from merchants passing through his home city to write a "world geography" that was famous as far away as Rome. The Roman emperor Augustus chose a Charax-born merchant named Dionysius as the chaperone for his grandson Gaius Caesar on an expedition into Armenia and Arabia. The North African Berber king Juba II (Cleopatra's son-in-law) also went on an expedition with Gaius, keeping an eye on him as they traveled into Arabia. His descriptions provided material for Pliny the Elder.[29] Pliny was killed by the eruption of Vesuvius near Pompeii, in whose ruins archaeologists later discovered a statue of the Indian goddess Lakshmi made in Bokhardan, India.[30] While there is no proof that it came through Charax, this artwork was undoubtedly obtained through the trade in luxuries from India and probably dates to around the time of Augustus.[31] It arrived in Rome via the Gulf or the Red Sea. In return, archaeologists have shown, glass vessels flowed from the eastern Mediterranean back into the Gulf from the second century BCE.[32]

The Gulf was not just a conduit, however. It was also the source of an important luxury. Gulf pearls were a primary export from the Charax region, and one fragment from Isidore's geography describes islands surrounded by banks "where many pearls are found; and . . . round about the island there are rafts made of reeds, from which men dive into the sea to a depth of 20 fathoms and bring up double-shelled oysters."[33] Moreover, ancient writers knew about Gulf oil long before companies starting prospecting for it in the early twentieth century. The Gulf's oil sands, *asphaltus,* were an important commodity, as the Greek geographer Strabo reported:

> Eratosthenes states . . . that there is a fountain of [dry] asphalt near the Euphrates River; and that when this river is at its flood at the time of the melting of the snows, the fountain of asphalt is also filled and overflows into the river; and that large clods of asphalt are formed which are suitable for buildings constructed of baked bricks. Other writers say that the liquid kind also is found in Babylonia. Now writers state in particular the great usefulness of the dry kind in the construction of buildings, but they also say that boats are woven with reeds and, when plastered with asphalt, are impervious to water.[34]

Strabo also described the paths of merchants who would pass through the narrow neck of the Gulf and go on to Terendon, near what became Basra, and then to Gerrha, a caravan city on the coast of what is now eastern Saudi Arabia that served a purpose similar to Dilmun's. Gerrha was led by independent chiefs and became wealthy from trade by both land and water, especially in spices from the east and in the frankincense from Yemen and Oman used in pagan temples and Christian churches. Strabo wrote that the Gerrhaeans "have become richest of all; and they have a vast equipment of both gold and silver articles, such as couches and tripods and bowls, together with drinking-vessels and very costly houses; for doors and walls and ceilings are variegated with ivory and gold and silver set with precious stones."[35] Gerrha's wealth, autonomy, and strategic location on the Gulf shore made it a target of the Seleucid king Antiochus III, who ruled Persia. He had a long reign, from the middle of the third to the beginning of the second century BCE. A letter from a Gerrha chief implored him to let the city remain independent: "Destroy not, O King, those two things which have been given us of the gods—perpetual peace and freedom."[36] For its liberty Gerrha paid Antiochus precious gems and silver; these riches, along with a survey of the coast, which was hard to approach because of its shallow waters and seemed not to offer many opportunities for extensive settlement, convinced him to abandon his plans. The would-be conqueror sailed home, and Gerrha remained a cosmopolitan meeting point between Greek, Persian, and Arab cultures. People from places as disparate as Greece, India, Africa, and Babylon mixed freely there. Business was conducted between ship captains from Oman or India and Arab merchants who took the caravan route from Gerrha through the desert and to the Mediterranean.

Greek, Persian, Arab, and Indian Ocean influences likewise converged on Failaka Island. Strabo tells us that this island, called "Icarus" in his day, had "a temple sacred to Apollo in it and an oracle of Tauropolus [Artemis]."[37] One of its temples, probably the one dedicated to Apollo, still embodies in stone an architectural order largely unknown in the West, a combination of Ionic and Persian. While the columns are crowed by classic scrolled capitals, they have fluted Persian bases. Such mixed Failaka styles of architecture are evidence of the meeting of East and West, what archaeologists call a "pastiche" of Asian and Greek cultures.[38]

The Gulf style, however, was far more than a mere pastiche. The melding of cultures created real opportunities for exchange in a region that was a crossroads for Arab, Greek, and Persian peoples well into the late antique period. At the geopolitical fault line between the Christian empire of Byzantium and Zoroastrian Persia, the Gulf became a destination for those fleeing persecution as well as those pursuing wealth. Most of the world history of Christianity has wrongly confined it to Europe and the Americas. In fact, especially in the third and fourth centuries, it was as much a pan-Asian and Middle Eastern faith as a Mediterranean one, spread by "heretical" groups who were exiled from Byzantium and Rome but found homes in central Asia and around the Gulf. In the fourth century, the Council of Nicaea conceived of God and Jesus as being of the same essence, and those who disagreed were eventually expelled from the churches that accepted Nicene Christianity, the official religion of Rome and Constantinople. One such group was the Nestorians, who were declared heretical by the Council of Ephesus in 431, banished from the Byzantine Empire, and settled in a tolerant and remote area on the Gulf's desert shore.

Meanwhile, the Sassanians, who had replaced the Parthians in Persia, were fighting with Rome and Byzantium for domination of trading routes from the Gulf and the Red Sea. But where the Roman and Byzantine emperors struggled to enforce particular Christian doctrine and to handle religious conflict between Christian and non-Christian communities in their domains, the Sassanians, practicing a form of Zoroastrianism that was primarily reserved for the elite, allowed most of the population under them to observe their own faiths—something close to the strategic tolerance of Cyrus the Great. The era of relative Persian dominance and tolerance lasted for almost half a millennium, from around the third century to the middle of the seventh. Persia's hold on at least some of the Gulf was occasionally threatened—by Rome under Trajan in the second century and by Byzantium under Heraclius in the seventh—but it managed to remain the local behemoth before the coming of Islam. That was possible, in part, because of its approach to religion. In Rome, the emperor was invested in doctrinal unity, and the Christianity of the Nicene Creed was focused on conversion. Sassanian Persian rulers, on the other hand, had little reason to engage in the theological squabbles between their Christian subjects. Instead, the Sassanian state religion was Zoroastrianism, an ancient faith already more than a thousand years old, rooted in the teachings of the prophet Zoroaster. His exact date of birth remains highly disputed, but he likely lived in the second millennium BCE, and in any case his writings and ideas were well established by the sixth century BCE, when Zoroastrianism became Persia's official religion under Cyrus the Great. The Gathas, a major Zoroastrian religious text, explains the human condition, particularly sin, evil, and suffering, as result of a cosmic struggle between good and evil, light and darkness, birth and decay. Light is the god Ahura Mazda, whose symbol is eternal fire. Ahriman represents darkness and death. There is a balance between these forces, but good will ultimately prevail. On the whole, the Sassanians allowed Jews, Christians, and members of other religious groups to fill important administrative roles, such as translator and diplomat. Some Nestorian bishops, for example, were paid and sponsored by the Sassanians, ensuring their ability to move throughout the Persian Empire and beyond.[39] Nestorians were persecuted by the Byzantine and Roman churches, but in the Gulf, under the Persian shahs, they had more—if not total—liberty.

Ardashir the Unifier founded the Sassanian dynasty in the first half of the third century, and his new empire managed to claim some command over the Gulf, thanks in part to the use of fortified ports. This was an attempt at monitoring trade that had been tried but not very successfully by previous empires. Perhaps the most important imperial Persian fort on the Gulf was Bandar Bushehr, which Ardashir built on the site of ancient Elamite Liyan. It provided access to the great Persian trading cities of Kazerun and Shiraz, allowing Sassanian trade to flourish. Elsewhere on the Persian coast, coins and remains of a fort have been found in Siraf, and there were Persian outposts on Kharg Island and at Kujaran Ardashir, near what is now Bandar i Lengeh. But even these explicitly imperial Gulf ports, founded by the shah, were never entirely Persian: they depended on

relationships between Persians and Arabs that could be both contentious and complementary. For example, the pre-Islamic hero Malik
ibn Fahim defied the Persians and forced them to recognize Arab
rights over much of Oman, and the Persians and the Arabs agreed at
various times before the seventh century to a form of shared administration of ports such as Julfar (in what is now the United Arab Emirates), as the Arabs were dominant in the surrounding country and the
Persians did not want to be constantly harried by raids. Better to join
with the Arabs in joint rule than to put up the resources necessary to
avoid constant siege.[40]

When the Persians tried to collect taxes, Gulf residents and mariners, both Arab and non-Arab, would take advantage of geography
to evade them. They could disappear into the mountains and desert
oases, set up alternative ports nearby, make deals with Persians in
other ports, or sail to distant trading centers in the Indian Ocean—at
least until a weaker ruler was in charge. This meant that the Persians
could not entirely extinguish the Arab presence in the Gulf or bend
the main Arab rulers and tribes to their will. For centuries, though,
the Sassanids maintained preeminence, but far from outright control, in the Gulf region.

The fourth-century Roman writer Ammianus Marcellinus was
well acquainted with the bustle of the Gulf: "All along the coast is a
throng of cities and villages, and many ships sail to and from." [41] However, ever since Hadrian had withdrawn the empire from Trajan's unwieldy Babylonian conquests in the second century, the Romans had
primarily used the alternative Red Sea route, with Ethiopia as a trading partner. The Sassanids, wanting to force this trade through the
Gulf, in response supported the Himyar Yemenis, who defeated the
pro-Roman Ethiopian Christians and their Arab Christian allies at
Mecca in the famous Battle of the Elephant mentioned in the Qur'an.
This war seems to have diverted merchants eastward and accelerated
trade through the Gulf, benefiting the Persians after all.

The Sassanids were interested in trade not only with the west. They also established concessions in Sri Lanka and Malaysia, and silver coins from the reign of Kawad I, in the early sixth century, have been found in Guangdong, China, having arrived via land and sea routes.[42] Persian horses were in demand around the Indian Ocean, and the Persians traded in Chinese silk, which came through the Central Asian realms that the Turks were increasingly conquering. Toward the middle of the sixth century, the Byzantine emperor Justin II again tried to go around the Gulf—the *qaghan* (an ancient word for *khan*) of the Turks in eastern Persia wanted to sell silk directly to the Byzantine Empire, bypassing the realm of the Persian shah. Both qaghan and shah were hungry for Byzantine gold.[43] The Byzantines had repeatedly banned the import of any silk that came through Persia and tried to have it made in and sent from India instead, but the tactic failed: illegal imports did not stop, and the logistics of connecting directly with India were too hard to manage.[44]

The Persian army, confident in its fortresses on the Gulf's mountainous shore, occasionally pressed into the desert realm of Arabia. During the fourth century, for instance, the Sassanian ruler Shapur II sent an expedition to Oman to punish Arab nomads who had raided a Persian base. The Persians then went after the Banu Tamim tribe, a group of Arabs who lived on the Gulf shore and had been blamed for attacks on Persian commerce and trade routes through the region. Among other things, the Persian troops destroyed vital wells needed for watering date plantations. Shapur's punitive campaigns finally reached Medina, deep in Arabia, the city that would later be ruled by the Prophet Muhammad and finally serve as his burial place. The Sassanian ruler also built a wall against the Arabs at al-Hira in Iraq and attempted to deport Arab tribes en masse to Persia.[45]

Shapur was forced into a defensive position as well. The defiantly pagan Roman emperor Julian, called the Apostate in Christian sources for refusing to embrace Christianity, tried to revive the pre-

Christian Roman Empire and defeat the Persians. As is always the case for would-be conquerors of Babylon, going downstream is the easy part. Julian personally led the Roman army to many heroic victories as it traveled along the Euphrates and the Tigris, but he failed to seal his conquest and take the Sassanian capital of Ctesiphon. At a strategic disadvantage, Shapur ordered canals cut and dams destroyed. The Roman army, unprepared to haul itself back up the river, suffered a disastrous defeat at the battle of Samarra on the Tigris, during which Julian was killed, ending the dream of a pagan revival. Even Shapur, however, who vanquished Rome's last pagan emperor, knew it was better not to fight the Marsh Arabs in their own backyard and, although he was one of the most powerful of Persian rulers, realized it was better to conclude treaties with the Arabs on the Gulf coast, giving them autonomy rather than attempting to crush them.

A couple of centuries later, the Persian ruler Khosrow I, also known as Anushirvan, or "Immortal soul," signed the Perpetual Peace with the Byzantine emperor Justinian I. To maintain the borders of his empire, Anushirvan formed alliances with some Arab tribes. Later Arabic texts describe him as a model of majesty, a wise administrator, and a philosopher king.[46] He built a great university and center of learning at Gundeshapur, accessible from the Gulf. He founded the *bimaristan*, one of the first kinds of hospital with wards, halls divided by type of disease. Some Arab writers believed the game of chess was invented in India to establish the relationship between its king and Anushirvan. Burzurgmihr, the main magus, or wise man and minister of his court, appears in later Islamic mirrors for princes, a genre of texts written to advise rulers. Anushirvan's Perpetual Peace, however, did not in fact last forever. Instead, the rivalry between the Sassanians and the Byzantines erupted into conflict, with Arabia in the middle of the two great powers.

Before the rise of Islam, the Arab tribes existed in a kind of tenuous borderland, pulled either to the east by Persia or the west by

Byzantium and lacking their own unified leadership. Byzantine emperors paid Ghassanid clients in the west of Arabia to fight frontier battles against the Persians and to ensure the security of their caravans. Persians likewise used the Lakhamid Arabs, based in the city of al-Hira in eastern Arabia, as allies in border skirmishes and wars with Byzantium. Their nearly constant rivalry destabilized both empires to the point that, when a new prophet unified Arabia, the Arabs managed to defeat both imperial behemoths. Arabia, Mesopotamia, and the Gulf were no longer war zones between Greeks and Persians, as the lines of battle shifted to the east and the west. Soon at the heart of the empire of Islam, the Gulf presented new opportunities: it was the launching point for the Arab conquests to the wealthy east.

Islam Comes to the Gulf

"Recite! In the Name of your Lord who created humanity from a blood clot" (Qur'an 96). The first revelations to Muhammad, brought down by the archangel Gabriel around 610 while the Prophet was meditating in the Cave of Hira outside Mecca, struck him with such power that he felt almost paralyzed. Each of the verses, which were eventually written down in the Qur'an, seemed to communicate a revolutionary idea from God. Chief among these were the absolute unity of God (Allah) alone and the need for a community—called *umma* in Arabic—that, despite its members being from very different economic, tribal, and cultural backgrounds, was united by belief. In 622—year 0 of the Islamic, or hijri, calendar—Muhammad and his followers left persecution by the polytheist merchant rulers of Mecca, the Quraysh, and went north to the palm-filled oasis city of Medina. In fact, Muhammad was a member of the Quraysh tribe, but he was orphaned in his youth and became alienated from Quraysh society. According to tradition, Muhammad was welcomed as a mediator and lawgiver by the various Jewish and pagan tribes in Medina, where he created the pillars of Islamic practice and belief. (These included rules for conversion; the *shahada,* the profession of faith, "There is no God but God and Muhammad is his prophet"; and the requirements of praying five times a day, giving alms, fasting during Ramadan, and waging war against polytheists.) He forced conversion upon polytheists and believers in tribal deities and punished members of some Jewish tribes who did not agree with his view of God, whom Muhammad claimed to be the God of Abraham. Yet he also allowed other Arab Jews and Christians to continue to practice their faiths when they agreed to his authority and did not come into direct conflict with him. The Prophet eventually defeated the elite Quraysh in 630, establishing himself as the ruler of Mecca, where he cleaned the tribal idols out of the Kaaba, the temple in the middle of the city, and gave sermons calling for the embrace of Islam by all. This idea of a universal community of believers, based not on a chosen people or race but on belief in the revelations to the Prophet, the Qur'an, as the indisputable words of God (not written by Muhammad but revealed by God himself), combined with the highly charismatic leadership and example of the Prophet, a great warrior, statesman, and religious leader, lit a fire of faith and political change. Later, Islam was adopted by increasingly diverse groups of people traveling through Arabia in caravans connecting Mecca and Medina to the Red Sea, the Indian Ocean, the Gulf, and the Mediterranean.

Islamic tradition holds that most of Arabia, including the Gulf, submitted to the Prophet's control during his lifetime. Arabic-speaking historians have called 630 "the year of the embassies," when Muhammad sent envoys and letters out to the whole peninsula to convince the rulers there to accept his authority. A version of one of these letters, dispatched to Iyas and Jafar, princes of Oman, and to Munzir ibn Sawa, then the Tamimi Arab governor of Bahrain, is currently housed in the Beit al Quran, or "House of the Qur'an," Museum in Hoora, Bahrain, with the apparent seal of the Prophet still intact:

In the name of Allah, the Beneficent, the Merciful: From Muham-mad the Messenger of Allah to Munzir bin Sawa, may peace be on you! I praise Allah, who is one and there is none to be worshiped ex-cept Him. I bear evidence that there is no God but Allah and that Mu-hammad is a servant of Allah and His Prophet. . . . My messengers have highly praised your behavior. You shall continue in your present office. You should remain faithful to Allah and his Prophet. I accept your recommendation regarding the people of Bahrain. I forgive the offenses of the offenders. Therefore, you may also forgive them of the people of Bahrain whoever want to continue in their Jewish or Majusi [Zoroastrian] faith, should be made to pay *Jizia* [a tax on Jews, Christians, and Zoroastrians].[47]

Unfortunately, few of the sources dated to the period of Muham-mad's life are considered reliable, and many of the details of that life were orally transmitted and not written down until centuries after his death in 632. Although these letters, which exist in many Gulf coun-tries, often written in a script that mimics early Arabic, may be based on earlier versions, there are scholars who question their historical authenticity.[48] What's more, we know that the spread of Islam to the Gulf was a complex and complicated affair. As this letter suggests, and as sources such as the early writer al-Baladhuri indicate, while Arabic speakers converted, Zoroastrians, Jews, and Christians re-mained in large numbers along the Gulf. Yet it is also clear that news of the Prophet and his success spread quickly there and that many Arab leaders were both inspired by his message and eager to liberate themselves from the Persian Empire. Allegiance to the Prophet made political sense.

Soon after the Prophet's death, many of the Bedouin, his former followers east of Mecca, began to rebel against Islam's new leader, the caliph. New prophets and even prophetesses, such as Sajah bint al-Harith ibn Suayd of the Tamimi Arabs, emerged to challenge the burgeoning faith. Although historical traditions imply that the Prophet's first successor, Abu Bakr, put down these rebellions during his brief reign, there are glimpses from later historians that the Gulf did not submit quickly or uniformly to the early Islamic caliphs, let alone the later imperial Muslim dynasties of the Umayyads and ʿAbbasids. The caliphs were soon engaged in a series of divisive battles, called *fitnas* in Arabic, concerning who was qualified to rule the Muslim community as a whole. These disputes created the first divisions among Shiʿa, Sunni, Ibadi, and other Islamic groups. The Shiʿa were the Shiʿat ʿAli, or "Party of ʿAli," supporters of the Prophet's cousin and son-in-law, whom they believed should have been chosen as the first caliph, or political and spiritual leader of Muslims—not Abu Bakr or ʿUmar, who were, respectively, the first and second, although not as closely related to the Prophet, and certainly not ʿUthman, the third, who was seen as a nemesis of the "Party of ʿAli." ʿUthman was accused of wanting to reestablish the aristocratic ways of the Quraysh, the Prophet's old enemies in Mecca, in the wake of his fantastically successful conquests in Persia, Egypt, and the Syrian provinces of Byzantium and the resulting flow of riches and prosperity into Mecca and Medina.

ʿAli was finally named the fourth caliph, after ʿUthman was killed. Many people, including ʿAʾisha bint Abi Bakr, the Prophet's youngest wife, accused ʿAli and his followers of ʿUthman's murder. At that point, the dispute over succession shifted westward from the Hijaz, the land of Mecca and Medina in eastern Arabia, toward lower Mesopotamia and the Gulf. As the staging ground for Islam's eastern conquests, it was Basra, not Mecca or Medina, that increasingly received their wealth, and ʿAʾisha fought pitched battles against ʿAli nearby. She was of the party of believers eventually called the Sunnis, or followers of the sunna, the example of the Prophet. ʿAli was assassinated in 661 in Kufa, a city now in Iraq, by a disaffected acolyte. The latter had left his party after ʿAli agreed to mediation to end the battle of Siffin against the Sunnis led by the wily general Mu'awiya in 657. Moreover, after a council of selected elders decided in favor of the Sunnis and Mu'awiya, a number of people broke away from both the Sunnis and the Shi'a, declaring that descent should have no bearing on who would be the leader, the imam, of the Muslim community. This group later moved to Oman and called themselves Ibadis. For the remaining Shi'a, the death of 'Ali was a major tragedy, alleviated by the hope that Hussein, his son and a grandson of the Prophet, might restore their dream of leadership. Hussein, however, fought a losing battle against the increasingly powerful Sunnis and was martyred, along with his band of followers, by the caliph Yazid I on the plains of Karbala in Iraq. The Shi'a have never forgotten that a Sunni caliph killed the Prophet's grandson, whose death they still commemorate with an annual ritual reenactment on 'Ashura, the tenth of Muharram. At the time, although many remained in Iraq, a number made their way down along the Gulf, on the eastern Arabian desert shore, where they could take advantage of the geographic challenges that the Gulf naturally posed and continue to cause problems for the Sunni caliphs in Damascus and later Baghdad.

The Gulf, therefore, with its geographic extremes, allowed Muslim groups to remain separate. Even so, the divisions between them did not make all contact or trade impossible. These differences were often fluid, and the importance of sectarianism in Islamic history can be overstated. The Arabic Qur'an is the core and holy book, the primary source of law and guide of faith, for all Muslims, and most of the hadith, the sayings of the Prophet that became a basis for Islamic law, are common to all as well. Members of all major sects go on hajj, or pilgrimage, to Mecca. Also, a large majority of Muslims follow one of the Sunni schools. Thus, while sectarianism may have divided Muslims politically, Islam as an overall culture had not been indelibly fractured. Instead, its conflicts were, and continue to be, between groups that interpret the religion differently but nonetheless share an aim: Islam's political unity under a single legitimate authority. As centuries passed and this dream faltered and failed, Muslims switched their focus to the idea of unity within the faith (*tawhid* in Arabic) and to the adjustments needed to take Islam from a primarily Arab context into the highly diverse cultural contexts of the rest of Asia. This allowed Islam as a culture, if not as a unified polity, to spread along the Silk Roads and across the Indian Ocean. As the next chapter will demonstrate, the Gulf was the staging ground for the creation of this cosmopolitan Islam.

The Gulf's story of political autonomy continued after the coming of Islam. An autonomous liminal maritime zone, the region adapted to this event just as it had adapted to previous great shifts in history, with a process that built on preexisting lifestyles and norms. The Arabs of the Gulf used their naval prowess, their connection to external markets such as India and Zanzibar, and the protection of the mountains, deserts, and marshes to avoid direct rule from Medina, Damascus, and Baghdad, the Islamic Empire's first three capital cities. Oman, which became home to the distinctive Ibadi community during Islam's first centuries, exemplified the role of the Gulf as a nursery of distinction. Abu Zaid, whom Muhammad sent to convert Oman, found its princes 'Abd and Jaifar on the coast at Sohar, engaged in long-distance trade. They accepted the Prophet's message, but after his death a group of Omani Azd Arabs rebelled against Caliph Abu Bakr, following a "false prophet" named Dabba.[49] Next, the Mahra tribe, famous for their large, dark camels from the Dhofar region, revolted against the Prophet's successors, but supporters of the caliphs soon defeated them. All the main Omani tribes eventually paid zakat, or charity, to Medina, even if they were mostly left to their own devices.[50] Then the 'Abbasid caliph Harun al-Rashid (who appears in *One Thousand and One Arabian Nights* as the ruler who threatens to slay the storyteller Scheherazade) sent a rapacious and oppressive governor to Oman. The Omanis rose up, refusing to pay homage or tax to Baghdad. Many adopted Ibadism, which rejects both the Shi'ite notion that Islam's leader should be a descendant of 'Ali and the Sunni idea of the caliphate in favor of the authority of the imam, who is elected by all the able Muslim males of a certain age in the community. Far from seeing themselves as having broken from Islam, the Ibadi claim to maintain the original spirit and intention of Islam as practiced by the Prophet.[51] They have not only survived multiple attempts to wipe them out or force them to submit to more centralized rule or to other Islamic legal and theological traditions but also formed a crucial trading network, merchants of faith who spread throughout the Indian Ocean.[52] Ibadis continue to make up a majority of the Omani population today, even though they are a small minority of all Muslims.

Far from instantly becoming Muslim, the Gulf continued as a home to polytheism during Islam's first century. Paganism and other pre-Islamic traditions, including the worship of horses and veneration of deities related to fresh underground waters, like Enki, did not immediately disappear. The historian al-Baladhuri describes the Asbadhi tribe in eastern Arabia as "horse worshippers." When Muhammad sent a man to govern the lands of Bahrain and Hajar, the coast of Arabia opposite Bahrain, the number of Magian Zoroastrians there was so extensive that, according to al-Baladhuri, the Prophet wrote directly to them, inviting them to Islam but also suggesting that Muslims could not marry their women or eat their food. Muslim men could, however, marry Christian or Jewish women. Large numbers of Jews and Zoroastrians, perhaps representing the merchants between the city walls as opposed to the Bedouin outside, who had already accepted Islam, paid the jizya, a tax on nonbelievers, instead of converting. A sizable amount of revenue, eighty thousand dirhams, was thus sent to Muhammad, "more than which sum the Prophet never received either before or after."[53] Following his death, however, Bahrain and Hajar also began to rebel against the caliphs, and new prophets promised to make these lands the center of pilgrimage and power. One named al-Hutam emerged, and many followed him until he was killed at a fort in Bahrain. Others favored Musaylima, whom later Muslim sources brand "the liar," before he died in the same year as Muhammad, 632. Musaylima was the most famous of the so-called false prophets who led tribally based resistance to Muhammad's spiritual authority. He declared his tribe, the Haniat, equal to the Quraysh, the tribe of the Prophet's family.[54] Later, a group of Zoroastrians on the Gulf coast refused to pay taxes to Mecca. Such signs of outright resistance to Islamic rule appear over and over again in the historical sources, even in those sympathetic to the religion.

Although Bahrain and the eastern coast of Arabia eventually gave tribute to the caliphs as their capital moved from Medina to Damascus to Baghdad, a new rebellion emerged in Bahrain and along the desert Gulf in the late ninth century, threatening to overturn the entire Islamic world. The Qarmatians (also called Carmathians) were founded by Hamdan Qarmat. Distinguishing themselves from elite landowners and imperial overlords and perhaps even trying to create a separate form of Islam based on Gulf and east Arabian norms, the Qarmatians deliberately disobeyed many standard Muslim precepts: women were unveiled, polygamy was outlawed, and men and women interacted freely with each other. Women weavers were an important source of revenue for the Qarmatians, who demanded a full fifth of the value of their products to contribute to the common purse.[55] Later, Qarmat's successor, the Persian Abu Said al-Jannabi, established a Qarmatian state, with its capital at Hasa (now in Saudi Arabia's Eastern Province). He attracted the date growers of the marshes of southern Iraq and Bedouin in northeast Arabia who had lost control of trade and no longer received subsidies from conquests. Al-Jannabi proclaimed 912/13 (300 in the hijra calendar) to be the beginning of the apocalypse, and his followers attacked pilgrim caravans, assassinated governors, and even threatened Baghdad. The motivations for this rebellion were economic as well as religious. The Qarmatians wanted access to Basra, in addition to their port in Bahrain, in order to get a cut of the lucrative Gulf trade into the Indian Ocean. They also wished to capture a portion of the revenue from the hajj by diverting pilgrims from Mecca to eastern Arabia.[56]

In the tenth century, a Qarmatian raiding party led by al-Jannabi's son Abu Tahir stole the Black Stone from the Kaaba, the square structure at the heart of Mecca, where it had been placed by the Prophet himself. Most Arab tribes worshipped stones before Muhammad arrived, and many continued the practice into the Islamic era. According to *The Book of Idols*, "Arabs called these stones baetyls (*anṣāb*). Whenever these stones resembled a living form, they called them idols (*aṣnām*) and images (*awthān*). The act of circumambulating them they called circumrotation (*dawār*)."[57] In Mecca, walking around the Kaaba is a devotional practice, part of the hajj. The Black Stone was both sacred and—as the traveler Nasir-i Khusraw, who visited Hasa between 1046 and 1052, called it—"a human magnet."[58] The Qarmatians of the Gulf took the stone to eastern Arabia because they were upset that the tribes of Mecca had a monopoly on it. They returned it only after receiving a huge ransom from the 'Abbasid caliphs.[59]

The Qarmatians extended their power from their independent state to the island of Bahrain in the tenth century and controlled the pearl fisheries along the east Arabian coast. Nasir-i Khusraw describes their capital, Hasa, as "a really splendid town," encircled by "strong walls," equipped with many wells, and protected by about "twenty thousand soldiers." He was struck by the Qarmatians' interpretation of Islam, which "relieved them of the obligations of prayer and fasting," on the orders of their founder, who declared himself "the ultimate authority on such matters." They awaited the return of this Mahdi, "who would bring about the end of time, and kept a horse

with a special crown tied up . . . to welcome his return."⁶⁰ When nearing death, "he directed that six of his [spiritual] sons should maintain
his role with justice and equity and without dispute among themselves until he should come again. Now they have a huge palace that
is the seat of state, and a throne accommodates all six kings in one
place, and they rule in complete accord and harmony. They also have
six viziers, and when the kings are all seated on their throne, the six
viziers are seated opposite on a bench." There seemed to be almost a
communal aspect to the economy, at least among Arab men, as "all
affairs are handled in mutual consultation," although they also "had
thirty thousand Zanzibari and Abyssinian slaves working in the fields
and orchards."⁶¹ As their pearl trading and mercantile focus grew, the
Qarmatians became more accommodating of difference, even favoring the settling of strangers: "Any stranger to the city who possesses
a craft by which to earn his livelihood is given enough money to buy
the tools of his trade and establish himself, when he repays however
much he was given." By the eleventh century, they even tolerated
non-Qarmatian forms of Islam: "They do not prevent anyone from
performing prayers, although they themselves do not pray." Also, a
non-Qarmatian Persian "named Ali Ibn Ahmad, who was a Muslim,
a pilgrim, and very wealthy, built a mosque in order to provide for pilgrims who arrived in the city."⁶²

In their ports, the people of the Gulf maintained their distance
from imperial power, allowing trade and commerce to take prece-
dence over religious orthodoxy and creating a distinctive form of
cosmopolitanism that propagated diversity within Islam and accepted different communities of faith. Ironically, however, it was the
Gulf's proximity to centers of power that made it a perfect setting for
exciting intellectual and cultural developments. The rise of Islam
may have even increased the Gulf's autonomy by destroying the
threat of Sassanid Persia.

The Fall of Sassanid Persia

At its territorial height in the early seventh century, the wealthy Sassanid Persian Empire was the envy of the world. However, there were hidden cracks in its foundations, made worse by centuries of war with the Romans and Byzantines, as well as threats and raids by various nomadic groups on its borderlands. At the midpoint of the seventh century, the Persian Empire, which had existed in one form or another for more than a thousand years, fell to a relatively small Islamic raiding expedition. It took almost another thousand years for Persia to rise to its previous heights again, under the Safavids, who emerged in the sixteenth century and made Shi'a Islam the dominant religion. While Arabs boasted of the extraordinary courage and unity that allowed them to defeat an empire that had reigned for more than a millennium, the toppling of Persia, like that of western Rome, was not just one event but a long process. In addition to its wars, Persia had been weakened by Justinian's plague, the world's first great pandemic, in the middle of the sixth century, and by intense internal criticism of its hierarchy and aristocracy and the state religion of Zoroastrianism.

In the sixth century, the old Persian order faced an onslaught of challenges both inside and out. Powerful revelations by the prophet Mazdak, many of them reactions against Zoroastrian ways, seemed to promise a great disruption in the Sassanid world-system: he preached an egalitarian and anarchist vision of communal property and the sharing of wives. Although he was hanged in 528, an apostate to Zoroastrianism, he seemed to tap into a growing popular desire for a new religion, one that was not bound by the tight strictures of class and caste and could be adapted to different cultures and contexts. Just a century after Mazdak, Muhammad began to preach a new dispensation, grounded in the well-established texts and traditions of Jews and Christians (the protected People of the Book, those who had a revealed scripture, the Torah and the Gospels, who should not be forced to convert but instead be taxed). Like Mazdak's teachings, Islam had an egalitarian promise—and provided social guidelines for life.

Persian writers—representing a wealthy and "civilized" empire—had depicted the Arabs as poor, unwashed Bedouin herders, divided by their tribal gods and other differences. The coming of Islam turned this stereotype on its head: thanks to the spoils of conquest, the Arabs became fantastically wealthy. After the death of the Prophet in 632 and the quelling of rebellions in Arabia, established Muslim Arabs and new converts sent out devastating raiding parties. Finally, a comparatively small group of Arab warriors, taking advantage of a dust storm, decisively defeated the Persian army at Qadisiyyah in 636, breaking through the "Wall of the Arabs"—a series of forts analogous to Hadrian's Wall in England, which was erected against the Picts—which Shapur II built to keep out Arab raiders. The triumph remains a major focus of nationalist narratives in both Iran and Iraq.[63]

If the Gulf's geography were easier to control, the Persian Empire might not have fallen to Islam so easily and world history might have been completely different. Instead of a launching pad for the expansion of Islam, the Gulf would have been the moat that prevented the overthrow of the great shahs. In the end, however, Persia was distracted and failed to establish an effective naval presence to secure the Gulf.[64] Merchant interests—not imperial ones—had tended to dominate its ports, making it vulnerable to Muslim conquests by sea. Tradition has it that western caliphs such as 'Umar, a nomadic Bedouin, opposed the use of ships, but Muslim Arabs in Oman organized a navy almost immediately. They used it to raid and otherwise take advantage of the declining Sassanian Empire's trading network. In 637, Omanis under Amir 'Uthman bin Abi al-Asi sailed from Sohar and Muscat to attack some Hindu merchants who had carried out commerce with the Sassanians, enriching the Arabs with a great booty. But they had failed to secure permission from the caliph, and he was enraged.[65] True or not, this story of overly eager maritime sailors from Oman defying the caliph and the shah encapsulates how the Gulf and its peoples maintained a great deal of autonomy even after the emergence of Islam.[66]

The Arab armies hunted down and killed the last Sassanid emperor, Yazdegerd III, in 651. Not since Alexander the Great had the region's status quo been so disrupted. The Persian Empire must have felt as old as the mountains on which the Persian shahs had carved their monumental likenesses, and now it had fallen.[67] Yet its culture did not disappear altogether. Even after converting to Islam, Persians retained their language and their culture, stamping it on their new faith. Muslim caliphs took on many of the courtly and governmental practices of the shahs while also integrating Greek and Roman models. For instance, the relative elevation and isolation of the ruler, the use of gardens and poetry to magnify his power, the bringing of tribute, and the layers of access between the leader and the rest of the population were all adopted, in part or in whole, from the Persian court. Arab caliphs were careful to keep Persian mints open and continued to circulate Persian coinage. The image of Yazdegerd III remained on Arab-Sassanian coins for decades, as did Sassanid Zoroastrian symbols of divine right. Soon after their conquest, Muslim caliphs added the Arabic bismillah ("in the name of God") or *la illaha illa Allah* ("there is no God but God") to their currency, but the shah remained. Later, the name and likeness of the early eighth-century Arab caliph 'Abd al Malik, holding a sword, replaced the shah.[68] Then, images of the caliph disappeared entirely, to be replaced with only Arabic script, breaking with centuries of Byzantine and Persian traditions of depicting the head of the emperor on coins. This shift happened at the same time when theologians were debating the power of word over image. Perhaps the caliphs concluded that the power of Arabic script alone, representing the word of God, was all that was needed to provide confidence in their currency. Regardless of what was on the coins, they were streaming in. Persia and the lands to the east of the Oxus River, such as Bactria (now Afghanistan), provided a bounty in tax revenue, mainly due to the boom in agriculture in early Islamic Iran.[69]

While the fall of Persia and the coming of Islam were monumental events, and monumentally profitable for those who held the caliphate, and while most Arabs in the region did eventually convert to Islam, the Gulf did not suddenly become a homogenous Sunni Muslim lake ruled by the Umayyads and 'Abbasids from their splendid capitals, first Damascus and then Baghdad. Almost every attempt to fully centralize control over the autonomous, multireligious, cosmopolitan, and liminal Gulf, to impose meaningful taxation on or conscript its peoples, was met with rebellion, evasion, or a shifting of trade to another port, returning the Gulf to its status quo as a region where the cities that practiced relatively free trade still prospered. Under Islam, the Gulf remained a place of intensive commerce, but its geographic extremes allowed both connectivity and isolation to exist at once.

Wealthy ports on the Gulf had often started as mere fishing villages, inhabited by Arabs who led poor, hard lives, during droughts even feeding dried fish to their camels and retreating to the mountains, deserts, or marshes to cultivate limited subsistence crops and find water. Such a small harbor might then be expanded for progressively larger shipments, merchants would arrive, and a connected city would arise, sheltered from taxes and from piracy by the same sea and desert, marsh, or mountain. The Muslim city of Basra was founded near an abandoned village and was used by Islamic conquerors as a garrison. Yet its main purpose quickly changed from war to commerce: it soon became a thriving port, a place for exchange and not simply to receive the spoils of war, sending ships out into the Gulf and taking in peoples from throughout the world, absorbing some ideas and beliefs and changing others. In fact, Basra was a scaffold on which Islam transformed and expanded into a world religion.

2 *Basra*

Where Islam Became a World Religion (632–1000)

Islam became a world religion in the port city of Basra, the main gateway connecting Mesopotamia and the Gulf. Basra's cosmopolitan mix of merchants, scholars, traders, Persians, Arabs, Africans, and Indians transformed it from a faith primarily imposed by Arab conquerors to one that appealed to converts, merchants, and mystics. From its founding in the seventh century to its ninth-and-tenth-century golden age, Basra was a cauldron in which many cultures and peoples mixed, the portal to the Eurasian world where Islam became a multiethnic and multilingual faith.[1] It was in Basra where Islam became accessible to peoples far beyond its homeland. As the previous chapter explains, Islam originated in western Arabia, in Mecca and Medina, in the first half of the seventh century, as a religion of Arabs and Arabic speakers. The Islamic conquest of Persia brought a major influx of Persian speakers into the religion, and Muslim expansion into south and central Asia, especially Sind (the land of the Indus River valley), sent flows of peoples into and out of Basra. The political capital of the Islamic Caliphate moved from Arabia to Damascus, which was previously under Byzantine rule, in the latter half of the seventh century, resulting in Greek influences on Islam. When Baghdad, in Mesopotamia, became the capital in the mid-eighth century, Basra, which had already grown rich as a staging ground and gathering place for the conquest to the east, enjoyed a further enormous increase in wealth. Although never the political center, Basra was Islam's economic and cultural powerhouse, a place of profound mixture of Arab, Persian, African, and south Asian customs, languages, and ideas.

Basra was full of peoples from highly diverse backgrounds who had converted to Islam. Many tried to learn Arabic, a requirement for reading and fully understanding the Qur'an. These non-Arab converts shaped Arabic culture, opening it up in ways that made it attractive to other nonnative Arabic speakers. In Basra, not Mecca or Medina, therefore, Muhammad's founding vision of Islam as appealing to all of humanity, not just to particular tribes of Arabs, was put to the test. According to a tradition established by the eighth century, the Prophet exhorted his followers to treat Arab and non-Arab equally in his last sermon before death: "O people, your Lord is One, and your father is one: all of you are from Adam, and Adam was from the ground. The noblest of you in Allah's sight is the most God-fearing: Arab has no merit over non-Arab other than God-fearingness."[2] The Prophet's dream of a postracial Islam has never been achieved: racial categorization remains a divisive issue within Muslim communities, including in the Gulf. Nonetheless, in Basra, groups of thinkers, mystics, and merchants created a humanistic Islam—a society and an outlook on humanity as a whole that at least approached the Prophet's ideal.

Two radically new approaches to Islam, both spiritual and intellectual, arose in Basra's diverse and polyglot streets. The first great force was Sufism, which focuses on the innate relationship between the soul and God, cultivating a realm for Islam in the interior mind. It did not, however, neglect the external world, also creating a sort of religious parallel state: nonpolitical structures of teachers and students, sheikhs and their followers, that spread from Basra throughout the Indian Ocean world. The spiritual mother and father of Sufism, Hasan of Basra and his friend Saint Rabi'a of Basra, reacting against the city's great wealth, established the foundations of an alternative vision of Islam, one that focuses on abnegation of worldly desires and the individual's spiritual relationship with God. The second expansion was Islam's opening to a vast realm of philosophical inquiry: Islamic humanism took root in Basra as a group of merchant-thinkers called the Brotherhood of Purity used a combination of Greek, Indian, and Persian ideas to speculate about the nature of the universe. The city was a haven where such societies of poets and philosophers, many of them educated merchants who had seen much of the world, could thrive.

Islam was initially spread by Arab armies, which achieved their conquests by unifying the warrior spirits of Arabia's Bedouin and oasis tribes. However, it was non-Arab converts and the imperative pull of Gulf trade and exchange in Basra that transformed the religion from a primarily Arab-centric faith into a global system encompassing culture, language, and commerce. For instance, as people from many backgrounds learned Arabic, poets, other authors, and mystics rubbing shoulders in Basra's famed markets and alongside its canals created a literary explosion by mixing ideas and methods of thinking and writing in ways that had never occurred before. In Basra, Islam broke out of its Arab-centric mold and became a world religion.

Strategic Location

As the acting capital of the Gulf's marshlands, Basra had many geographic advantages. The Arab and Islamic armies established it as the first great *amsar:* a walled garrison outpost of conquest, a fortified settlement. Just six years after Muhammad's death, 'Utba bin Ghawan, a companion of the Prophet, built this first military encampment to support Islam's rapid march into Asia, on the orders of the just caliph 'Umar. Like other walled settlements set up by Arab armies in Islam's early years, such as Kufa (in Iraq), Kairouan (in Tunisia), and Fustat (which became Cairo in Egypt), Basra was settled as a new and separate Islamic city and as a deliberate, strategic choice.[3] As 'Umar and 'Utba knew, Basra's location was nearly perfect for rallying troops on their expeditions east into the rich lands of Persia, Khorasan, and central Asia. Warriors returned to Basra laden with wealth after every victory, and the city rapidly attracted merchants and converts, including some of the brightest lights of early Islam. On the hip socket of the Islamic world, near the Shatt al-Arab if not right on it, Basra was not built directly on the Gulf. Instead, it was far enough upriver to avoid most pirates and seaborne conquests—to warn of impending raids, large bonfires would be set in lighthouses built upon marshy banks —but this protected position required special arrangements for the shipment of goods, a logistical challenge for traders. Cargo on the larger ships that went to India or China had to be offloaded at Siraf on the Persian shore or at 'Uballa, a bit closer to the Gulf, and then relayed on pack animals or on smaller boats through the canals that traversed the marsh, likely dug out and maintained by a combination of both Zanj (Black African) slaves and free labor. While large merchant ships and pirate warships could not sail so far them, smaller rivercraft may have been able to dock near the hearts of various markets during periods of high water in the winter. This infrastructure had to be maintained, but conquest and other upheaval meant the breakdown of the dikes and levees that held back the rivers. In Basra's first years, a flood created large inland lakes, including Lake Hammar between the city and Kufa. On the edge of this floodplain, Basra seems to have shifted its location several times, but it always maintained its connections to maritime and desert routes.[4]

To early sailors, the Shatt al-Arab, the main channel that carries the waters of both the Tigris and the Euphrates into the Gulf, was the "One-Eyed Tigris," owing to the Island of the Unwary close to its mouth, which made it look like an eye. Although one would expect abundant drinking water at the watershed of two of the world's greatest rivers, silting caused challenges, as it prevented the flow of freshwater from upstream. Not only was the Shatt al-Arab shallow and shifting—its width has ranged from 1,200 to 3,600 feet— but sandbars would develop along its course from the Gulf. Basrans sometimes navigated up to the main branch of the Tigris River for freshwater during droughts. But there were also benefits to living near a marsh. The river silt brought great riches as well, especially the many date trees lining the banks of the Tigris. Basra's soil was so good that orange trees grew under the vast date canopy.

Remains of early Islamic Basra still exist in the neighborhood of Zubair, about seven miles to the south of today's city.[5] Basra was connected to the larger Tigris system by two main canals, one to the north and one to the south, creating a kind of circle around the city. A network of smaller canals crossed to and through the port, in much the same way that Venice is built into its lagoon. In between were mud-brick houses, like those that of the ancient Babylonians, and stone houses, built by wealthier Basrans. *Funduqs,* or hotels for merchants, and khans, or storehouses, lined the roads and channels. Shrines and mosques commemorated the many famed Muslims who lived in its warren of streets. There were quarters with churches and synagogues and places for Hindus and those of other religions. The Mandaeans, sometimes called Sabaeans of Saint John (a name given by Europeans), following ancient rites but protected as People of the Book, worshipped in the city and would have been seen baptizing in the waters. The larger canals and the al-Kalla' river harbor on Basra's eastern side welcomed shallow-bottomed boats transporting the wares of deeper-draft, ocean-worthy merchant crafts that had made their way through treacherous shoals to 'Uballa, farther down the Shatt al-Arab, guided by lighthouses made of wooden scaffolding and lit by fire at night. The city's western side, with the Mirbad market and streets in place of canals, faced the desert. Outside town were the graves of great Sufi Basrans such as Hasan of Basra, which can be seen to this day. Farther on, caravans linked Basra in multiple directions to a huge range of markets. In the middle of the seventh century, more were set up along newly dug canals for the sale of spoils and other goods from the Islamic conquest of Persia and lands farther east. As they moved from the canal zone to the higher, drier parts of Basra, merchants went from selling goods on the ground to trading in traditional markets without canals and stored precious items in large khans.

Basra, unlike many other Gulf ports, could grow its own food, and even exported some of the surplus. In *One Thousand and One Arabian Nights,* the narrator Scheherazade tells the story of the caliph Harun al-Rashid's three forbidden apples, grown in his orchard near Basra. The city also became famous for its dates, used as ballast in merchant ships well into the twentieth century, and for its involvement in the thriving textile trade that linked the port to every major urban center within the Islamic world and beyond.[6] There was a massive circulation of products within the lands of Islam, and Basra was known for silks and embroidered linens of various kinds even as it imported cotton textiles and fabrics from Khuzistan, Nishapur, Herat, and Samarkand. Many of these goods then made their way from Basra straight to Damascus or Baghdad.[7]

In addition to being tied to rivers and the Gulf, Basra was a desert port connected to the great routes going west to Mecca and the Mediterranean. To the southwest, the desert could creep up to the irrigated land where great caravans were outfitted for the hajj on routes maintained by the queens and sisters of the caliphs. Like the marsh, the desert was a vulnerability and an opportunity. Bedouin raiders streamed into the region from the desert in recurring waves of invasion. Yet Arab raiders who had sacked so many Persian metropolises were also Basra's founders and went from being poor herdsmen to the city's upper crust: in the span of one generation, its Bedouin conquerors were transformed into some of the wealthiest people in Asia, receiving enormous windfalls from the spoils of war.

Arabic poetry and other literature celebrated Basra as a city of the first warriors of Islam: the new Arab aristocracy. At the time of its founding, however, many of them would have been "barefoot and naked," except perhaps the most elite.[8] *The Shahnameh,* the Persian epic, has the hero Rustam exclaim, "I have a sharp arrowhead that penetrates iron, but it is no use against the naked [Arabs]."[9] Although these Arabs may have been respected among their tribes, they were still looked down upon by Persians, and Persia still had a monopoly on what it meant to be elite. But aristocratic status for the Arabs has always meant more than just outward appearance. Even in Islam's earliest years, "high tribes" used their names to identify districts of the city. Many were from the highlands of the Hijaz, the plateau of the holy cities of Mecca and Medina, including the Tamimi, Bakr bin Wa'il, 'Abd al-Qays, and Azd, which were each given control of one of Basra's five zones. Over time, a near constant stream of wealth transformed the city's buildings, but outlines of the original social structure of tribal or sectarian affiliation remained even as fired brick replaced reed huts and walls went up between family and tribal areas.

With their wealth, the new leading Arab families attached networks of slaves and clients, converted non-Arabs, to their tribes. Conquered Persians, central and southeast Asians, Indians, and Africans often won their freedom quickly—sometimes within just one generation if they converted to Islam or married a Muslim warrior and had his children. They began to settle in distinct neighborhoods near Basra's markets and canals, adopt Islam, and learn Arabic. Interestingly, as we will see below, it was mostly non-Arabs, who suddenly needed to know the language, both to read the Qur'an and to cater to the city's elite, who became the most important grammarians and poets of Arabic. By the beginning of the eighth century, Basra's streets and canals were full of poets and storytellers, thieves and officials, soldiers and merchants, schismatics and Sufis, all meeting in one great, colorful mixture of human possibility. This influx of peoples and ideas led to the rapid elevation of the Arabic language, making Basra the most celebrated heartland of Arabic cultural and literary expression along the entire spectrum from sacred to profane.

The city's wealth made it hotly contested by different Muslim factions. As the site of a great *fitna,* or Islamic civil war, between the Party of 'Ali and the proto-Sunnis, it also had a reputation from its beginning as full of civil strife. The death of 'Ali in the middle of the seventh century and the victory of the Umayyads, who governed as caliphs from Damascus, did not end the conflict. Eventually, as we saw in chapter 1, Yazid I, the second Umayyad ruler, in putting down a rebellion by 'Ali's son Hussein, the Prophet's grandson, massacred him and his family and supporters at Karbala. Remembering this and other martyrdoms at the hands of the Sunni caliphs, the Shi'as, the "Party of 'Ali," continue to struggle with Sunnis to this day. To be sure, they have also enjoyed many years of peaceful coexistence. Yet the pain of the original conflict in Basra and southern Iraq was etched into the historical memories of Basrans and added a layer of complexity to the city from the start. Always known as a way station on the route to Medina and Mecca, it became a pilgrimage destination itself for Shi'a Muslims commemorating the life of 'Ali. The Mosque of Imam 'Ali was likely the first Friday mosque, a large structure meant to hold the whole town's population for Friday sermons, built outside the Arabian Peninsula.

The rise of the Umayyad dynasty after 'Ali's death meant that the center of Islamic power moved from eastern Arabia to Damascus. Mediterranean, especially Greco-Roman, culture became a predominant influence, fusing with Arab culture. Then, in the very middle of the eighth century, the capital shifted eastward, closer to the Gulf, Persia, and Sind, when the 'Abbasids assumed power and the caliph al-Mansur built Baghdad, which he called City of Peace, upstream from Basra on the Tigris River at a point where it turns and comes close to the Euphrates. With this move, Basra's importance suddenly increased: being nearby and having already existed as a Muslim city for more than a century, it naturally became the port of Islam's new political center.

Throughout its first two centuries, multiple rebellions rocked Basra, even after it was connected to Baghdad: its marsh protected it from centralized control. Clients, slaves, and former slaves of the "high tribes" quarreled with and revolted against their masters. Another instance of rebellion involved the Zubayrids, followers of the alternate caliph Ibn al Zubayr, who even set up their own dynasty and ruled Basra as a virtually independent city within the caliphate until the end of the seventh century. Elite Arab families, supposed to uphold Arab rule, also led revolts, such as the noble Arab Ibn Ash'ath, whose insurrection was put down only by direct intervention from Damascus. With a mix of excellent administrative skills and persecution, the famous Umayyad governor of Iraq al-Hajjaj bin Yusuf was able to quell rebellion—but for only a decade. Called a tyrant and even a pharaoh by the locals for his heavy-handed style, he died in the early eighth century. Like clockwork, the Muhallabid faction rose in defiance of the Umayyads (719–20).[10] Even with this constant contestation of central power, however, Basra continued to thrive economically and expand its urban footprint.

Despite being so rebellious, Basra benefited from Baghdad's wars, which sent yet more Muslim armies to push eastward into the depths of central Asia, all the way to the borders of China. While raids westward brought the Islamic world into contact with Europe and Latin Christianity, the lands of the western Mediterranean were not as wealthy as those to the east. But Islam was expanding and the caliphate filling its coffers not only by the sword but also through trade and the creation of Muslim merchant networks in the Indian Ocean. The port cities of Tang China were also flourishing in the seventh and eighth centuries, thanks to the open policy toward foreigners of early Tang emperors. Just as cosmopolitanism drew incredibly diverse peoples from around the world to the Gulf, so did it attract Gulf merchants to the Far East, a journey that could take two or three years with the monsoons. Thousands of Arab merchants who started their voyages in the Gulf, in Basra or Siraf, resided in China at that time.[11] Harun al-Rashid sent embassies and gifts to China and a fabulous gift to his distant Frankish ally Charlemagne, who was fighting the Umayyads: an elephant named Abu al-'Abbas.[12]

In the ninth century, the 'Abbasid caliphs in Baghdad, confident in their position, upped the ante. They tried to completely solidify their claims to both political and religious authority, combining the political power of the Persian shah with the spiritual claims of the first Arab caliphs. The palace in Baghdad had layers of encircled walls so large that it was called the Round City. Each circle was overseen by a chamberlain who jealously guarded access to the caliph. This model, a fusion of influences from the courts of both the Persian shah and the Byzantine emperors, was diametrically opposed to that provided by the Prophet and the Arabs, who preferred a more informal, personal approach from their leaders. By the end of the tenth century, however, the caliphs' political and religious authority was split asunder. Having overreached, they saw their golden age come to an end as the ulama, or teachers of Islam, wrested theological authority from them. The caliph's claim to military command was also diminished, with the use of non-Arab mercenaries such as the Buyids, who took over many other aspects of government, leaving him a figurehead. The reasons for this decline in both religious and political power are complicated, but many scholars agree that some of the major problems emerged during and after the reign of al-Ma'mun, the son of Harun al-Rashid, who died in the early ninth century. Al-Ma'mun embraced Greek learning and claimed to have met Aristotle in a dream.[13] He even tried to impose a form of Aristotelian theology on all Muslims, setting up an inquisition to make sure all Muslim scholars were on board. This highly centralized approach to Islam backfired, though, handing power to the very scholars who resisted the caliph's top-down imposition. The danger to philosophers and theologians was particularly high in Baghdad's House of Wisdom—where scholars would debate and translate works from Greek and other languages—which could be a dogmatic prison as much as an incubator of thought: Al Ma'mun could be a fickle patron and was famous for his purges of those who disagreed with his favored philosophy, such as Ibn Hanbal, the founder of what is known today as the Hanbali school of Islam.[14] In the end, the posthumous success of Ibn Hanbal's interpretation led to the rise of an independent class of religious scholars, who were not completely controlled by the caliph like their peers. By the tenth century—when an alliance of convenience between the naval forces of the Ibadi ruler of Oman Ibn Wajih and the army of the Bedouin Qarmatians managed to invade Basra, threaten Baghdad, and temporarily control much of the Gulf's maritime trade—the power of the 'Abbasid caliphs was a mere shadow of its ninth-century splendor.[15]

Throughout this period of the caliphate's decline, Basra was a thorn in Baghdad's side: an annoyance if not an almost constant source of worry and rebellion. It was home to many of the Buyid elite, who effectively ruled, if not reigned, in the name of the caliph from the middle of the tenth to the eleventh century. As Daylamite Persian chiefs who controlled the 'Abbasid Empire's government, finances, and military, they revived hopes of a restored Persian culture. Instead of crushing the Sunnis or their rivals, the Buyids were content to accommodate the realities of handling the diversely sectarian peoples of the Gulf to keep trade flowing. Poetry and other literature portrays them as epicureans, pursuing pleasure rather than the enforcement of creed. Buyid silver vessels from Basra, including one with a poem about wine, show their embrace of the bacchanal.[16] With the Buyids in Basra, which was connected to the port of Siraf and their capital in Shiraz, the 'Abbasid caliphs in Baghdad could maintain their titles and some of their religious authority, if not their real power. Uncooperative caliphs were simply blinded, retired, and replaced with a more pliable alternative.

As the marshes shielded it from the turmoil in Baghdad, Basra still had the bustle of opportunity and exploration. It was a place where relative freedom of mobility and imagination led to a cultural awakening in Islam. From the eighth to the tenth century, Basra was the center of a humanistic renaissance in language, letters, and science. It was the clearinghouse of the world's peoples and ideas on their way to Baghdad.

Economy and Markets

While shifts in religious and political power kept the caliphs and their ministers in Baghdad busy, the spoils of conquest and trade flowed almost continuously into Basra's storehouses and markets. At first, its neighborhoods were controlled by noble chiefs and populated mainly by their clients and slaves. Slaves, having been captured by elite Arab warrior tribes during campaigns in Persia, Mesopotamia, and elsewhere, were brought back to the garrison city of Basra. Many were eventually freed, converted to Islam, and became mawali: non-Arab Muslims with a lower social status than that of the ruling tribal class but faith in Muhammad's promise that all Muslims are equal before God, regardless of blood. Filled with rich fighters and flush with their victory over the Persian Empire, one of the greatest upsets in military history, Arab families must have seen little need for a wall or other defensive works for the city in its early decades. War prizes came in from Fars (the heartland of the Farsi, or Persians), Khorasan (a great land with legendary trading cities such as Merv and Balkh), and Sijistan (around what is now southern Afghanistan), all provinces with resources far beyond the wildest dreams of the first generation of Muslim Arab fighters.

According to early Islamic law, these Arab conquerors could claim those distant lands and their revenues for themselves. Ibn al-Balkhi, a tax accountant (*mustawfi*) for the province in the twelfth century, wrote that when Fars—also called Pars, from which we get "Persian"—was the center of government for the Persian kings, "all the world paid them taxes and tribute." When Islam arose, however, proud Fars "became the camping-ground of . . . 'Irāq, for no sooner had the Moslems come hither than they took up their quarters permanently in the land, on the one part the troops from Kūfah, on the other those from Baṣrah, and from this base they went forth to the conquest of all lands and to subjugate the [eastern] world."[17] Elite Arab Basrans were thus able to collect taxes and tribute from the vast and cosmopolitan collection of territories within their *mah*, or "camping-ground," tracts of land in Persia. As the center of Persian imperial culture and splendor, Fars was the greatest prize. Once taken, Persian lands and peoples became a direct concern of the Arab victors, who needed help managing Persian revenues and estates. Many generations of Persians went to Basra to aid with this task, and some of these people then converted to Islam, learned Arabic, and added a very Persian influence to the city. As for Khorasan, on a rich plateau in Persia, it directly influenced Basra's history: without their newly converted Khorasani troops from the east, the 'Abbasid caliphs never would have come to power.[18]

Eventually, the era of easy booty met insurmountable barriers and came to an end. The Muslim armies' eastward progress was stemmed after a defeat by China at the battle of Talas (751) on the Silk Roads in Transoxiana. As spoils from war in Persia diminished, a more sustainable economy emerged in Basra, based on port and commercial services, on the selling and exchange of goods through networks of Arabs and non-Arabs alike, who would spread Islam even more effectively than the raiding warriors who had departed from the city during Islam's first century.

Conquest and trade also connected Basra to south Asia and India.[19] In the early eighth century, the Muslim general Muhammad ibn al Qasim led a group of warriors into Sind, capturing it and linking it, through Basra, to Baghdad. In those cities, Arab warriors, merchants, and mystics were exposed to the major achievements of the Mauryan and Gupta Empires of India, which preceded the rise of Islamic Mesopotamia. Adherents of Buddhism, a belief system that spread throughout India during the time of those empires, started streaming regularly into the Gulf. The Barmakids, the most famous family of wazirs (ministers) ever to manage the affairs of the caliphs, were once Buddhists. Rock-cut monumental reliefs right on the Gulf near Khormoj in Iran's Bushehr province point to either Buddhists or Nestorian Christians.[20] This "southernization" did not mean that influences from the Mediterranean, coming south from Syria along the Euphrates, stopped. In fact, ideas and writings of Greeks, both Christians and Islamic converts who translated their works into Arabic, spread like wildfire through the schools and seminars of Basra and Baghdad. The ancient, pre-Islamic traditions, astrological knowledge, and secrets of the Mandaeans also had a lasting influence on Gulf culture. From Armenians through Vikings to Jews, Greeks, and Africans, the streets were full of bustling exchange in Basra, a new Babel of its age.

Focused on profit, Basran merchants and craftspeople were adept at cultural adaptation and attempted to copy successful manufacturing techniques from China. Chinese ceramics, were highly prized throughout the Indian Ocean and incredibly expensive, so Basrans, who wanted in on this market but did not know how to produce these premium goods, developed their own Chinese-style pottery.[21] One ninth-century earthenware bowl found in Basra deliberately emulated the "luminous quality" of Chinese stoneware using a "tin-opacified white glaze" to mask the lack of whiteness.[22] The Basran ceramics makers used a hoard of imperial Chinese ware given by the Muslim governor of Khorasan to the caliph Harun al-Rashid in the

FIGURE 8. Basra bowl emulating Chinese stoneware, ninth century. The text in the center is the Arabic word *ghitba*, "happiness," twice. Metropolitan Museum of Art, New York. Harris Brisbane Dick Fund, 1963.

ninth century as their model.[23] The lateen sail, paper, and other vital technologies were also spread through Basra. Although Baghdad, as the 'Abbasid Caliphate's capital, was more famous, Basra remained, from its foundation to around the thirteenth century, the front door of the caliphs and a center for commercial, intellectual, and technological exchange.

In Basra the overland Silk Roads met the maritime routes to Africa and Asia. The tenth-century Persian geographer and bureaucrat Ibn Khurdadhbih mentioned trade conducted by Frankish (European) Jews who sailed for Oman, India, and even China from Basra.[24]

In the ninth century it was already an economic powerhouse. Al-Muqaddasi (d. 991) said, "Have you not heard of the Khazz (silken stuff) of Basrah, its Bazz (cotton stuff) and its rare remarkable wares? Basrah is a mine of pearls and jewels, a port of the sea, and an emporium of the land."[25] It was even a place for the preindustrial refinement of certain minerals, such as red lead and cinnabar. And there seemed to be markets for almost every service or good, plus khans in which to store them: markets for camel sellers, leatherworkers, locksmiths, coppersmiths. There was a separate market for vendors of vinegar and pickles, and the Suq al-Saqat, for the sale of "unworthy items." The Mirbad market was famed as a gateway to the desert route to Mecca and for the many poets, storytellers, and grammarians who filled its streets, seeking to gain knowledge of the Bedouin's "desert Arabic," which became the basis for a great cultural awakening from 700 to 900. By the late ninth century, as many as two thousand boats left every day from Basra's Suq al-Kalla' near the Fayd canal, across which thick ropes were laid to prevent them from passing without paying tax.[26] Boats could be repaired using the special asphalt sold in the Suq al-Kalla' or disassembled and reassembled at the suq of the vendors of old ships. In short, one could find whatever one's heart desired in Basra's sprawling markets, which were spread out around the city, some close to the canals, some close to the desert.

Armenians, Jews, Mandaeans, members of elite Arab tribes, Sufis, Ikhwan al-Safa', Zanj, Zutt—all used or even attempted to control Basra as a type of headquarters at the head of the Gulf. Crucial to the city's importance, however, was the way that such groups and their networks encountered one another, sharing spaces even as they all tried to find a place of prominence. Thanks to Basra's relative autonomy from Islam's political center in Baghdad, these encounters sometimes led to organized resistance. The marshes and natron salt flats around the city, which protected it from raids and conquests, could also offer ideal conditions for rebellion and revolt. Two such movements had the potential to overthrow the entire 'Abbasid Empire. First came the Zutt revolt, starting in 810.

The identity of the Zutt, a people famous for their migrations from market to market and called "gypsies" in some translations, is debated to this day. In Islam's first centuries, the term probably referred to the Jhat people from northern India, who were brought into the Gulf region by slave traders or migrated there for work. In Oman there is still a group called Zuti, or "gypsies," whose name might have meant "prisoner of war" in Islam's first centuries. The Zutt have worked in leather tanning and masonry and were often relied on for circumcision in certain rural areas.[27] There were south Asians in the Gulf for millennia before Islam, but the Zutt probably arrived during the reign of the fifth-century Sassanid emperor Bahram V Gur. Many of these locals converted to Islam after the Arab conquests, and some became clients of noble Arab families, such as the Hanzala of the Tamim. Others chafed against Arab rule. Those in Basra who did not wish to work as servants set up communities beyond the city's walls, becoming outlaws who demanded payment for safe passage through their the canals they controlled. In the middle of the ninth century, the Zutt rebelled openly, besieging Basra. The caliph was forced to intervene, and one successful amphibian campaign by his general saw almost thirty thousand Zutt deported north to Anatolia, perhaps to to help with the war against Byzantium or to settle territories taken from the Greeks. Nonetheless, many avoided deportation, remaining part of the fabric of southern Mesopotamian as well as Gulf society.

The Zanj, mainly black slaves brought from the coast of east Africa by Gulf traders, tried to end their oppression by overthrowing the cultural and religious system of their masters. Instead, just as new forms of Christianity in the American South served as means of organizing slaves against their owners, so too did a new Islam that emerged among the Zanj in the area around Basra in the ninth century. So successful was their rebellion and so many were the new system's adherents that for several years it seemed they might actually succeed against the caliphs, the most powerful rulers in their world.

The leader of the Zanj, 'Ali bin Muhammad bin 'Abd al Rahim, was not from Africa. In fact, he claimed to be a descendant of the family of the Prophet.[28] He grew up in the Persian city of Rayy before moving to Baghdad, which was about eighty miles from Samarra, then the court of the caliph, place of refinement and ceremony.[29] 'Ali, tired of the sycophancy in Baghdad and having obtained religious knowledge in Samarra, went to the island of Bahrain (then also the name of much of Arabia's Gulf coast). In the town of Hajar, which was in the orbit of the Qarmatians, he claimed judicial authority—the ability to interpret cases using the Qur'an and the hadith—and through his rhetoric and charisma gained many followers. He had just as many enemies. He eventually had to flee to the desert and seek the protection of the Bedouin. He had several lieutenants, including a grain weigher called Yahya al Bahraini, a merchant and possible financier named Yayha bin Abi Tha'lab, and an African (perhaps a Zanj) named Sulaiman bin Jami', who became the commander of 'Ali's small army.

'Ali told his followers of a dream: "I was lying down, musing about the place I should be heading for to set up residence. The thought of the desert and its recalcitrant inhabitants dejected me, but then a cloud cast a shadow upon me; thunder crackled and lightning flashed. A thunderclap resounded in my ears, and a voice addressed me saying, 'Head for al-Baṣrah!' I said to my companions who were assisting me, 'A voice from the thunder has commanded me to go to al-Baṣrah.'" While in the salt flats outside that city, 'Ali falsely claimed to represent one of the caliph's sons, who was in charge of handling the sale of *sibakh,* the nitrogen-rich topsoil harvested as fertilizer around there. He gained the trust of the Zanj slaves who transported flour and dates, as well as those who worked on the salt flats. During several meetings with them, 'Ali promised a new life to whomever joined him. He wanted not to end slavery as an institution but to free his African followers and give them slaves of their own, money, women, and houses. Moreover, each new Zanj brought into the movement would be attached as a client to the person responsible, replicating the system of the Arab-conquest aristocracy. In this way, 'Ali convinced the hundreds of slaves of the salt flats, who far outnumbered their masters and foremen, to join him in revolt. As they raided, they freed the slaves who joined their ranks. They also captured slave masters, to whom 'Ali said, "I wanted to behead you all for the way you have treated these slaves, with arrogance and coercion and, indeed, in ways that Allah has forbidden, driving them beyond endurance."[30] He and his army traversed the many villages and channels of southern Iraq, picking up followers and dispatching enemies along the way. Soon, towns surrendered before he arrived, and he promised protection to those who acknowledged his authority.[31]

After several bloody campaigns, 'Ali consolidated his forces in the canals around Basra, which they besieged. The Zanj built a parallel city called Mukhtara southeast of town. Although intended as an ephemeral encampment, it soon had walls, palaces, and many other accoutrements of a city. There they coordinated with other rebels in the marshes. The Zanj enslaved as many as five thousand elite or middle-class Muslim Arab women and managed to seize several large boats in a flotilla on its way to Basra. At the height of their revolt, the Zanj controlled a vast territory around the city, including some of the richest date palm groves and most important strategic waterways. The caliph finally sent a full army from Baghdad, commanded by his own son. Suddenly faced with certain defeat, 'Ali couldn't continue his miracles. He was finally captured and executed at the end of the ninth century, ending one of the most existential threats to the 'Abbasid caliphs, titular heads of the Muslim world.

The near success of the Zanj revolt proved the power of African Muslims and inspired a reconsideration of racial assumptions. Al-Jahiz, born in Basra in the early ninth century and one of the greatest authors in the Arabic literary canon, wrote *The Book of the Glory of the Black Race,* embracing the virtues of Black skin and the Zanj of Africa. According to one popular story, he was killed by his love of books: while deep in thought, he died instantly when the overstocked library in his study fell on him.[32] No longer relegated only to labor in the salt flats, Africans became full members of the Gulf's mixed and cosmopolitan environment, including its intellectual class. Through intermarriage and other alliances, many Zanj and also Zutt became merchants and social leaders even as they maintained links to ancestors in Africa or south Asia.

In addition to ethnic diversity, Basra was a site of religious difference. In the twelfth century, Rabbi Benjamin of Tudela, who traveled to the Gulf from the Iberian Peninsula, mentioned that a Jewish official "controlled" the pearl trade of Qatif, which was on the eastern shore of the Arabian Peninsula near Bahrain and had as many as five thousand Jews, a thriving community. Jews believed Qatif to be the "Havilah" of Genesis 2:11–12, a city with gold, bdellium, and onyx.[33] Benjamin described Basra as also having a sizable Jewish population, far above the mere two hundred or so people in the great European cities such as Rome: "Here there are 10,000 Jews, and among them are scholars and many rich men. . . . 1,500 Jews live near the sepulchre of Ezra, the priest, who went forth from Jerusalem to King Artaxerxes and died here. In front of his sepulchre is a large synagogue. And at the side thereof the [Muslims] erected a house of prayer out of their great love and veneration for him, and they like the Jews on that account. And the [Muslims] come hither to pray."[34] The prospect of Jews and Muslims praying together seems extraordinary today, but it was a relatively common sight in the twelfth century. These shrines were particularly significant points of juncture: interfaith destinations that emphasized the region's importance and shared holy topography. In Susa, in Khuzistan, great numbers of Muslims, Christians, and Jews gathered to see the sepulcher of Daniel of the Lion's Den. But there was such wrangling between two synagogues on different sides of the river over which should hold it that the sultan al Faris, according to Benjamin, had them hang the tomb from an iron chain from the middle of the bridge between the two, so that whoever wished to worship could do so, "Jew or Gentile."[35]

In Europe and North Africa, Jews acted as tax collectors and emissaries for kings and princes, and there were some instances of this in the medieval Gulf. But unlike in the Mediterranean, where they were often treated as outsiders, Jews in Basra were not alone among minorities: they could blend in with the many other religious groups who made themselves useful in commerce. For example, the city's Muslim ruler often sold the position of head of the customhouse to the highest bidder—usually, but not always, a Hindu Indian merchant of the Banian caste. Their specialized trade knowledge became an indispensable feature of any successful port. Mandaeans spread throughout the Gulf and Indian Ocean world as ministers for Gulf rulers. Armenian Christians were also known as an important migrant-merchant minority, as were the Muslim Ibadis of Oman. The networks of these groups were therefore not only integrated into the economy but indeed a fundamental part of the Gulf's political and institutional structures.

Basra's many ethnic, religious, and merchant communities exposed the Arabic language to a wider world and made it accessible to different cultures and peoples. Often, it takes a nonnative speaker, somebody from outside the tradition, to understand and standardize the rules of a particular language. This was certainly the case for Arabic, teachers of which were very much in demand, especially among ambitious new converts. Arabic was the language of the Qur'an: "We have sent it down as an Arabic Qur'an" (Qur'an 12:2). Any Muslim scholar, regardless of native tongue, needed to learn Arabic well to be respected. The language's structure was formalized and written down in Basra—not in Mecca or Medina, not in Baghdad, but in Basra. In the eighth century, the grammarian Sibawayh codified many of Arabic's rules. He was Persian, not an Arabic speaker by origin, so he could view the language from the outside, systematically. He was also something of a protoanthropologist and linguist. He recruited Bedouin from the desert who spoke "pure" Arabic, such as al-Khalil ibn Ahmad al-Farahidi and Yunus ibn Habib, assuring the success and acceptance of his work. Titled *Al-Kitab,* which means simply "The book," it is the earliest written comprehensive Arabic grammar. Sibawayh used his native knowledge of Persian to represent the "Basra school" and offer a comparative understanding of Arabic.[36] He debated the language's structure at the court of the caliphs, and his rules on grammar—which really represent the rules of the speech of God, since Arabic is the language of God in the Qur'an—spread throughout the Islamic Empire and became the standard for interpretations of the Qur'an worldwide. In fact, his book is still used today as a basic reference by Arabic-language scholars and linguists. It is no accident that Sibawayh wrote his grammar for Basra's scholars. The city was home to some of Arabic's greatest poets and other authors—and many of them were non-Arabs who had learned the language as adults or were descendants of parents or grandparents who did not speak it at all.

In Basra, Arabic was shaped into a language that could produce world literature expressing experiences, beliefs, and other ideas outside the institutionalized, orthodox, religious realm. Soon the majority of Arabic speakers were no longer Arabs. Ibn al-Nadim, probably a Persian, compiled his *Al-fihrist* in the tenth century to catalog all books in Arabic and their authors, creating a kind of literary who's who that traces vast nets of connections among disparate lives, high and low, refined and rough, Arab and non-Arab, slave and free.[37]

One example of the diversity of literary characters is the blind lothario Bashshar ibn Burd, who lived in the eighth century, a Persian from eastern Iran. His father was freed from slavery only after working in drudgery for an Arab bricklayer in Basra. Having grown up among the varied sounds and textures of the Basra markets, Bashshar was gifted, as if by magic, with a poetic tongue at the age of ten. Although he was blind from birth and called exceptionally ugly, he captivated women with his mind and his mastery of Arabic. Eloquence in Arabic was good for more than just romance: it also opened doors to the homes and courtyards of the most important families of that time, especially those in the city's elite quarters, and the powerful feared his biting epigrams. Bashshar was outwardly pious in dress and manner, but his poetry contained secret hints of Zoroastrianism, praising the fire-worshipping ways of his ancestors.[38] Although not a native speaker of Arabic, Kutrub, a freed slave and tutor to the son of Basra's military commander in the eighth century, specialized in Arabic's puzzling contranyms: words that have opposite meanings. Al-Khubza'aruzzi, "the Rice-bread maker," who was homosexual, had a large group of admirers who were attracted to his ghazal poetry, verses on the beauty of young men and boys. Espousing love for young men in the streets was not so shocking for Basra, and unlike Bashshar, this bread and verse maker wisely shied away from political controversy. Shariya, the renowned singer, chef, and storyteller, was born in Basra to an Arab father and a non-Arab mother at the beginning of the ninth century. Like her male counterparts, she embraced the Arabic language and her non-Arab ancestry, creating a mixture that continued as a model through the centuries.

Basra was also home to the greatest theological and political minds, some of whose works Muslim lawmakers use to this day. Al-Mawardi, "The son of a rose-water seller," was born there in the tenth century. His writings on Islamic law became so famous and respected that he was named the qadi of qadis (judge of judges) and even stood up to the Buyids who were then in charge of Iraq. Al-Mawardi bolstered Sunni orthodoxy in a way that has become a model for subsequent theologians. His *Treatise on the Laws of Governance* is still the classic work on Islamic public law, and his list of the required qualities for a caliph remains influential. The impact of even this expert on Islamic orthodoxy and Islamic law, however, pales in comparison to that of the great spiritual thinkers and experimenters who founded Sufism and preached it in the dense markets of Basra.

Birthplace of Sufism and Islamic Humanism

Although its origin is still hotly disputed, the term *Sufi* probably comes from the simple woolen (*suf*) garment worn by the sect's first members.[39] This etymology captures the essence of the religion as practiced by its founders, who were surrounded by the wealth of Basra and wanted to present another way of life: Hasan of Basra and Rabi'a of Basra, Islam's best-known woman saint. Both flourished in the early eighth century, just as Muslim armies were spreading into Sind and sending a stream of riches and luxuries back to the Gulf region. As a magnet for these spoils, Basra had become enormously prosperous, but there were great disparities of wealth between believers, especially between Arab aristocrats and non-Arab converts and slaves, which made many disaffected. Moreover, it seemed that the spiritual purpose and meaning of Islam were being neglected, leaving an opening for Hasan and Rabi'a to preach a doctrine of abstention and renunciation of worldly goods and comforts. Hasan's disciples founded a settlement of ascetic Sufis, dedicated to the denial of all earthly pleasures, in Abadan, a city downstream from Basra on the Shatt al-Arab. They practiced a discipline of abstinence and "perpetual sadness."[40]

Rabi'a of Basra steeped herself in the Qur'an and the sayings of the Prophet and the companions, impressing all with her knowledge.

Probably the daughter of a slave of Persian or other nationality, she showed that ethnic or tribal background did not determine one's spiritual bona fides. In fact, she too was a slave, released by her Arab master because of her holiness. One day, according to one of the many traditions associated with her, she left Basra to live on her own in the desert. Abandoning life's comforts, she wished to strip away distractions and find herself close to God. She even remained unmarried, keeping her virginity for God. She and Hasan of Basra, who became the trunk of a many-branched tree of Sufi masters, showed an alternate path to the truth in their way of life, not just in their theology. When she returned to Basra, she had gathered a following of both men and women. But distinctions of gender and even of heaven and hell faded into irrelevance for Rabi'a when one approached the greatest mystical union. Her most famous statement expresses this complete abandonment of what she saw as merely façades: "I am going to light fire in Paradise and to pour water on to Hell so that both veils (*i.e.* hindrances to the true vision of God) disappear and it becomes clear who worships God out of love, not out of fear of Hell or hope of Paradise."[41] More than a thousand years before John Lennon sang, "Imagine there's no heaven," a female mystic said similar words on the streets of Basra. Love of and union with God should motivate the believer, not worldly or otherworldly rewards. For Rabi'a, what the Qur'an promises will be found in paradise only obscures a deeper connection with God.

Although most Sufis wanted to add to religious law, not reject it, there were instances when some stepped beyond the confines of Sunni orthodoxy. Sufism existed outside governmental control and was often led by people in everyday professions, such as al-Hallaj, "the Cotton carder," who was famously condemned to death because of a profound misunderstanding of one simple phrase.[42] Orthodox jurists believed he was equating himself with God when he said, "I am God." Instead, he was merely expressing the possibility, after complete submission, of unification with God. He thus became a martyr for divine love. Al-Hallaj's life story also demonstrates how Sufism followed trade routes from Basra to the Indus valley. In the early tenth century, he took a ship to India to convert nonbelievers to Islam. From Sind he went with the caravans that brought brocade from Tustar (in what is now Iran) and returned to Basra with Chinese paper. While in Sind, he is supposed to have met with a branch of the Qarmatian Muslims of Bahrain who had a base in Multan. His possible connection with the Qarmatians caused the government of Baghdad great concern and may have been one of the main reasons for his death sentence.[43]

The impact of the stories and legends of Basrans such as Hasan, Rabi'a, and al-Hallaj on both Arabic and Islam was profound. Basra, having birthed a new culture and a new experience of faith, was a city at the threshold of heaven and the world. Spirituality and philosophy flourished there. The city was a hotbed of experimental thinking, radical ideas that tried to reconcile Islam with Greek, Indian, and Persian intellectual traditions. The resulting debates shaped Arabic into a language of sophistication and precision. In Baghdad, the caliph sponsored—and controlled—most scholarly activity. In Basra, by contrast, philosophy and literature were the product of self-supporting writers or those with the patronage of locals or passing merchants, so they were freer to pursue their own interests. Seekers of the wisdom of Hermes-Idris, for example, seemed to thrive as much in Basra as in the court of the caliph, if not more so. According to classical mythology, Hermes, or Hermes Trismegistus (Thrice greatest), was the transmitter of secret knowledge. The Hermetic tradition was guarded and passed on to those deemed worthy of it by various scholars, alchemists, astrologers, and Masonic societies in Europe. Some Muslims identify Idris with Hermes and with Enoch in the Hebrew Bible (Qur'an 21:85). They believe he was born in Babylon, near Basra, and had knowledge of divine mysteries. In Basra,

Idris became something of a patron saint to the merchants who encountered a cosmopolitan variety of faiths while traveling the world. They sought an explanation for this multiplicity, some universal interpretation of God beyond external doctrine.

The Ikhwan al-Safa', Brethren of Purity, were based in Basra. Their members wrote anonymously, believed that human values exist outside the constraints of any one religious or ethnic identity. In a number of popular works, which wove its philosophy into the fabric of Mesopotamian and Persian culture and intellectual thought, this secret society showed itself to be the heir of Plato and Aristotle.[44] Their most famous realization, an idea also espoused more than fifteen hundred years earlier by the Greek philosopher Plato in his dialogue *Timaeus,* was that the universe has a soul and humanity is a mirror of the entire creation:

> Know, O my brother, that by saying 'world' the wise men mean the heavens, the earth, and all the creatures of them, and they called it a 'macroanthropos' because they think that it is a single body with all its spheres, the strata of its heavens, the elements of its matrices and of the begotten beings, and they think that it has a soul, whose faculties are diffuse in all parts of its body as the faculties of the soul of a single man are diffused in all parts of his body. So, we want to recall in this epistle the form of the world, and describe how its body is composed, as the composition of the human body is described in the *Book of Anatomy.*[45]

In this ultimate expression of a humanistic world view, the workings of the human body and of the universe reflect each other. By studying the world and humanity itself, the Ikhwan wished to uncover the secrets of the universe, put into motion by the Prime Mover.

The Brethren were usually associated with the merchant classes and often with the Fatimids who conquered Egypt at the end of the tenth century. This would make them inclined toward Ismailism: a branch of Shi'a Islam whose followers believed in the secret or hidden meaning of religious texts such as the Qur'an and the hadith. One Abu Hayyan al-Tawhidi, writing in the eleventh century, claimed that many Brethren were ministers of the Buyids. If the Ikhwan did include political and religious leaders along with merchants, there may have been important connections formed among them. At one point, their leader was a qadi who worked for the Buyids, named Abu'l-Hasan al-Zanjani. Still other people linked the Brethren with the Qarmatians, famous for relocating Mecca's sacred Black Stone to the shores of the Gulf.[46]

The Brethren's writings point to a desire for encyclopedic knowledge, for a universal understanding of creation. Their work is in the form of letters, which they divided into four sections: fourteen epistles on mathematics, seventeen on natural sciences, ten on rational sciences, and eleven on theology. Some letters also include treatises on magic and the occult. The Brethren of Purity reflected the diversity they saw all around them on the streets of Basra. Reaching far beyond the realm of Islamic tradition, they studied Judeo-Christian, Iranian, Indian, and Hellenistic writings and even remnants of Babylonian astrology.[47] As Neoplatonists, they viewed the world in terms of its spiritual significance: scrutinizing it would reveal clues not simply to how things worked but to the structure of God's greater plan. This created the all-embracing interest.

Although not animal rights activists in the modern sense, the Brethren extended their understanding of spirits and souls to nonhuman creatures, even placing them on the same level as humans: "the animal degree is adjacent to the human [degree], not only from one side only, but from various sides" in the hierarchy of beings. "In fact, as the animal level is a place of origin for virtues and a source for noble traits, these cannot be contained by one animal species only, but by several species."[48] Their most compelling dialogue gives voice to animals in Arabic, allowing them to share the primacy of humanity itself, if only to make a point about humankind's universal aspects. In *The Case of the Animals versus Man before the King of the Jinn,* the animals, represented by many species, from donkeys to lions, tell the king of the jinn of their unjust enslavement, oppression, and slaughter by humankind and ask for freedom. How can this brutality by one species against another be allowed? Humans argue that it can only be part of God's plan, one that elevates all of humanity above the animals. The Ikhwan put this claim in the mouth of a so-called universal man, who was conceived in the milieu of Basra's literary and philosophical scene, a meeting point between Islam and the world, and embodied many identifying societal traits: "Finally arose a learned, accomplished, worthy, keen, pious, and insightful man. He was Persian by breeding, Arabian by faith, a *hanif* [a follower of a pure form of monotheism in the spirit of Abraham] by confession, Iraqi in culture, Hebrew in lore, Christian in manner, Damascene in devotion, Greek in science, Indian in discernment, Sufi in intimations, regal in character, masterful in thought, and divine in awareness." [49] It was thus with this extraordinary creation that Basra's intellectual life reached a level of global understanding. In the end, the king of the jinn, inspired by the message of the universal man, rules against the animals and declares that it is just for humans to have dominion over all other beings.

The Golden Age Fades

At some point in most literary and artistic cycles, the outward form and design become just as important as the content or meaning. In Basra, the result was the creation of word puzzles. One book of such baroque wizardry, called the *Maqamat,* or *Assemblies,* is full of formulaic tales meant to illustrate both moral and grammatical points. All the lines end with the same sound, double and even triple puns abound, and words with unusual double meanings are put together into a word puzzle. The idea is to show off the author's mastery of Arabic's lexicon and grammar. The *Maqamat* spread quickly from Basra, copied and redone with similar word puzzles, puns, and other tricks, many times throughout the Islamic world.

Yet even in the literary maze of the *Maqamat,* a deeper philosophical and mystical message is communicated. At the climax of one story, Abu Zayd, who in previous tales had filled the role of the trickster, reveals from within his soul a higher truth and deeply universalist sentiment:

> Weep not for a friend that is distant, nor for an abode, but turn
> thyself about with fortune as it turns about.
> Reckon thou all mankind thy dwelling-place, and fancy all the
> earth thy home.[50]

The fictional Abu Zayd was the quintessential Basran, actively challenging the past through a venerable means: in his case, the qasida, the Arabic ode. Instead of employing the classic *nasib,* the nostalgic "weeping for the abode" opening used by almost every other Arab poet to display pride in tribe and family, Abu Zayd advised that one "weep not" over the loss of any particular place. Rather, he called on his audience to consider humanity in its entirety, regardless of creed or race, as their family, to see the whole world as their "home." Such transcendent Basran literary achievements transformed Islamic culture from one that expressed purely Arabic roots and traditions to one compatible with Abu Zayd's vision of "all mankind."

While there were many sources of the extraordinary ideas floating around Basra, none of them could have emerged without the networks of different peoples, faiths, and languages that sustained the city's many links with the outside world. Basra was the place where a global Islamic culture assumed its form, a result of the city's global reach, independent urban spirit, and cosmopolitan character at the height of its intellectual golden age.[51] But while Islam was certainly the larger framework within which Basra developed, it was just one of many faiths and influences in the city. Basra resisted being the center of any one world view, religion, or imperial project. From its rather ramshackle inception as a small *amsar,* or fortress town, it had grown to attract the world to its gates and canals.[52]

Arabic was the lingua franca of Basra's cosmopolitan streets, standardized by Persians and shaped into odes, riddles, and philosophies by non-Arabs from distant lands, becoming a language of world literature and culture. The city's golden age, in the eighth, ninth, and tenth centuries, continued to shape the imaginations of educated Muslims everywhere, even after the Mongols invaded and trade shifted westward in the thirteenth century to that great rival of Gulf fortunes the Red Sea. In the fourteenth century, Ibn Battuta traveled from Tangier in north Morocco to Basra, expecting to find the marvelous and intellectually stimulating milieu he had read about in the great works of grammarians, poets, and philosophers. But when he arrived, he was astonished at how much its literary edifice had crumbled:

> I was present once at the Friday service in this [Basran] mosque and when the preacher rose to deliver his discourse he committed many gross errors of grammar. In astonishment at this I spoke of it to the qádí and this is what he said to me: "In this town there is not a man left who knows anything of the science of grammar." Here is a lesson for those who will reflect on it—Magnified be He who changes all things! This Basra, in whose people the mastery of grammar reached its height, from whose soil sprang its trunk and its branches, amongst whose inhabitants is numbered the leader whose primacy is undisputed—the preacher in this town cannot deliver a discourse without breaking its rules![53]

The slow shift of patterns of power and trade had ended Basra's cultural heyday.

The Mongol leader Hulagu Khan besieged Baghdad in the middle of the thirteenth century, smothering the last caliph in a blanket and trampling him under the foot of an elephant. The Mongols effectively ended the 'Abbasid dynasty, a line that had occupied the caliphate for almost five centuries. Also destroyed was the city of Baghdad, its population devastated and many of its great books burned and drowned.[54] Destruction and economic decline fell upon Basra, which lost a main purpose as a port for the Islamic capital. Over time, however, the Mongols acculturated to the societies of the peoples they vanquished, which was especially true in the lands around the Gulf. Just a few decades after the Mongols killed so many Muslims, their descendants became Muslims themselves. As the Mongols converted, power shifted to their court, in the uplands of Persia. Interestingly, the Mongol adoption of Islam was far from guaranteed. The Mongol khans, many of whom worshipped the Mongol god Tengri and some of whom embraced Buddhism, were besieged by ambassador missionaries who attempted to convert them to Christianity or Shi'a or Sunni Islam. Mahmud Ghazan, who ruled the Ilkhanate (in what is now Iran), converted to Islam at the end of the thirteenth century after meeting the famous Muslim scholar and jurist Ibn Taymiyya at his court. The rise of the Ilkhans and later the Seljuks, a Turkish dynasty, may have increased Basra's prosperity by connecting it to their overland empire, although the city remained far from its heyday.

In the sixteenth century, after the Seljuks had replaced the Mongols and then the Ottomans had established their empire, the Portuguese made an agreement with Basra's Arab and non-Arab leaders to maintain the city's independence from direct Ottoman rule. This allowed Basra to trade with the Ottomans and the Portuguese at various times. Basra remained diverse and was sometimes prosperous. Ambrosio Bembo, the eighteenth-century Italian traveler, remarked, "There are many bazaars, rich rather than beautiful, because of the quantity of merchandise from India that arrives there, carried not only by Gentile merchants but also by French, English, Portuguese, and Dutch, who every year dock there with their ships loaded with spices and jewels. These goods are sent throughout Turkey, and from there some go to Aleppo and then also to Venice." The monsoon trade was very much alive: "All the ships from India arrive in the month of July and leave at the latest in November so as to be in India before the winter, which begins there in May and ends in September."[55] Edward Gibbon described the air of Basra, which he called Bassora, as "excessively hot" but also "pure and healthy; the meadows are filed with palm-trees and cattle; and one of the adjacent valleys has been celebrated among the four paradises or gardens of Asia . . . and the vessels of Europe still frequent the port of Bassora, as a convenient station and passage of the Indian trade."[56] But Basra lost its primacy to Bushehr on the Persian shore, the location of the main British residency from the eighteenth century until 1946, when it moved to Bahrain. Even so, in the eighteenth and nineteenth centuries, the Naqibs and other of Basra's notable families engaged in trade with India by sea and overland with Syria and the Najd (in what is now Saudi Arabia).[57]

Basra has been the world's main gateway to the heart of Islam. It embodies the Gulf's distinctive cosmopolitanism, a model copied by later ports and other cities. Basra's rich history and heritage as the crucible of Islam have never been forgotten, and it has been continuously inhabited, even after economic decline. Today it is a major city on the cusp of resurgence. In contrast, the empty ruins of its medieval sister on the Persian shore, the once great city of Siraf, the port of larger, deeper, ocean-voyaging ships, are a stark reminder of prosperity's fickle nature in the Gulf. Sustained by its marshes, dates, and connections to the Mongol, Portuguese, Ottoman, and British Empires, Basra continued to live after its golden age, whereas Siraf became an urban ghost: when its merchants left, there was little reason for anybody else to stay behind.

3 *Siraf*

Boom and Bust in the Medieval Gulf (1000–1500)

Siraf hugged the coast, a thin line of habitation on the beach, a narrow bit of flat land hemmed in by mountains. The city embodied the challenges and opportunities of ports of the Gulf's mountain realm, the Persian shore. Built on a natural harbor, or *bandar*, called Tahari, Siraf was sometimes confined to just one street parallel to the sea. Much of the Gulf is very shallow, only 115 feet deep on average, but its waters are deeper on the Persian side, allowing larger ships to come into port and avoid the sandbanks found on the Arabian side. In Siraf, there was so little flat land available that the dead had to look down on the living: cemetery plots were dug into the cliffs surrounding the town because the shore, covered in tightly packed apartments for sailors, traders, and merchants, was too valuable for the deceased. On the northwest side was a gradual slope that climbed up to the main road, which wound to the city of Jam and, eventually, over a hundred miles of mountainous passes to Shiraz, one of the great market cities of Persia and the Silk Roads. In the eleventh century, Shiraz was the capital of the Buyid dynasty, the Persian Shi'a who patronized the Brethren of Purity in Basra and had gained effective control over the caliphs of Baghdad by working as their mercenaries. In addition to being a starting point for a road to Shiraz, Siraf was a place of maritime transit, a layover port where cargo from the larger ships suited for the Indian Ocean and the monsoon was transferred to smaller craft that could make their way up the river route to Basra.

Because of its connections to these two cities, Basra and Shiraz, Siraf was prosperous in the tenth and eleventh centuries, bursting at the seams with long-distance traders, merchants, and other travelers, for whom it could not build enough housing. It also had to import freshwater on ships. Although Basra could usually rely on its constant freshwater supply and on its fruit orchards and date palms for subsistence agriculture and local trade during economic downturns, Siraf, like most other cities along the Gulf, was not as well provisioned. A deep-water port connected to Basra and almost entirely reliant on long-distance trade, Siraf suffered along with it as the power of the 'Abbasid caliphs and Buyid sultans declined. As Baghdad's population fell, there was less need for a transfer port near Basra, and some trade shifted away from Iraq and toward the great magnet of the Indian Ocean. With the rise of the Fatimids in Egypt, a competitive route expanded in the west, sending commerce to Egypt, Venice, and the Red Sea ports. Having lost its function, Siraf was abandoned—but its end did not mean the collapse of trade in the Gulf as a whole. In fact, other primary transit ports emerged there in the medieval period, often on islands and bandars in the southwest.

Siraf's story is one of transience, of boom and bust, symbolizing the fickle nature of the Gulf economy. It went into decline at the height of its prosperity, in the tenth century, and had mostly disappeared as a major port by the twelfth century, after earthquakes and other natural disasters damaged its economic foundations. Siraf came to life almost wholly dependent on a global network of trade and died as that trade declined and relocated. Many islands and cities tried to take its place as the Gulf's main port, and those that succeeded for a time, such as the island of Kish and the semi-independent Kingdom of Hormuz, embodied both the precariousness and the perseverance of the medieval Gulf. Lasting from around 900 to 1500, this medieval or middle period of Gulf history, best represented by Siraf and its successors, again displays the resilience of the Gulf model of distinctive cosmopolitanism and autonomous ports, even as the metropole, Baghdad, was in decline and much of the Islamic world around it in disarray. These ports were able to conduct their cosmopolitan trade and remain tolerant of the practices of foreign merchants by maintaining relative independence from the Persian shah and the Turkish sultan, but that lack of centralized oversight could also mean intense competition from one another.

For the Islamic world as a whole, the medieval period was crucial in the formation of what Marshall Hodgson termed "Islamicate" culture, the product of Muslims and non-Muslims alike, inspired by Islamic and Arabic arts and society. The caliphate had been broken apart for many centuries, but a growing cultural unity, based on religious legal practices and Arabic literature, existed across the Muslim world, from Morocco to Malabar.[1] Although rooted in Islam, this connection encouraged a point of view beyond the simply religious and provided an awareness of humanity as a whole. In the Gulf, communities of Muslims, Jews, Persians, Mongols, Armenians, Sabaeans, Banians, Ibadis, and others continued to interact, shaping the local merchant ethos in their writing and ways of doing business. It is little wonder that the medieval study of comparative religion flourished there. Scholars such as al-Shahrastani (d. 1153), who wrote *The Book of Sects and Creeds,* obtained their information about the many peoples, languages, and faiths of the world from traders and other travelers who made their way through the Gulf.[2] Meanwhile, fortunes rose and fell and ports emerged from the desert shore only to disappear back into the sands in response to regional power changes and more distant global events.

City of Sailors

Siraf was packed with merchants, traders, and sailors from different realms. Some felt so tied to the water that they considered it better than the shore, as the tenth-century Persian geographer Abu Ishaq al-Istakhri related: "A man from Siraf went for trade to the sea and stayed in the boat for forty years and did not come to land. And when he came to the coast, he did not desire to leave the sea. He sent his workers to conduct trade and make profit and come back to him. And when the ship was in ruins, he moved to another one."[3] Siraf's mariners were famous for their love of the salt water and their intrepid voyages to distant ports. They were as comfortable in Canton (Guangzhou) as in Basra. Abu Zayd al-Sirafi, a tenth-century traveler to East Asia, compiled stories from mariners in Siraf who had voyaged to India (*Hind* in Arabic), China (*Sin* in Arabic), and east Africa (*Zanj* in Arabic). Accounts of the splendor and wealth of China in particular challenged the Arab world view. There were so many Muslim and Arab merchants in Canton that the Chinese ruler appointed a "Muslim man . . . to settle cases arising between the Muslims" at the port.[4] Likewise, the Chinese knew about the Gulf and its important cities. Zhao Rugua (d. 1228), an official in Quanzhou, wrote a record of foreign peoples in Arabia and Persia based on information from Arab mariners.[5]

Sailors made regular, often biennial trips between Siraf and China. The predictability of the Indian Ocean monsoon and Siraf's oppressive heat and other weather created a certain annual rhythm. The winds that blew from the northwest in the summer made for easy voyages east across the Indian Ocean. In the winter, winds from the opposite direction allowed for an equally easy return to the Gulf, in the months when the temperature was relatively cool. The geographer Ibn al-Balkhi wrote that Siraf was "very populous and full of merchandise, being the port of call for caravans and ships." The scents of roses, camphor, and sandalwood wafted through its markets, where merchants made "immense sums of money," especially after Siraf was connected to Shiraz.[6] In the summer, when merchant ships were heading east, wealthy shipowners and traders who did not want to risk the voyage themselves would shutter their shops and homes in Siraf and make their way into the mountains to their retreats around the Buyids' capital.

Archaeology has revealed clues to Siraf's prosperity. Excavations of the medieval city are ongoing near the small village of Taheri, with its rock-cut graves and crumbling dwellings and cisterns. Like many other abandoned ports along the Gulf, the site is desolate and windswept, with barely a boat at anchor. Signs of its former splendor have long been preserved in the dry air. James Morier, a British traveler, in 1809 saw "extensive ruins and sculptures." The entrance to the harbor was marked by "two large white spots . . . formerly covered with glass," according to local accounts. They served as guides for the hundreds of ships that used to make their way into the great port, and, as Morier noted, "the reflection . . . produced by the sun's rays [on each circle] rendered the object visible to a great distance at sea."[7] In the early twentieth century, the British writer Arnold Wilson described broken cisterns and pottery, including large amounts of Chinese porcelain "strewn about." Slightly inland, human remains in caverns and other mysterious monuments led some to believe that Siraf was founded as a Zoroastrian town or even by Persia's legendary Kayanian dynasty, supposed contemporaries of King David.[8] In the latter half of the twentieth century, international teams of archaeologists recognized Siraf's importance as a naval base under the Persians, who ruled the Gulf before the coming of Islam.[9] Thus, it already had the ships and shipbuilding infrastructure necessary to take off as Basra and Baghdad grew more prosperous and demanded goods by sea.

Even more commerce oriented than Basra, Siraf was a deeper-water port that could welcome large ships without the need to transfer goods to vessels with shallower hulls. It made possible—and was almost wholly dependent on—the long-distance global trade that fueled the imaginations of Basra's poets and other writers. The people of Siraf were known for their business acumen and willingness to bend their customs to meet the requirements of visiting merchants. With this practical attitude and with high demand from Baghdad for luxuries from China and all the ports in between, Siraf prospered. The tenth-century chronicler al-Mas'udi noted it as one of the wealthiest places in the entire Islamic world, due to the large sums earned and spent there by mariners of many faiths and origins. He recalled the city as the crucial node of the trade web, the port of call immediately after Basra.[10] Al-Istakhri wrote about its multistory teak homes (some of this wood would have been from old, deconstructed ships) and fine buildings along the Gulf: "The most important town of the district of Ardashir, after Shiraz, is Siraf, which is almost as large as Shiraz; its houses are of teak wood, or of other wood from Zanzibar; they have several stories. The town is situated on the sea coast, is covered with fine edifices and is very populous. The inhabitants take such great pride in the elegance of their houses that some spend 30,000 dinars in constructing a house and surrounding it with gardens." The geographer also indicated that there was a limited source of water from the mountain of Jamm, or Hum, probably captured by a Persian qanat, or dug-out, underground system. He counted a rich array of imports coming into the city, many from the east coast of Africa and throughout the Indian Ocean: "aloes wood (for burning), amber, camphor, precious gems, bamboos, ivory, ebony, paper, sandal wood, and all kinds of Indian perfumes, drugs and condiments." Surrounded by steep mountains, Siraf had little room for agriculture beyond some private gardens. Instead, the whole city was given over to commerce. A clearinghouse for merchandise from the Indian Ocean making its way to Mesopotamia, Siraf also produced some of its own items for export. As al-Istakhri noted, "In the town itself excellent napkins are made, also linen veils, and it was a great market for pearls."[11] Ibn Khaldun mentioned that the clay stamps of the caliphs, used to seal the red wax of their letters, were all manufactured in Siraf, "a specialty of this city."[12] By the time this fourteenth-century historian was writing, in faraway Tunis, the memory of the Gulf port's greatness had faded, and he makes little mention of its role as the linchpin of trade between the Gulf and the East.

Siraf's story of rise to great prominence followed by dramatic fall was repeated by many Gulf ports. Success could be both fragile and fleeting as trade moved from one city to another along the fickle Gulf's shores. This also meant that, as in much of the world where ports often became centers of power, those of the Gulf remained on the periphery of empires.

Decline

All was booming in Siraf until a series of earthquakes, starting with the great quake of 977, threatened its reputation as a safe port. While the city tried to rebuild, savvy rulers of rival ports took advantage of its misfortune. The port of Kish, on an island about two hundred miles to the southwest, was often Siraf's bitter competitor.[13] While Siraf was governed by the autonomous atabeg (Turkish governor) Rukun ad-Dawlah, he attempted to capture Kish and add the island to its trading network. Abu al-Qasim, the merchant-ruler of Kish Island, was similarly envious of Siraf's prosperity. His strategy was to kidnap the traders there and force them to use his port instead. This didn't quite work the way he'd hoped for Kish, but the effect on Siraf was exactly what he wanted: "No merchant would bring his ship into the port of Sīrāf to refit, nor for shelter would any anchor there on the voyage to Kirmān [an inland region and city] from Mahrubān or Dawraq or Baṣrah, wherefore no goods but leatherware and pots, and things that the people of Fārs alone had need of, now passed by the road of Sīrāf, and thus the town fell to complete ruin."[14] But it was not earthquakes or the ambitions of Kish's leaders alone that led to the end of Siraf: far more important was its vulnerability to changing trends in world commerce and to the competing factionalism and political disunity that led competing warlords to try to lure its merchants away. Marco Polo, writing in the thirteenth century, mentioned Kish, not Siraf, as the main stopping point in the Gulf: "Baghdad is a very great city. . . . Through the city flows a very large river, and on this river on can well reach the Indian Sea. There merchants come and go with their merchandise. Know that, from Baghdad to the Indian Sea, the river is a good 18 days' journey long; merchants who wish to go to India follow this river down to a city [island] called Kish . . . and from there enter the Indian Sea."[15] The island also linked trade between the Ilkhanids (Mongol successors in Persia who had converted to Islam) and Genoa, which had been increasing its commerce through the Gulf.[16] Kish, however, had a growing rival: surrounded by irrigated streams and date palms, the port of Hormuz was founded on the Plain of Hormuz, the mainland at the narrow opening of the Gulf. Its merchant-princes, not as interested in date farming as in trade, decamped to a more easily defended island offshore after being attacked by a prince of Kerman, the base of a Seljuk sultanate in the twelfth and thirteenth centuries from which regular, if unsuccessful, raids tried to bleed Hormuz of its commercial wealth. Polo went to Hormuz, not by ship as most sensible merchants of the region would do, but by way of Kerman, down a treacherous twenty-mile descent. In this mountain pass, travelers were continually assaulted by "robbers," who seemed not to be under the control of Kerman.[17] Hormuz paid tribute to Kerman under the Seljuks, but their successors the Ghuzz Turks had little ability to exact much more from Hormuz's wealthy merchants, who had moved to the island by then. Regardless of the prevailing Turkish overlord, Hormuz traded pearls and silks with cities as far away as

Venice, forming a connection between the booming Mediterranean cities and the markets of the Indian Ocean.[18] With commerce shifting from port to port, the Gulf exhibited the same pairing of political decentralization with local social and cultural vibrancy seen in many other regions in this period, such as the Mediterranean. In the Gulf, this meant the flourishing of unique literary expressions and celebrations of a nonimperial form of cosmopolitanism, typically without the interference of overweening powers inland.

Thus, as Hormuz rose, Kish went into decline. It was replaced just as quickly as it had replaced Siraf. There were several possible reasons. In the eleventh century, the cotton boom in Iran, which had been ongoing since the rise of Islam and which used Kish for the export of cotton goods, seemed to peter out. This was once an engine of great productivity and of the cloth trade throughout the Gulf region, and the economy suffered greatly.[19] Around the same time, a military commander from the Persian mainland invaded Kish and pillaged its stores and the homes of its wealthy merchants. The prince of Hormuz in 1230 took advantage of Kish's weakness to secure his city as the primary Gulf port. To do this, Hormuz expanded outposts on the Arabian shore and formed an alliance with Qalhat in Oman, and as the two cities "became dominant in the Gulf-Omani trading patterns, . . . Kish's days were numbered." Hormuzis seemed to triumph not only from eliminating a rival in Kish but also from their strong connection to the powerful Nabhani dynasty, which brought Oman's abundant agricultural products to the trading table.[20] The sources on the kings of Hormuz provide important insights into the rise of this later medieval Gulf port as it moved from the mainland to its namesake island for both greater security and more autonomy. Most traders who went there used it as a transit point between Africa, Arabia, and India, avoiding the potential hazards of going deeper into the Gulf. However, there were still plenty of dealers traveling through the Gulf.

One of them was Ibn al-Mujawir, probably a businessman from Khorasan, Persia, who traveled through Arabia in the thirteenth century and wrote between 1226 and 1230, just as the Rasulids were coming to power in Yemen, where they took advantage of a boom in Red Sea trade. Indeed, Ibn al-Mujawir gave the impression that the western side of the Arabian Peninsula was becoming more dominant. Nonetheless, he did not indicate a catastrophic decline in Gulf commerce and in fact showed how Red Sea trade was connected to Gulf trade, both of which may have benefited from the rise of Aden and the Rasulids. He also mentioned Gulf ports, including Kish, whose "people . . . have great esteem for strangers and take great care of them," and where, he claimed, "women dominate" the men.[21] Instead of being a disparaging statement, this reinforces the idea of Kish as primarily a long-distance port of call, since its women were commonly put in charge when the men went on trading missions far away.

Resilience of Trade

The Gulf, although facing several crises, remained an integral site in the mixing of faiths and goods in the medieval Indian Ocean trading system.[22] One almost unacknowledged and still underexplored part was east Africa: evidence of Gulf trade has been found in the Lamu Archipelago off the coast of Kenya, and scholars have called for a "new thalassology" of the Indian Ocean that better incorporates the Gulf-African economy into world history.[23] Horses raised in Arabia, prized as far away as Bengal for their endurance, were one of the most important exports from the Gulf to the subcontinent.[24] This trade was facilitated by Jewish, Hindu, and Muslim ship-owning merchants, whom their passengers called *nakudas* and *nauvittakas* (Gulf and Indian Ocean words for "ship captains") and who "illustrated remarkable cooperation and social amity."[25] Similar cosmopolitanism may have existed among the famed Karimi businessmen, of Yemeni, Egyptian, and Indian extraction, who made the Red Sea spice and slave route between Egypt and India highly prosperous. While it was once believed that most of them were Muslims, there is no reason why Christians and Jews could not have been part of their ranks.[26] One of the nauvittakas, Nuruddin Firuz, starting from the port of Hormuz, traveled to and traded in India's Kathiawad Peninsula in 1264. His career is a case study of pragmatic interactions between people of different faiths. This Muslim worked with Hindu friends and other contacts to build a mosque in India. Moreover, he was highly successful at his business of equine export: six years after the fall of Baghdad, literal horse trading was still happening between the Gulf and India. Nuruddin's fellows called him *malik ul tujjar,* "king of kings of merchants."[27]

The rise of the Red Sea route, therefore, was not necessarily the death knell for the Gulf. In the fourteenth century, in fact, the autonomous Kingdom of Hormuz created a thalassocracy of connected ports and islands from Bahrain to the strait. Such was the fame of Hormuz's "fish-eyed" pearls that Abraham Cresques of Majorca, a Jewish mapmaker from the western Mediterranean, depicted pearl fishers in the lower Gulf in his *Catalan Atlas* of 1375.[28] Even Baghdad, demoted and without its caliph, continued to be a center for trading pearls, as Marco Polo remarked: "Almost all the pearls brought from to Europe from India [and the Gulf] have undergone the process of boring, at [Baghdad]. . . . It is the noblest and most extensive city to be found in this part of the world."[29] Ibn Battuta noted that things improved for the Gulf after the Mongols converted to Islam and created a cultural center in Persia.[30]

For some historians, global cosmopolitanism did not emerge until well after 1500 and is set within a Western frame. What, then, explains the world of Nuruddin Firuz, the "social amity" and remarkable acknowledgments of universal human experience that seem to verge on the "modern" concept? Part of the answer, perhaps, was the end of imperial hegemons, the decline of the 'Abbasid caliphs and the resulting lack of centralized imperial power able to enforce a singular doctrine. Their fall seemed fated by God and the stars as punishment for excess and luxury. Ibn Khaldun predicted this collapse. He claimed that al-Kindi, the astrologer of the 'Abbasid caliph al-Ma'mun, composed a book on the future of Islamic empires: "It indicated that the end of [the 'Abbasids] and the ruin of Baghdad would take place in the middle of the seventh hijri/twelfth century and that its destruction would be a consequence of the decline of Islam." This work disappeared, he said, "without a doubt because it perished along with the books thrown into the Tigris by Hulagu."[31] So famous was the fall of Baghdad that it entered both Islamic and European history as a morality tale. Marco Polo repeated the fictional story of the Mongol Hulagu locking the last 'Abbasid caliph in his tower of gold and other treasure without food.[32] Interestingly, in describing Baghdad after its sacking, Polo still called it an important city and part of the wider Gulf trade, now that the Mongols were interested in expanding their power and commerce.[33]

Once the Mongols had crushed the 'Abbasid caliphate in Baghdad, the economies and culture around the Gulf shifted but remained fairly steady. Scholars of the pearl trade have shown that it seems to have increased in the century of Baghdad's decline, evidence for a narrative of resiliency, not collapse. In 1225, during the Song dynasty, a customs official from Canton recorded pearls and horses from Kish and Oman. In that period, "the Gulf, previously established as one of the two most important sources of pearls in the world along with India, gained a reputation as *the* leading provider of the most and the best pearls . . . with Bahrain being the premier market and fishing ground." Competitors were emerging on the Persian shore as well.[34] Instead of being beset by problems due to Baghdad's collapse, independent rulers and migrant merchant communities in this era prospered in ports such as Siraf, Kish, Julfar, Qalhat, and Hormuz. Some have even theorized that the Qawasim, a tribe that will play an important role in chapter 5, founding the emirates of Ras Al-Khaimah and Sharjah in what is now the United Arab Emirates, originated as immigrants fleeing Siraf when it went into decline. Moving across the Gulf over many generations, they settled in various ports and were often called Banu Sirafi. They may have been members of the so-called Bani Huwalah, or Nakhilu, a group of Arabs who vehemently resisted any central authority and moved from the Persian to the Arab coast in the eighteenth century.[35]

Medieval Gulf ports arose on whatever space along the shore was most convenient. Their politics were slippery, transient, diffuse, detached from imperial centers, and, for dogmatists, sometimes dangerous, as they did not fit the usual religious paradigms of the Shiʻa Buyids and Safavids, the Sunni Seljuks and Ottomans, or, in the sixteenth century, the Catholic Portuguese. This autonomy was a feature of life outside the capitals and other great cities. In fact, the Gulf ports may have been even more decentralized. Ibn al-Balkhi described the "extremely torrid" regions along the coast as inhabited mainly by Arabs. There was no Friday mosque in any town and very little central government. In Irahistan around the port of Bandar Lingeh, the Arabic-speaking people were "always in revolt against the Government, since no army can stay in these parts for more than the three months of the springtime, for they cannot hold out the winter here by reason of the rains [and torrential flash floods through the steep valleys], with the consequent lack of fodder [for their animals; the local Arabs adapted theirs to eat fish in these circumstances], nor during the summer by reason of the heat." Hoping to collect rain runoff, the locals dug trenches so great in which to plant their palm trees that only the tops could be seen above ground.[36] Again, the extreme climate frustrated imperial ambition. The Arabs of this region—whose descendants still live near the Gulf, a Sunni, Arabic-speaking minority in modern Iran—rarely paid any sort of tribute to the Persians. The autonomy of these lands and the cosmopolitanism of the medieval Gulf ports continued under the Portuguese, thwarting attempts at forced conversion or the full control of trade.[37]

While Siraf declined and almost disappeared, the medieval Gulf as whole did not share its fate. The thirteenth and fourteenth centuries were a time of prosperity for the autonomous Kingdom of Hormuz, for instance, which even managed to control the island of Bahrain and other ports along the Gulf. Pearls, a luxury good, provided a main source of income, bringing money into, not just through and out of, the Gulf. Its global trade nexus was very much on the minds of mariners at both ends of Eurasia: the famed Chinese court eunuch and admiral Zheng He (d. 1433), born a Muslim but also a worshipper of Mazu, goddess of seafarers, sailed impressive ships into the western Indian Ocean, and as we have seen, the Venetian Marco Polo visited the port of Hormuz and commented on its intense commercial and maritime orientation. Although it faced challenges including the fall of Baghdad and the hollowing-out of important markets (such as cotton), the medieval Gulf was far from a backwater. From 1000 to 1500 it was an important node in a network linking markets throughout Eurasia and Africa. While individual ports were vulnerable to shifts in world trade and large historical events, such as the Mongols' defeat of the 'Abbasid caliphate in 1258, the Gulf itself persisted in its role as a transit point in global commerce.

The Portuguese discovery of the route around the Cape of Good Hope, navigated by Vasco da Gama in 1498, allowed Europeans to bypass the Middle East on their way to India, but the economic impact on places such as the Gulf, which became part of the trading system of the Portuguese after they captured Hormuz, was much less than has been thought. Trade in spices, silk, and other commodities continued to flourish throughout the Middle East in the sixteenth century. During Europe's "age of discovery," the Islamic Ottoman

(Turkish), Safavid (Persian), and Mughal (Indian) Empires reigned in western Asia. Many of these powers saw European as their inferiors. When Portugal came to Arabia, unlike the first Europeans in the Americas, it was not completely unaware of the peoples and traditions it would find there. European traders were already relatively common in the markets of Siraf, Kish, and Hormuz. Indeed, it was the wealth streaming from the Gulf trade through the great city of Hormuz that the Portuguese were so eager to obtain.

4 *Hormuz*

How the Gulf Shaped a European Empire (1500–1793)

On Atlantic shores from the Azores Islands to Brazil, the sudden arrival of Portuguese ships, some built as fortresses on water, was a tectonic shock. New diseases, new weapons, and new technologies brought by the Europeans wrecked and sometimes nearly extinguished local populations, power structures, societies, cultures, and economies. In places with vast resources and agricultural potential, such as Brazil, conversion, colonization, and commodity exports changed the landscape. The Gulf was different. Although it would put a Christian, Catholic ruler in control of Hormuz and the regulation of Gulf commerce for the first time, Portugal's Gulf arrival was marked more by continuity than by disruption. The king of Hormuz stopped sending tribute to the shah of Persia and instead paid it to the king of Portugal, and while the Portuguese built an impressive fort and factory on the island, almost everything else about Hormuz remained the same. With little valuable land for farming, Hormuz served the Portuguese as a stopping point, a transit port, maintaining the role it had played for centuries. Despite almost three hundred years of rule in the Gulf, beginning in 1507, Portugal did not overturn its society or leave much of a mark beyond defensive architecture, artillery, and shipbuilding. The history of Portugal in the Gulf is interesting because of how much the latter did not alter, especially when compared to other parts of the Portuguese Empire around the world.

Disease resistance is one explanation. In the New World, pandemics introduced by European sailors ravished native armies and rulers. The people of the Gulf, in contrast, were already exposed and relatively immune to Eurasian diseases when Portugal arrived. Gunpowder was also already known, and artillery was used regularly in the Indian Ocean sea battles between Muslim empires before Vasco da Gama made it to India. Even Christianity was a familiar faith, practiced by many traders from India. Europeans were not new to the Gulf either: from Nearchus to Marco Polo, merchants from the west had been traveling and trading there for millennia. In the Gulf, instead of fundamentally displacing the local economic and social system, the Portuguese added another layer. They conquered a few strategic ports and erected bigger, stronger forts, trying to tax as many ships as possible to maximize revenue. Although they used important new technologies in maritime architecture, these advantages were soon copied by the enterprising people of the Gulf, such as the Omanis. Familiar with guns, cannons, and gunpowder, Omani shipbuilders modeled some of their warships and forts on Portuguese designs while modifying them to use local materials and even improving them. Some local rulers obtained Western-style artillery and even took over Portuguese forts for a time. Interestingly, many of the cannons found during restorations of Gulf forts from Oman to Bahrain still bear the royal stamp of Spain or Portugal. But the stamp of both is not much deeper than that.

Portugal's approach to slavery in the region around Hormuz is another reason for its lighter impact there. In the Gulf, European rulers did not systematically enslave the locals, destroy or replace previous structures, or impose their hegemony in a deep way.[1] While there were some outbursts of intolerance—moves to convert the king of Hormuz, to tear down mosques, to impose the Inquisition—these initiatives failed to stick. Early attempts to sell the freedom of the people of the Gulf, mainly merchants and others tied to commerce, were counterproductive and not that profitable, as this immediately killed trade in the area. Besides, the area around Hormuz did not support large plantation farming, and the date groves on the Plain of Hormuz on the Persian mainland were already supplied with labor. On the whole, Portugal behaved like previous Gulf powers: the main interest was in maximizing customhouse revenue. Hormuz under Portuguese rule became cosmopolitan and relatively tolerant, open to merchants from many backgrounds. The Portuguese population on Hormuz tended to be deaf to commands from the churches in Goa and Lisbon. When orders came from Goa—the headquarters of the Portuguese viceroy in India, who held titular sway over Hormuz—to destroy the mosque or to convert more people to Christianity, they were often simply ignored. While there were a handful of true believers in conversion, most of the Portuguese speakers who went to the Gulf were there to increase their fortunes, not to spread faith. Although some crusading evangelists tried to impose Catholicism, they did not succeed in disrupting or displacing varied Gulf customs or religious beliefs. Rather than the Gulf being fundamentally shaped by them, the Portuguese largely shaped themselves to the Gulf, becoming more tolerant of its cosmopolitanism as they realized that trade was more lucrative than the typical pattern of conquest, conversion, and control.

The Portuguese came to the Gulf with a great knowledge of strategic architecture, including how to leverage forts both defensive and offensive. Centuries of building fortress-like cities on the border with Spain, sieging and being besieged during the conquest of the last Muslim cities in the Algarve in southern Portugal in 1249, and another two and a half centuries of attacking Muslim coastal forts on the north African shore, including the taking of Ceuta in 1415, had refined Portuguese offensive and defensive systems. In the Gulf, the fort was even more the center of power for the Portuguese—getting a cut of trade revenue, not agricultural surplus, was the point—who built many throughout the region to enforce the payment by local ships for the *cartaz*, the official Portuguese permit to sail. The fort on Hormuz, the most important jewel in the necklace, was raised by Afonso de Albuquerque on the high point of Modrona. There the Portuguese could be separate from the rest of the bustling and diverse town, where most merchants and sailors remained in the winter while waiting for the change in the monsoon. The large Hormuz Fort is considered one of the "most important military accomplishments of Portugal."[2] It sits on a foundation that extends under water, using the cutting-edge design of Francisco Pires, the great architect known as the Master of the Works of India.

Freshwater made all the difference in siege warfare, especially in a place like Hormuz, where there were almost no sources on the island or the nearby shore that the attackers could use. In addition to new types of strategic defenses and the use of stone rather than mud brick in construction, the most important innovation of the Portuguese was the introduction of very deep and large cisterns to avoid this perpetual weakness of ports near the Persian shore. They could hold almost 240 tons, enough to withstand a prolonged siege. Albuquerque also had an enormous underground reservoir dug out and built a type of "water cathedral," a large, complex bastion that was located in the southwest of the fort alongside the keep and supplied yet more water.[3]

Another tactical advantage for the Portuguese was the shock value of their large, iron-fastened ships rigged up for long voyages from the tempestuous Atlantic. In fact, as early as the thirteenth century, Marco Polo noted the surprising difference between ships in the Gulf and those in the Mediterranean:

Ships [built at Hormuz] are very bad and many of them perish, for they are not nailed with iron nails but are stitched with thread made from the bark of Indian nuts [coconuts]: they soak it and it becomes like the hair of a horse's mane; then they make thread and stitch their ships; it is not damaged by salty seawater but is quite durable. The ships have one mast, one sail, and a rudder. They have no cover, but when they are loaded, they cover the merchandise with leather; and after they've covered it, they put the horses they are taking to India to sell on top. They have no iron for making nails; therefore they make wooden pegs and thread stitching. For this reason it's quite dangerous sailing in these ships. I tell you that many of them sink, because the Indian Sea is often very stormy.[4]

This nail free-construction, using mangrove or palm wood, which was readily available, was still being used in the sixteenth century and even as late as the twentieth century by traditional ship builders. While these vessels may have seemed inferior to European ones to Polo, he did not consider the cost calculus of local builders and merchants: these ships were often less expensive to make and had been developed over centuries to fit the conditions of trade in the Gulf and the Indian Ocean. Lightweight and dedicated to the transport of cargo and passengers, they used local materials and were adapted to the monsoon, which allowed for faster, cheaper voyages.[5] Even the use of ropes instead of nails may have had advantages, as some flexibility between the planks might have helped in shallows and around sandbanks. Unlike Portuguese carracks and galleons, locally built ships traced a well-known path and had little room for instruments of war. They could thus not as easily be gunboats, fortresses outfitted for Atlantic missions to the unknown. This put them at a distinct disadvantage during head-on conflicts with Portuguese ships. But their lighter construction allowed for greater speed, useful when trying to escape the imposition of Portuguese taxes on the high seas or along the shores of the Gulf.

Although it introduced great new cisterns, impressive armadas that often overwhelmed local populations, and strings of strategic forts on both sides of the Strait of Hormuz, Portugal still could not fully control the Gulf in the same way that it controlled parts of Brazil or even Goa, India. However, it did manage to build maritime forts in all three of the Gulf's geographic realms: the mountainous regions of Muscat and Hormuz, the desert in Bahrain, and the marshes of Basra. But these were really just small pockets of Portuguese power, meant to extract revenue from trade, not to directly administer the surrounding country. Instead, they commonly entered into practical power-sharing arrangements. In Basra, for instance, Portugal agreed to maintain an autonomous Arab tribal leader to limit the power of the Ottomans. From their capital in Istanbul, the Muslim Ottoman Turks ruled an empire stretching from north Africa to Aden. Their great navy, commanded by famous admirals like Piri Reis, a Greek convert, was the main military threat to Catholic Portugal and Spain, whom they also rivaled for trade with India. Thus, it was not surprising that the Portuguese sought such accommodations against the Turks. The same was true in Oman, after temporary truces. Although Portugal captured the port of Muscat, much of Oman, including the rich agricultural areas of the Batinah coast, was still held by local Ibadis, who regularly besieged small Portuguese forts along the shore. For the most part, however, the Portuguese benefited from the markets outside their forts as much as any other trader. Even as they held the high ground, they also bartered, bought, and sold. A fort could secure local value-added production or refinement of goods such as silk. Thus, the next priority after building a major fort like the one on Hormuz was to set up what was called a factory, a type of storehouse with some assembly activities, to which the Portuguese sent various kinds of merchandise to be sold to the local traders at a cheap price to gain their goodwill.[6]

Before the Portuguese took power, Hormuz at the end of the fifteenth century was already an important, globally networked port, a necessary stop for merchants on the monsoon route from Africa and

Arabia to India. The island's king paid tribute to Persian rulers, buying some stability, but was never really under the direct control of the imperial mainland. Hormuz had existed for centuries with one primary purpose: commerce. As the Portuguese would realize, the only benefit that it could provide their empire was the management of trade and the customhouse's enormous revenue—which was great but tenuous, liable to decrease if exclusionary or otherwise intolerant policies scared away the fickle merchant community. For the Muslim kings of Hormuz, it was necessary merely to switch allegiance from Persia to Portugal and become vassals of the distant Catholic kings in Lisbon and Madrid. An intensely cosmopolitan population of traders and merchants passively resisted attempts by Portuguese missionaries and moralists to Christianize and homogenize Hormuz. Outnumbered by the port's heterogeneous population and not wanting to discourage trade, the Portuguese found it necessary to tolerate practices that were banned in other parts of their empire. If they did not, merchants would simply decamp and even join one of the many "pirate" settlements established nearby to evade taxes. Of course, they saw themselves not as pirates but as armed competitors to the Portuguese.

Like the inhabitants of the Gulf, the Portuguese were a maritime people, with a seafaring culture dedicated to long-distance trade. Portugal was a small kingdom in Europe, using its attachment to the sea to expand far beyond its natural boundaries. It built forts along the coastlines of Eurasia, Africa, and Brazil, which allowed it to resupply ships on distant voyages and engage some in local trade without having to invest in the armies and people needed to control larger territories. By 1700 there were 244 major Portuguese forts around the world. Twenty were set up on the east African coast and the Gulf to control the western Indian Ocean, supported by many minor watchtowers and smaller forts nearby.[7] Hormuz was a piece of a globally interconnected network of forts in ports.

Part of the overarching goal of Portugal's King Manuel I was to circumvent the Ottoman Empire, Portugal's great rival, by establishing a direct link to the Indian Ocean trade in spices and the central Asian and Persian trade in silk. In addition to Hormuz, Portugal originally had its eye on capturing Aden, the port that controlled Red Sea trade and eventually gave access to the two Muslim holy cities of Mecca and Medina, then under the patronage of the Ottoman Empire. But Albuquerque failed to take it, so Hormuz was the primary Portuguese fort on both the Gulf and the Arabian Sea.[8]

Around Hormuz, however, the Portuguese always had to be on guard. Many naturally protected sandy coves (*khors* in Arabic) practically invited "pirates." The Nakhilu, or Banu Hula, were Sunni Arabic speakers on the Gulf coast of Persia whose descendants still inhabit the Gulf coast of Iran. For decades they set up pocket ports in the many hidden bandars and byways of the mountainous shore and created an underground economy that rivaled Hormuz's.[9] These "pirates" were a major drain on Portuguese revenue, regularly attacking ships that paid the fee for the cartaz, and docked at Hormuz. The Nakhilu's boats could retreat into the shallows and were faster and more agile than the much bigger and heavier Portuguese galleons and carracks. These sailors had a fearsome reputation and appear regularly in Portuguese chronicles. One Portuguese captain, determined to stamp them out, commanded fifteen ships "against the Niquilus [Nakhilu], now dangerous Neighbours, who hindered the carrying of Provisions to Ormuz [Hormuz], from whence 5 Vessels more were sent him, with which he made up 600 Men, many of them Men of Note. Scarce were they landed, when the Enemy rising from an Ambush fell on them with such fury, that breaking those who were drawn up, and hindering the others from forming themselves, they slew 250, forcing the rest to swim to their Vessels, many whereof were drowned. This was one of the greatest and most shameful Losses we sustained in *India*."[10]

On the eve of its capture by the Portuguese, Hormuz was an intensely cosmopolitan, globally connected, and multilingual city, densely packed with multistory apartments for merchants, sailors, and traders of all types. Its rulers were incredibly wealthy: despite being under the dominion of the Persians, they maintained diplomatic contact with distant powers and even sent envoys with gifts of horses to the Ming court in China.[11] Many Europeans went there, including the Italian explorer Ludovico di Varthema, who learned some Arabic to try to pass as a native and arrived after a daring journey on a locally sewn ship, blown by the monsoon winds along the Indian Ocean. He visited just a few years before the Portuguese conquest: "We departed from Meschet [Muscat] and went to the noble city of Ormus [Hormuz], which is extremely beautiful. It is an island, and is the chief, that is, as a maritime place, and for merchandise. It is distant from the mainland ten or twelve miles. In this said island there is not sufficient water or food, but all comes from the mainland. Near this island, at a distance of three days' journey, they fish up the largest pearls which are found in the world."[12] This center of global commerce was the destination of an astonishing number and diversity of ships and merchants: "Sometimes, as many as three hundred vessels belonging to different countries are assembled at the said city, the Sultan of which is a Mahommedan [Muslim]. . . . You must know that there are generally in this city four hundred foreign merchants, who traffic in silks, pearls, jewels, and spices."[13] The Portuguese did not bring the world to Hormuz. Instead, Hormuz was already a crucial node of the "world-economy" when Afonso de Albuquerque arrived demanding submission from its king.[14]

The Conquest

Knowing of its riches, Portugal had planned to take Hormuz for years. It sent a spy there in the late fifteenth century to gather intelligence about the island's wealth and strategic location, more than a decade before Vasco da Gama reached India in 1498 and proved there was a maritime route south of Africa. Traveling secretly on local ships owned by what he called "Moors" (a blanket term for non-Christians), Peres de Covilhão sailed from Aden, which he reached by caravan, to Calicut, to Goa, and back to Hormuz. Having heard his account of the busy trade there, Manuel I of Portugal pushed for a route to India that would circumnavigate Africa and not require embarking on any Moorish ship, as Covilhão was forced to do.[15] When Da Gama returned to Lisbon on the eve of the sixteenth century, having rounded Africa, there was a great celebration—not because he had discovered places that were not previously known but because he showed a way for Portugal to circumvent its greatest rival: the Ottoman Empire. Manuel I, with the blessing of the pope, became "King of Portugal, Lord of Guinea, and Lord of the Conquest, Navigation and Commerce of Ethiopia, Arabia, Persia and India."[16] King Francis I of France pretended to be unimpressed, derisively calling him "the Grocer King."[17]

Afonso de Albuquerque, a brave naval commander who proved himself in campaigns against Muslims in north Africa, was the descendant of an illegitimate member of the Portuguese royal family and eager to claim the nobility denied to him by birth. To gain the title he so desperately sought, he had to perform a daring deed for his king. Connected to the court, Albuquerque had formed a secret plan to control Indian Ocean trade with Manuel. Their idea was to capture Hormuz and Aden, classic choke points, depriving the Islamic world of trade from the east. Seeing his mission as a type of crusade, it was no surprise that Albuquerque later called the multiethnic population of Hormuz, regardless of origin or faith, "Moors," just like those who had finally been driven out of Iberia in 1492, ending the Reconquista. This term was a relic of those seven centuries of campaigns, used for the largely north African and culturally Arab Muslim rivals of the

Christians on the Iberian Peninsula and beyond. Portugal, like Spain, was hardened by that period of conflict and expansion. It was "a society organized for war," based on militias that had developed over hundreds of years, often tactically superior to their enemies, overwhelmingly brutal, and capable of taking down vast numbers of rivals.[18] With their light caravel ships rigged with lateens (maneuverable triangular sails) and their mastery of the winds and currents of the sea, the Portuguese had centuries of naval expansion and decades of rule over predominately Muslim ports under their belts, having captured cities along the north African coast. They did not believe that sailing around Africa was somehow better than going through the Red Sea or the Gulf—indeed, they would have preferred the latter. It was a disappointment when Albuquerque failed in his ambitious goal to take Aden, invade Mecca, and attack the Islamic world at its heart, but Hormuz and the Gulf trade were still a valuable prize. The Portuguese sent regular armadas, often galleons and carracks, to the state of India after 1505, and between 1500 and 1650, over one thousand sizable ships sailed from Lisbon to the Indian Ocean. Many if not most needed a place to dock on the Arabian or Persian coast while traveling with the monsoon, hence Hormuz's importance. It could also be used as a vice to squeeze the heartlands of Islam, blocking Ottoman ambitions in the region, including a desire to control all Indian trade to the Mediterranean and Europe.

On his way to Hormuz in 1507, Albuquerque attacked and set fire to several small fleets that were approaching the port. In trying to cut it off and surround it, he attacked its sister cities on the Omani coast, including Qalhat, another important port. While eighty of the Qalhat defenders lost their lives, only three Portuguese were killed. This deadly ratio seemed to favor the Portuguese in almost every battle, including against Hormuz. Another Omani port, Quriyat, was burned when its leaders failed to produce ten thousand xerafims (siler coins). The captured men and women of Quriyat, who were not kept as slaves, had their noses and ears sliced off. They were then sent "to Ormuz to bear witness to their disgrace."[19]

Despite being a hodgepodge of merchants and traders of many loyalties and faiths, the people of Hormuz banded together to resist Albuquerque's brutality. They knew the Portuguese were coming and prepared for the siege. The young, if precocious, king of Hormuz, Saif al-Din, who was a mere twelve years old, assembled more than two hundred galleons, plus mariners from the surrounding regions. His regent, a slave named Coje Atar, was subtle and courageous. He organized an embargo of all ships in the harbor, forcing them to fight for the city, and hired mercenaries and gathered volunteers. Up to thirty thousand Persians, Arabs, Baluchis, Indians, and others in boats large and small— sixty of considerable size, full of archers and guns, and a ship of one thousand tons, laden with cannon sent by the king of Cambaya in India—represented interests from around the Indian Ocean. But despite these impressive preparations, the Hormuzis had many reasons to fear the Portuguese, who had already established a reputation for fierceness at conquered ports.

Driven by a crusading spirit and assured of his tactical superiority, Albuquerque did not back down when faced with the overwhelming number of defenders at Hormuz. Even though his captains protested against going into battle outgunned, Albuquerque still abandoned negotiations with Saif al-Din, who refused an offer to become a vassal of Portugal. Leaving his main ship with his top men, Albuquerque brashly headed for shore, sailed under the jetty, and disembarked, then marched through the gates and started randomly "firing into all the houses": "This battle, which our men had with the Moors on the sea, lasted from seven o'clock in the morning until three in the afternoon, and in it there perished an infinite number of Moors, and the gunners so managed that day (for Our Lord was thus pleased to help them) that there was not a single shot fired that did not send a ship to the bottom and put many men to death."[20] With the benefit of surprise, Albuquerque could now make several demands. In addition to fifteen thousand xerafims a year in tribute, Portugal received land for a fort and a factory.[21] Also, all vessels passing through the Straits of Hormuz without a cartaz would be seized. Albuquerque began building the fort's principal tower immediately but was soon called to India. He returned to Hormuz in 1515, the last year of his life, to rescue the same king whom he had once besieged, now held by the shah of Persia, who wished to retake Hormuz. On his way back to Goa, Albuquerque grew ill and died, leaving his nephew Pero as the caption of Hormuz's fortress. Pero and subsequent governors solidified the fort, part of their attempts to further monopolize trade going through the strait.

At first, it might seem that Portugal's conquest of Hormuz and subjection of its king would upend the whole Gulf–Indian Ocean system, destroying its freedom of trade: merchants would avoid paying for the cartaz and might have feared being enslaved or forcibly converted. However, not all Portuguese governors and admirals were as religiously inspired as Albuquerque. Many had pragmatic motivations. In fact, after Albuquerque became the viceroy of India on the orders of Manuel in 1509, the previous officeholder, Francisco de Almeida, wrote a letter protesting the choice. Unlike Albuquerque, Almeida had used this appointment as a means of enriching himself and other merchants, setting up trade and factories, not pursuing a Catholic agenda. Albuquerque, in contrast, was an idealist and a crusader and always had a larger strategy at heart, one closely aligned with Portugal's new, ambitious role. He saw himself as the tip of a spear of Christian expansion, as Luiz de Camões, the Portuguese bard who flourished in the middle of the sixteenth century, recognized:

Albuquerque's hand shall tame
the Hormuz Parsi's heart which be his harm,

refusing gentle rule as yoke of shame.

. . . .

. . . For our God shall aid,

who holy faith of Mother Church would spread.[22]

The promised spread of "Mother Church" in the Gulf failed to materialize. After his death, Albuquerque's fervent mission was replaced by the pursuit of profit over prophecy, immediate gain over grand strategy. Hormuz was again a hub of merchants from many lands and religious backgrounds. This was Portugal's strategic and commercial beachhead. In the sixteenth century, wanting to increase trade there, the Portuguese even pursued an agreement with the Ottomans, sending an ambassador to the Sublime Porte in Istanbul after the autonomous pasha of Basra, where Portugal had a fort, proposed free trade between them and the Turks. Unfortunately for those pursuing this imperial reconciliation, the overture was rebuffed by the grand vizier in the palace, who seemed more interested in taking bribes than in taking peace offerings seriously:

> The [viceroy of India] Count de Redondo . . . sent Antony Teixeira, a Gentleman sufficiently qualified Ambassador, to Constantinople. He entered the Palace this Year [1564], scattering gold Coin. The Grand Signior to receive him was seated on the ground sewing Caps, which his Grandees bought at excessive Rates. The Ambassador told him that the Pasha had proposed a Peace to the Viceroy, and a free Trade for the Subjects of the Turkish Empire. The Great Turk, without lifting up his head from stitching, answered, I ask Peace of no Body: If the King of Portugal desires it, let him send some Great Man of his Court, and he shall be heard. The Ambassador brought a Letter containing this Answer to Portugal, and it was thought fit not to reply to it, because they found the Turk did not speak like a tailor.[23]

This story provides important evidence of the tensions inherent in the Portuguese presence in the Gulf. While peace may have benefited Portuguese, Persian, and Ottoman traders alike at a pragmatic and local level, that interest was stymied by a larger, imperial interest in maintaining conflict on a global level. Even as their subjects traded with one another, the Shi'a Safavids of Persia, the Sunni Ottomans of Istanbul, the Hanafi Mughals of India, and the Catholic Portuguese all fought on land and at sea for domination of the Indian Ocean economy. Great-power conflict usually got in the way of profit. Still, the Gulf, not under the immediate control of any of them, still found a way to benefit during this era of the so-called gunpowder empires, becoming an ideal space for trade in smuggled firearms.[24]

Portuguese power in the Gulf seemed even more assured after they defeated the Ottomans off Muscat in 1554 at the Battle of the Gulf of Oman, not too far from Hormuz. This was as important for Indian Ocean military history as Lepanto, a couple of decades later, was for the Mediterranean. But even as Portugal won battles at sea, it hardly won the loyalty of the people of Hormuz and other port cities under its control.

Four Holidays a Week

The Portuguese Inquisition reached Goa, India, in the middle of the sixteenth century.[25] But while enforcing Catholic orthodoxy, burning non-Christian books, and conducting trials of those accused of witchcraft were common in other outposts of the Portuguese Empire, Hormuz largely avoided many of the Inquisition's impacts. The main reason for this, it seems, was a desire to maintain trade and customhouse revenue, a great portion of which went directly to the church.

This unspoken reality offended some of the more conservative Catholic clerics who visited Hormuz on their way to Goa. They noticed that there was no real enforcement of Catholic morality on the city's streets, at least outside the fortress walls. The chronicler Manuel de Faria e Sousa, for example, was dismayed that the Portuguese chose gold over God in the Indian Ocean: "Till this time the Gentlemen had followed the Dictates of true Honor, esteeming their Arms the greatest Riches; from this time forwards they so wholly gave themselves to trading, that those who had been Captains became Merchants, so that what had been Command became a Shame, Honor was a Scandal and Reputation a Reproach."[26] The cleric P. de Herédia described Hormuz as hot and infernal, a hell on earth where segregation of faiths could not be maintained because of extremely narrow shadowed lanes and close quarters: "There are houses in the city where Christians, Muslims, Jews and Hindus live, and they all use the same door." This moralist tried to intervene, personally setting up a cordon to confine Christian women to two streets of the town, afraid they may have been selling themselves as well as their wares.[27] In Hormuz, a place where people came and went, often far from their homes and often away from their lovers for months, mores were relaxed. Descriptions of sexual relations between members of different faiths at the port indicate that the city was a fluid, transparent, and transient site of cultural mixing.[28]

Further offending Catholic purists were Hormuz's burial practices: even the dead of different faiths were put together, all buried in the graveyard just outside the city walls. As García de Silva y Figueroa, a Spanish diplomat who visited Hormuz in the first decades of the seventeenth century, just as the Portuguese era was nearing its end, remarked, "The rest of the plain [near Hormuz] is [a cemetery] containing the graves of Moors, . . . [Hindus] and Jews, without distinction of place, one along with the other indifferently." Like Herédia, Figueroa was also surprised to see Muslims and Hindus sharing homes, thanks to the island's lack of space, especially during the monsoon's high seasons.[29] Wealth and commerce, not religion or ethnicity, it seemed, determined one's ability to live in particular neighborhoods.[30] Moreover, Hormuzi society was frothy, diffuse, and dissolvable. As the population waxed and waned with the monsoon cycle, the city was largely abandoned some months, then full of merchants and bustling trade. It housed people of many diasporas, many identities, ethnicities, faiths. Nor was it a site of wholesale population replacement, as occurred in the wake of diseases that were brought to the Americas.[31]

Being small in number and unable or unwilling to settle in the harsh climate of Hormuz, the Portuguese only threw off the light grip of the Persian mainland instead of destroying and rebuilding everything in a Catholic mold. For the first decades after their arrival, the collecting of trade customs and the title of *malik*, "king," were in the hands of families with Arab ancestry, creating what political scientists like to call a "condominium" power arrangement. These Arab kings had paid tribute to Turkish, Perso-Mongol, and Persian rulers farther inland, Timurids and later Safavids. Although it was said that "the custom-house of Ormuz is a conduit of silver that is always running," the Portuguese, perhaps revealing a novice understanding of the Gulf economic system, did not take over this main and only substantial source of revenue outside the cartaz until after Albuquerque captured the port.[32] In almost every previous case in Gulf history of a port's being taken by force, the seizing of the customs revenue was the immediate and most important first step. This threat to his income, however, drove the king of Hormuz to plot against the Portuguese. He secretly organized simultaneous rebellions in Hormuz, Bahrain, Muscat, Quriyat, and Sohar, hoping to divide and distract the few Portuguese in the region, many of whom were killed. The rebel Hormuzi king was soon defeated by a Portuguese detachment of ships with accurate artillery. They set fire to part of the city, and he fled, succeeded by his thirteen-year-old son. Even after this revolt, however, the Portuguese still did not fundamentally change the way business was done on the island.

Hormuz's customs revenues, even when skimmed by corrupt administrators, were substantial, as high as those in Malacca, the eastern Indian Ocean gateway to China.[33] Importantly, the Portuguese realized they could raise funds from intra–Indian Ocean trade, including the sale of strong Arabian horses to India, not just trade with Europe. Even church workers were paid by customhouse revenue: the administrator, the priest, the treasurer, the organ player, two choir boys, and four unidentified beneficiaries all received money directly from this source, which also provided alms to the poor distributed by the House of Mercy and the cost of upkeep for the Augustinian and Dominican convents.[34] From the needy laity to the abbot, the church in Hormuz was dependent on commerce, not on land revenue. Although perhaps loath to admit this openly and despite its mission to convert, it found itself pragmatically tolerating the great diversity of religious groups on the island. This tacit acceptance must have been multilayered. For one thing, there were many forms of Christianity: Catholics, Eastern Orthodox, Armenians, Georgians, Jacobites, and Nestorians would have had to negotiate the building or sharing of worship spaces. This was unlike Goa, where the Inquisition imposed Roman Catholicism more successfully.

Hindus were one of the major groups of traders in Hormuz, and their religious practices shaped the city. They allowed holy cows to walk in the streets with a card of immunity that was handed out to prevent the animals from being claimed, sold, or slaughtered by beef-eating Christians or Muslims. Visiting Hormuz in the middle of the seventeenth century, Pietro Della Valle, an Italian who traveled in the region just as the Portuguese were losing their hold on the city, explained that "in some cities under divers princes, where there are many Banian merchants, large sums of money are paid each year to ensure that the cow cannot be used for meat; and others needs must put up with this, and offenders are punished rigorously with their lives." He had also heard of "weddings between cows and bulls" that were paraded through the streets.[35] Even the Muslims, according to Della Valle, adopted the notion that these beasts held special power and should be respected, probably due to a long-standing need to tolerate these Hindu practices. But he had some odd ideas about Islam, claiming that its adherents "believe that the fabric of the world is sustained on the horns of a cow, or ox, called by Mohammedans [Muslims] Behemoth."[36]

Occasionally, individuals of one faith put on the garb and identity of another to pass and gain advantage in commercial, social, or, presumably, sexual relations. This could lead to cross-cultural comedies of errors on the streets of Portuguese Hormuz:

As for their religious rites, the Indian idolaters are very diverse, for the most observant and the most rigorous of them neither eat nor kill any living thing. Rather, they regard it as a great sin to destroy even unclean creatures, such as fleas and so forth. On the other hand, they believe that it is good and holy work to give life and liberty to animals, and thus very often they buy, at great cost, birds that others have caged and that have been hunted for food, only to free them from death and give them, as they do, their liberty, for the love of God.

This practice is frequent among them, and once it led to a very charming event in Ormuz. A Christian, who was dressed like an Indian, bought from a huntsman some birds to eat at home, but the huntsman believing that he was in fact an Indian, who wished to make the charitable offering of freeing the birds, as soon as he had taken the money, opened the cage and let them go. The Christian started to shout, and when the huntsman was informed how he had been misled, he had not only lost the birds but had to return the money to the Christian, amid roars of laughter from the bystanders.[37]

At sea, religious rites were shared by Muslim and Hindu mariners—although, interestingly, not those of other religions—when they left the

FIGURE 9. Musandam *batil* with goatskin, Khasab Fort Museum, Musandam, Oman, 2016. Photo by author.

Gulf, sailing through the Strait of Hormuz and out to sea amid treacherous currents and rocks.[38] In the ceremony to exit Hormuz, a toy model ship appeared on deck, outfitted to look like the actual ship in every detail. Then, according to one Portuguese priest's account from 1663, "a sailor beat the drums and the ship's master blew his whistle and everyone on board, both Hindus and Moslems, got together, each with samples from the goods he carried in the ship, and placing these in the tiny ship, they put it out in the sea with much rejoicing. . . . It was a tribute all ships paid to Cape Mosandam [Musandam], which was otherwise so evil that those who failed to do it on the way to India would undoubtedly consider themselves lost on their return journey."[39] On their ships, the Dhahoori and other maritime families of the Musandam Peninsula still adorn the *batil*, a decorative element of the bow, with the skin of a goat and cowrie shells for good luck, to secure a safe passage through the difficult waters of the strait (see figure 9).[40]

Back on the island, charismatic yogis and holy men of other faiths were visited by Muslims and Hindus alike in Hormuz. It seems that this crossing of lines upset religious leaders on all sides but was impossible to stop. Even if these groups had kept to themselves, some people would have been happier if the island had been home to fewer. One Jesuit, for instance, lamented that on Hormuz "we have four holidays each week: the Hindus on Tuesday, the Moslems on Friday, the Jews on Saturday and the Christians on Sunday. It appears to me as if every day is a holiday." [41] Hormuz stood out as a multisectarian middleman, a point of transition for both peoples and goods.

One year in the second half of the sixteenth century, the governor of Goa ordered the destruction of the mosque of Hormuz, including its minaret. Interestingly, it was the intervention of King Sebastian himself, the head of the Portuguese Empire, that saved it. Portugal was in a great deal of debt, and he may have wanted to maintain the customs and tribute coming from Hormuz. Although Sebastian is often portrayed as a dreaming crusader for his forays into north Africa, it appears that even he realized the importance of Hormuz's Muslim community and its trade as a source of revenue. Other attempts to destroy Hindu temples, demolish Muslim mosques, and raze Jewish synagogues in Hormuz were made after the Third Provincial Council of Goa. They were also largely unsuccessful. At the start of the seventeenth century, Hormuz's non-Christian houses of worship were still bustling. Even if knocked down, they were quickly rebuilt. Hormuz seemed ever ready to flout the intolerant decrees of the church, often with the tacit support of local Portuguese officials.[42]

Exasperated by the lack of support they received in Hormuz, some Portuguese Catholics tried a new strategy: making converts of or into the Hormuzi ruling family. The hope was to create a Christian dynasty that would pay tribute to the Portuguese king. Matias de

Albuquerque hatched a plot to replace Farrokh Shah I, the king of Hormuz, with a Catholic convert named Sheikh Joete. The plan dissolved when Joete died, assassinated in Goa at the end of the sixteenth century, but his son, taking on the fully Portuguese name Don Jeronimo Joete, continued to claim his right to Hormuz's throne. Although a daughter and a son of a Hormuzi minister were convinced to convert to Catholicism, probably under the influence of the island's powerful Augustinian monasteries and Albuquerque, backlash from the local population and intervention from the hinterlands stymied the attempt to catholicize the Hormuzi elite. Badr al-Din, a local chief from the Iranian mainland, amassed his troops and threatened to cut off supplies to stop the plot to Christianize Hormuz's royal line and thus tie it to a deeper dependence on Portugal. What few Hormuzi converts to Catholicism there were ultimately moved to Portuguese India, where they received income from the viceroy.[43]

Portuguese administrators used Hormuz as a machine to amass personal wealth, often at the expense of the crown and the island. "Much of the money" meant for defensive batteries and strong forts, for instance, "was pocketed by unscrupulous high Portuguese officials."[44] While certainly a source of moral and physical decay, this widespread corruption may have been precisely what prevented the Portuguese from imposing more intolerant policies on the population. Bribes to Portuguese officials represented far more money than their salaries and allowed Asian traders to pass through Hormuz without paying full taxes or duties.[45] Corruption softened the already soft shell of Portugal's presence and may have given it the malleability to remain longer than it could have otherwise. It is a testament to the power of the port, the pull of the customhouse, the climate of commerce, and access to wealth that the Portuguese persisted on the island despite rampant mismanagement.

The End of Portuguese Rule

The seventeenth-century English poet John Milton in *Paradise Lost* invoked Hormuz as a byword for sinful decadence.

> High on a Throne of Royal State, which far
> Outshone the wealth of Ormus and of Ind[ia],
> Or where the gorgeous East with richest hand
> Showrs on her Kings barbaric pearl and gold,
> Satan exalted sat, by merit rais'd
> To that bad eminence . . .
>
> (2.1–6)

Hopes, desires, wealth, splendor, and decadence: Hormuz under the Portuguese helped prime the European colonial imagination. But even while offering symbolic significance as modern Europe's first real gateway to the riches of Asia, Hormuz, in the vein of Gulf ports before and after, resisted becoming an effective colonial outpost. As a center of trade and cosmopolitanism only barely controlled by imperial power and dependent on the cooperation of local rulers and other actors, Hormuz still had all the main characteristics of the global Gulf port after more than a century of Portuguese rule.

Portugal's presence was not without consequences, however. Its legacy went beyond its administrative imprint or even the physical stamp of the forts it constructed around the Gulf. The technical advances it introduced in guns and other weapons, mapmaking, and shipbuilding—all had their impact. The Portuguese experience in the Gulf contributed to a body of knowledge and a template used by later European and non-European powers. Even the Portuguese language was employed for some time as a lingua franca among Indian Ocean traders traveling back and forth from Africa to Arabia, India, and Indonesia.

As the Portuguese expanded their alliances and zones of influence in the Gulf, they changed Europe's spatial awareness of it. The Portuguese cartographer Fernão Vaz Dourado, for example, who was born in India and traveled back and forth between Goa and Portugal, created a beautifully stylized map in the sixteenth century that shows a great advance in awareness of the shorelines, ports, and islands of the Gulf, depicted as a correctly oriented, narrow-necked, and distinct body of water, not just a continuation of the Indian Ocean, as in previous maps.[46] The Portuguese were building on centuries of local Indian Ocean expertise. One of the most famous of the pre-Portuguese navigators was Ahmad Ibn Majid. Although scholars dispute whether he sold or otherwise revealed his information to the Portuguese, his *Book of the Benefits of the Principles of Seamanship,* written around 1489, reveals a sophisticated and extensive knowledge of the ports, winds, and currents of the entire Indian Ocean world.[47] Afonso de Albuquerque's *Commentaries* describes how he learned as much as he could about the surroundings before attacking Hormuz, including studying a map made by a Muslim navigator:

> [He was] always keeping in sight of the coast, with the determination to leave no place in the whole of the land ignorant of what he could do to it; for he held it a most important part in his plan for getting possession of Ormuz, first to make himself master of all those places and ports which he might find along the coast, and to burn all their ships to prevent their assisting the [Hormuzi] king. And going along thus within sight of land, he told the Moorish pilots that he had a chart, made by a Moorish pilot named Umar, when he accompanied Vicente Sodré [a captain of the Portuguese naval patrol and uncle of Vasco da Gama], and containing all the harbours, towns, and places of that coast.[48]

To take Hormuz, the Portuguese depended on captives, traders, and other local partners, just as they relied on the island's king to maintain internal control once they had it.

In their turn, the Portuguese provided illustrated guides to the peoples and practices of the Gulf and the Indian Ocean. Medieval stories of headless men and monsters in foreign lands, while still inhabiting the imaginations of many, were gradually replaced by depictions of the customs, clothing, and habits of real people. Works such as the *Codex Casanatense* offered intimate, humane, and even sympathetic portrayals of diverse ways of life. While meant to excite the reader—an image from Muscat depicts nude women bathing, while one from India has a Hindu man willingly being crushed in a religious procession—this codex shows that the Portuguese were beginning the process of collecting and disseminating specific knowledge about the world beyond Europe, replacing myth and sea chantey with the descriptive, the illustrated, the categorized. Interestingly, the Persians also painted stereotypical views of the Portuguese. A pale and handsome Portuguese youth in one seventeenth-century manuscript, probably a visitor to the Persian court from Hormuz, reveals that observing and desiring went both ways (see figure 10).

Back in Europe, however, Iberia was facing several wars of succession, and the English and the Dutch were chipping away at Spanish and Portuguese possessions. As Lisbon and Madrid declined, Amsterdam and London rose to become world economic powers.[49] Peace treaties ending wars among Spain, the Netherlands, England, and France mandated a cessation of hostilities in the zone north and east of the "lines of amity," the Tropic of Cancer and an imaginary boundary in the middle of the Atlantic. European powers that wanted to fight would now have to take their imperial disputes overseas, outside this area. This system lasted until around 1680.[50] Far beyond the lines of amity and therefore fair game for rival European powers,

FIGURE 10. Young Portuguese man in a manuscript from Safavid Iran, seventeenth century. Metropolitan Museum of Art, New York. Rogers Fund 1955.

Hormuz, like many Portuguese possessions, was too ripe and seemingly too easy to take for British traders and merchants to ignore. England, which had defeated the Spanish Armada in 1588, felt confident at sea, and it rushed to fill the void as Portuguese and Spanish influence waned in the Indian Ocean.

Della Valle chronicled the dramatic last days of Portuguese rule over Hormuz. An Italian Catholic with Portuguese sympathies, he was in Shiraz, attempting to travel to Hormuz, when his path was cut off by the Persians:

> A huge army [of Persians] had come to the sea coast to await the arrival of . . . English ships, with which the Persians wished to prevail by force in this way. They, the English, could not refuse to [take Hormuz from the Portuguese], for otherwise they would not be allowed to ship [their] silk; but on the contrary, if they served [the kind of Persia], he had ordered that they were to be given whatever munitions and provisions might be needed, and that they should also be paid for all the losses they received through the war; and even for the delay in transporting the silk, with interest.[51]

English silk merchants, thousands of miles from home and without any authorization from the Crown, were thus compelled into an alliance with the Persians against the Portuguese, to take Hormuz, in order to secure their merchandise. Finally, the Persians could reclaim their suzerainty over Hormuz, even if it came at the cost of depending on another Christian and naval power, the English.

Historians often think of European powers as possessing agency, "choosing" and dominating their colonies, selecting ports for exploitation and setting up a mercantile system that prioritized the metropole—Lisbon or London, say. The colonized port is the passive party, bending to the will of the imperial power. The classic case of Commodore Matthew Perry sailing to Japan to demand its opening to trade was the opposite of what happened in Hormuz in 1622. Instead, the Hormuzis, along with the mix of Persian, Arab, Jewish, and Hindu merchants participating in the Hormuz market, were here the active party. Good navigators who sensed the changing winds, Hormuzis chose the British over the Portuguese as their new naval protectors. It was was in the interest of Hormuz and Persia alike for the English navy to protect their lucrative Indian Ocean market, even if this came at the marginal cost of ceding some power—and they may have felt, as Della Valle wrote, that they "have only changed . . . Christians for Christians, the Portuguese for the English."[52]

The Persians, English allies, celebrated the most. Although it conceded shipping rights to England, Persia not only benefited from direct trade with this rising power—and without having to pay protection money to Portugal—but had also finally retaken Hormuz as its vassal, allowing the Safavid shah ʿAbbas the Great, who reigned for the first three decades of the seventeenth century, to centralize some aspects of his empire's economy. One big change was that Persia now controlled the Gulf trade in silk, which it exported to regions not under Ottoman power—thanks largely to Christian Armenians whom the shah had resettled during a war with the Ottomans. As the Ottomans advanced, ʿAbbas had ordered mass evacuations and devastated the lands north of the Aras River. Many of the evacuees, originally Christian, later adopted Islam. In Isfahan, the important inland trading city that ʿAbbas restored and chose as his capital, non-Persian Georgian and Armenian Muslim converts staffed the bureaucracy. Isfahan remains a great center of Muslim architecture and art, financed by Armenian trading networks that stretch around the world. New Julfa was its suburb built by the shah to house Christian Armenian refugees from Ghilan, an Iranian city south of the Caspian. Armenian merchants connected overland and sea routes across the whole of Eurasia.[53]

While Persia and its shahs were more than happy to benefit from the economic expertise of their Armenian subjects, their dependency on the English and English ships was a serious handicap. Lacking an effective navy, Persia was not able to take charge of the entire Gulf, even at the height of Safavid power. The last of the Safavids, who continued struggling in their remaining territories against Russians, Afghans, and Ottomans, was deposed in 1736. The new and powerful ruler of Iran, Nadir Shah, of the Turkoman Afshar dynasty, which had effectively taken Isfahan from the Safavids in the 1720s, tried to rectify Persia's long-standing lack of a good navy. After buying European-style ships and setting up a naval dock at Bushehr, he captured Bahrain and even Ottoman Basra, but only fleetingly. Nadir Shah also wished to end the centuries-long rift between Shi'ite and Sunni Islam. With typical bravado, he convened a conference of clerics to smooth out their differences and bring universal peace to an empire that spanned the Gulf.[54] He was murdered by his troops in the middle of the eighteenth century, however, leaving his plans for reconciliation unrealized and his ships to rot away.[55] More than one hundred years later, in the middle of the nineteenth century, Iran's Qajar ruler also attempted to create a naval force in the Gulf, seeking but failing to acquire effective armed steamships. It was not until the last decades of that century that Persia began purchasing vessels, at the slow rate of one per year, from Germany. In the end, just two were sent: the *Persepolis* and the *Susa*. They rusted, hardly used, anchored along the Karun River in Arabistan, sent out only on dispatch missions.[56] Iran's inability to exert effective and controlling power across the Gulf, a body of water that defines its southern border, continues to be its most immediate strategic handicap.

The story of the Gulf in the sixteenth and seventeenth centuries does not fit the pattern of rapid Western domination that occurred elsewhere. Certainly, the Portuguese created some ruptures, but the Gulf did not change as much as other parts of the world impacted by European commercial and imperial projects. Despite some dramatic Portuguese victories, including the taking of forts dotted along the

shore, the cosmopolitan and autonomous Khaliji way of life continued to flourish, even within Portuguese cities and strongholds. In
contrast, the Gulf significantly transformed the culture of the Portuguese, as well as their Asian and Afro-Portuguese descendants, absorbing them into a global system of trade and contacts that had been
running for millennia. In Hormuz, the Portuguese came to accept
that they were just one group of many, part of a multiethnic, multilingual, and multireligious society. Although they had taken over that
society and may have had dreams of bringing its people to Christ
when Albuquerque captured Hormuz in 1507, they realized that con-
versions by force would only lead to the exodus of the main population and reason for the port's existence: merchants, who had a choice
of whether to come or not. While many Portuguese, perhaps especially those fresh off the boat from Lisbon, persisted in the fantasy
that they might convert Gulf Muslims and Hindus to Christianity
well into the seventeenth century, most Portuguese governors, merchants, and missionaries understood that far greater profits and far
greater access to trade would come from bending their rules and allowing the system of the Gulf and the wider Indian Ocean to continue as it had before. Instead of exacting taxes from vast estates, the
Portuguese in Hormuz relied on customhouse revenue, and trade ne-
cessitated toleration. While Hormuz was not a possession great in
size, it was great in wealth, and this was why the Portuguese put so
many resources into keeping it and were willing to compromise or
look the other way when it came to cultural norms. The chronicler
Faria e Sousa put it well: "The City Ormuz, a Kingdom more famous
for its Trade than extent."[57]

Portugal's experience in Hormuz also upsets some of the deepest
assumptions of world history. Many of the discipline's scholars identify 1500 as a significant turning point in the human narrative, the beginning of modernity. Some claim that global history itself, which is
about connections and exchanges across the whole world, started

only around 1500 with the European discovery of the trade winds and shipping methods that made global commerce possible.[58] The reasons given for the pivot on this date—rounded up from 1492, when Columbus sailed, and 1499, when Da Gama returned from India—are many. In the Atlantic and elsewhere, European intervention and the opening of global exchange created great alterations, tearing deeply into the fabric of societies and stitching together peoples and histories that had rarely before been linked. Peoples from the Americas to India and Indonesia were impacted in dramatic ways as European explorers and conquerors landed on their shores. Small European states ruled global empires. Wealth and power shifted worldwide as local and regional actors rose and fell. Germs killed off non-European populations, allowing a relatively few organized Iberians, equipped with superior military ability and weapons, to crush resistance. With so many successes for Portugal around the world, Albuquerque, Manuel, and their successors thought they could use Hormuz as part of a plan to conquer Islam itself, to establish a Catholic stranglehold on the Indian Ocean. Although Portuguese was spoken as a lingua franca of the Indian Ocean, used between groups of people who had no connection to Portugal, the ocean and the Gulf overwhelmed the Portuguese ambition to impose Catholic culture and religion on them as had been done in the Atlantic. The few Portuguese who settled in Hormuz eventually adopted its cosmopolitan ethos.

In the end, Portugal's main threat in the Gulf was not the English, the Persians, or the Ottomans but local Omanis, who had learned from the Portuguese, incorporating and improving on some of their tactics. With the rise of Oman, the Gulf unexpectedly produced a homegrown empire at a time when the rest of the world was losing to European expansion, again defying the typical narrative of world history. Its sultans and imams built a navy with Portuguese methods and local materials, which they used to take over Portuguese forts and ports all along the Gulf and the African coast. Muscat, an Omani city that had a natural harbor and was protected by two impressive bastions built on steep bluffs on opposite sides of the city, became the next great Portuguese stronghold to fall after Hormuz. From there, the Ibadi Omanis, in cooperation with South Asian and African partners, did not just control much of the Gulf. They also built a western Indian Ocean domain.

5 *Muscat*

Oman, the British, and the Long Nineteenth Century (1793–1945)

At the end of the eighteenth century, a "great divergence" in economic and military power was emerging between the West and the rest of the world, and it only grew during the nineteenth century.[1] While Europe could still be distracted by internal conflicts—such as revolutions and the Napoleonic wars—it seemed that little could stop the advancement of Western power, military technology, or economic prowess. New trading opportunities and markets opened up as explorers and merchants made their way deep into Africa and into the heart of Asia. Financed by investors throughout Europe, the joint-stock company was supreme. The most famous of these, the East India Company, took over much of India during the first decades of the nineteenth century.

In the Gulf, however, there was a divergence from the great divergence, as an exceptional local dynasty defeated a European empire in the middle of the seventeenth century and established a large maritime realm that would last centuries: Oman, whose rulers were initially based in Muscat, arose at the expense of Portugal, whose forts it took over along much of the western Indian Ocean. Its southern reach, on Africa's Swahili coast just above Mozambique, was ratified when it signed a highly favorable treaty with the Portuguese in 1829.

The Omanis were Ibadi Muslims. They practiced a form of Islam different from those of both the Shi'a and the Sunni. Although the

Ibadi faith was centered in the mountains of Oman, the Omanis were also a highly maritime people, dependent on trade and on relationships with other Muslims and non-Muslims. Their most important non-Muslim partner was the Banians. These Hindus were consummate merchants and were often given control of the customhouses and financial activities of the Omani Empire. The Omanis and their allies established a series of ports from the Gulf to south Asia. Oman reached its apogee under Sayyid Saʻid bin Sultan, who saw so much profit from trade with Africa that he shifted his capital to Zanzibar.

After the Persians captured Hormuz in 1622 with the help of a British fleet, the British presence in the Gulf grew alongside the Omani Empire, and often their interests merged, especially as the British were reluctant to rule directly over territories along the Gulf and Oman was happy to serve as an intermediary. As Oman expanded its trading empire in east Africa in the eighteenth and nineteenth centuries, the British gradually established an effective strategy to secure their primary interest: the flow of goods, information, and people from the Gulf to India. Their method worked much better than the Portuguese or Persian system: instead of having to station battalions or maintain forts to dominate Arab sheikhs, they formed alliances with those along the shore, conceding power and autonomy over land that was not viewed as particularly valuable. By signing the treaties they were offered, whose simple aim was to provide security for British shipping, these sheikhs became the ancestors of the princes and kings of today's Gulf. After the 1850s, however, British steamship technology and the separation of Muscat and Zanzibar into two realms governed by two rival sons of Sayyid Saʻid caused a rapid decline in Omani power just as the British crown was establishing its formal presence in India and creating the protectorate system in the Gulf. Britain began relying more on agreements with coastal Sunni Arab sheikhs, not just its relationship with the Ibadi Omani sultan, to ensure the security of shipping between the Gulf and the subcontinent.

Climate and geography stifled Britain's ambitions, limiting any long-term or large-scale intervention on land in the Gulf before World War II. There were a very few British "political residents" in the region, often East India Company men, who meticulously gathered intelligence, trying to learn as much as possible about the intricacies of intertribal relationships.[2] But while the political resident may have been from England or Scotland, many of the British representatives were from Persia, Arabia, or south Asia. The British especially favored low-cost "native agents" from India who could write in English and Arabic.[3]

Controlling the Gulf from the water was a brilliant solution to the problem faced by every empire that tried to find a way in. The British policy also encouraged a peaceful environment in which local shipping and pearl trading could flourish. One issue that complicated relations between some sheikhs and the British was the abolition of slavery, but although it was important in London, the Gulf was far away and full abolition was only variously enforced there. By the middle of the nineteenth century, the British had treaties with most of the tribal leaders along the Arabian coast, but their strategy changed after the unexpected discovery of Gulf oil in the 1930s, focusing more on infrastructure and bureaucracy building. Even in the last decades of their presence, however, the British maintained a relatively light touch in their dealings with the Gulf.

The Rise of the Omani Empire

In many ways, Muscat is a perfect Gulf port, although not strictly inside the Gulf. Located on the Gulf of Oman, that funnel-shaped body of water just outside the Strait of Hormuz that seemed to direct all ships into the same choke point, Muscat was a primary and crucial harbor, a safe alternative to the shallows of the opposite coast. Finding the city from the water, however, was a challenge. Called *Cryptus*

Portus, "Hidden port," by the ancient geographer Ptolemy, Muscat has the unusual feature of being invisible from the Indian Ocean, thanks to high mountain cliffs.[4] It is only when a ship comes near that the obvious way in can be seen. Extremely well protected by nature, old Muscat's harbor is a small horseshoe with a height on each end, on which were built two impressive forts, al-Mirani and al-Jalali. Although forts were here before, these twins were constructed mostly by the Portuguese and then improved by the Omanis. They stand today as sentinels over the palace of the sultan of Oman, built directly on the harbor below. All around the city of Old Muscat, which huddles against a small cove, are the precipitous, almost impassable Hajar (Stone) Mountains, forming the great wall of a natural fortress, capped by watchtowers. A gate on the inland pass allowing access to Mutrah, the main market town outside Muscat, was closed at night. While dates, horses, and other commodities could trade hands in Muscat, Mutrah, which lies along a harbor that is much larger but still protected by massifs, was where most merchants bought and sold their wares. Up the coast from Muscat and Mutrah, the summits begin receding from the shore, and a vast open plain spreads out. This is al-Batinah, "the Stomach," Oman's agriculturally rich lands, fed by wells, cisterns, and channels. Even the mountainous areas of Oman, however, are not barren: deep within the Hajar range are green -terraced valleys fed by the ingenious qanat system, which the Omanis call *falaj,* channels for bringing groundwater to dates and other crops. Some of these plots are concentrated near the high peaks of Jabal Akhdar (Green mountain) and Jabal Shams (Mountain of the sun). The same kind of channel also irrigates the flatland, the plateaus of Nizwa, where the Ibadi imam is elected, and, even farther from the sea, the "interior" to the west of the mountains. In this way, Oman, unlike much of the Gulf, has been supplied with a self-sustaining amount of food and water. It even exported large numbers of dates. But agricultural production was not the main concern of the

Omani rulers in Muscat. Instead, from the beginning, the port was dedicated first and foremost to long-distance commerce, made possible by its advantageous position on the coast. Many Omanis, even those born in mountain villages, went seafaring to far-flung places, especially in Africa and India. But Oman and its trading empire were not built by Omanis alone. They could not have been successful without alliances and collaborations at home and overseas, the result of centuries of contact across the Indian Ocean and between religious groups, including Hindus and Muslims.

The Omani and Banian taking of Muscat from Portugal in 1650 shocked Europe. A major imperial Western power had been bested not by another Western navy but by an emerging Gulf coalition between the Muslim Omanis and the Hindu Banians. One of the most important events in the history of Oman and Arabia, this was a new beginning for Oman and the Gulf. The Muslim Ibadis who captured Muscat were not given full credit, however. Rather, a Hindu was said to have opened the gates, as the Danish cartographer and explorer Carsten Niebuhr, a member of the eighteenth-century Danish Arabia Expedition, related: "The Portuguese made themselves masters of [Muscat] in 1508. Two churches, one of which is now a magazine, and the other the house of the *Wali* or Governor, still remain to show that *they* were once established here. An hundred and fifty years after their conquest of Maskat [Muscat], the Portuguese were driven hence by the Arabs, through the treacherous aid of a Banian, who had been robbed of his daughter by the Portuguese Governor."[5] The story goes that in January 1650, the outraged father rallied his fellow Banians against the Portuguese governor, named Pereira, who had sexually assaulted the Banian's daughter and held sway from the steep heights of Fort Jalali. He convinced the governor that it would be good to "drain the water from the garrison and discharge the gunpowder, since its 'shelf-life' had expired," then told the newly elected Ibadi imam, Sultan bin Sayf al-Ya'arubi, what he had done, effectively handing over the city.[6] In recognition of their aid, Sultan bin Sayf exempted Banians from paying the poll tax. This policy continued under later imams.[7]

It was cooperation between Omani Muslims and Hindu Banians over centuries that the story really celebrates. According to Niebuhr, "In no other Mahometan [Muslim] city are the Banians so numerous as in Maskat; their number in this city amounts to no fewer than twelve hundred. They are permitted to live agreeably to their own laws, to bring their wives hither, to set up idols in their chambers, and to burn their dead. If a Banian intrigues here with a Mussulman [Muslim] woman, government does not treat him with the same severity as he would meet with elsewhere."[8]

Despite their numbers in Muscat and their eventual role in expanding Omani trade along the African coast, Banians were not always aligned with the Omanis and seem to have had a complicated relationship with the Portuguese, sometimes shifting their loyalty as the fortunes of each shifted. The Banians—also spelled *Baniyas* or *Vanyas*—were a community of mostly Hindu and some Jain moneylenders, merchants, and bankers. Today they also manage large commercial enterprises. They came from all over Bengal and India, but the name appears to have spread to highly successful traders and money managers of many geographic origins.[9] The Kaphot Banians of Diu, a port city in what is now Gujarat in the northwest of India, were famed for their wealth and connections around the Indian Ocean.[10] Other Banians were from elsewhere in Gujarat. Not all engaged in high finance and trade—some were shipbuilders or carpenters. In the seventeenth century, Oman's Ibadi rulers allowed Banians, who kept many of their shops outside Muscat's walls, to trade with the tribes of the hinterland. By the middle of the eighteenth century, the Banians had moved squarely into Mutrah and become invaluable business partners of the Ibadis, all the way to east Africa.

Most Omanis were Ibadis, neither Shi'a nor Sunni. Instead, they claimed to be the original Muslims, had their own legal school, and believed that the imam, the political and religious leader, could be any pious man, not just a member of an elite tribe or a descendant of Muhammad. A large number of Ibadis from Basra found refuge in Oman's mountainous interior, escaping persecution by Sunnis and caliphs or perhaps simply a lack of economic opportunity in Gulf cities. While traveling for trade, some were forced to practice taqiya, dissimulation, to avoid being revealed as Ibadi and punished as heretics by Sunni or Shi'a authorities. They themselves have a pacifist philosophy regarding nonmembers. One branch of the Ibadis fled to north Africa, to the island of Jerba in Tunisia and to the Mzab plateau and mountains in Algeria. Some Ibadis went to port cities around the Indian Ocean, the beginning of their global network. Nonetheless, the main population was—and remains to this day—in the region around the relatively isolated Nizwa and Rustaq in Oman's Hajar Mountains. Ibadi identity was maintained and strengthened in the mountains even as trade in the ports opened the community to cosmopolitanism and as diverse expressions of religious practice informed the architecture, culture, and even daily life of those from the "heartland."[11]

By the seventeenth century, the Ibadis in Nizwa were electing powerful imams. Although ancestry was not supposed to be a requirement, it was typical for the imam's son or another relative to be selected after his death, and this passing of the title still occurred in the eighteenth century. In the seventeenth century, the practice allowed the Ya'arubis to establish a dynasty of Ibadi imams. As they grew in power and spread down from the highlands, they clashed with the Portuguese and the Persians for control of the Omani ports that were gateways to lucrative trade in coffee, dates, slaves, spices, and silk. Many Ibadis left Oman to pursue commercial success, going all the way to the east coast of Africa or to Bombay. But to succeed, they had to work with other groups. While the Ibadis who were nestled in summits maintained a cohesive religious message, it was the Ibadi merchant rulers on the coast who partnered with the Banians, who managed the customhouses and opened up markets for their allies. This agreement, a Hindu-Muslim union like none other, was profitable for both groups. Despite their religious differences, they created an interconnected migrant merchant community in ports all along the Gulf and the Indian Ocean. The Ibadi imams thus oversaw one of the most extraordinary expansions of commerce in the history of the Arabian Peninsula. In the seventeenth and eighteenth centuries, Oman was a region with fluid borders, sometimes extending well into the Gulf. From there its empire spread into southern Asia and eastern Africa, controlling various ports throughout the Indian Ocean and leveraging the desire of multiple Western powers—including the United States, which signed a treaty with Oman in 1833—to enter its markets.

In the sixteenth century, Portugal had expanded its empire along the coast of Africa with a series of *prazos*, trading posts, which were controlled by Portuguese merchants and their descendants or Afro-Portuguese or Goan *prazeros*. These agents acted almost like independent rulers, buying and selling slaves and collecting gold and ivory for export in exchange for textiles from India, fine china, and other goods. Sometimes the prazos were more vibrant and successful than official Portuguese government posts. But by the eighteenth century, the prazo economy was in decline, along with Portuguese fortunes throughout the western Indian Ocean, due to increased competition from other European powers and dynastic troubles in Lisbon. This was an opening for Banians, who managed customhouses and built businesses, and the Omanis, who ousted the Portuguese from both Muscat and Fort Jesus in Mombasa, a coastal city in what is now Kenya, where they formed an alliance with the Yao people near Lake Malawi. The Yao captured slaves, whom they sold to work in clove plantations in Zanzibar and as far away as Brazil. Omanis established themselves in Zanzibar and near Kilwa on the Swahili coast, setting up an economic system in competition with the Portuguese merchants from Goa who traded ivory and slaves along the Zambezi River.[12] Moreover, they were able to take advantage of growing global demand for east African commodities as "a new pace of economic change became evident over the period from about 1780 to 1820. . . . The sheer quantities of goods entering trade, and especially those exported overseas, increased manyfold."[13] At the same time, Africa proved to be a rich market for international manufactured goods and textiles, far more extensive than Arabia.

Also in the eighteenth century, Oman defeated Persia, which was expanding into Oman after the English helped it to capture Hormuz (see previous chapter). Sayf bin Sultan II, a member of Oman's Ya'arubi dynasty, formed an alliance with this local hegemon and urged it to interfere in Oman against an internal rival of his. Persia decided to conquer the divided population and started to take over Omani ports and forts, imposing its rule on the local population and sending resources back to Persia. Sayf's poisonous agreement with Persia tainted his reputation, and Ahmad bin Sa'id, the governor of the port city of Sohar, rallied Omani tribes against them and the Persians and became the undisputed sultan in 1749. He established his capital in Muscat, where trade and the customhouse provided him with revenue—with the help of Banian and other merchants. At the same time, he maintained important commercial and political connections to the religiously conservative Nizwa. Recognizing his growing power and wanting him to provide them with security, the British signed a treaty with Ahmad on the eve of the nineteenth century to guarantee their access to the Gulf: not only was trade important, but official and secret communications needed to be maintained between British East India Company agents in Basra and India.

Ahmad's eventual successor Sayyid Sa'id bin Sultan reigned for fifty years, almost the entire first half of the nineteenth century, and focused even more on trade, greatly expanding Oman's influence in the western Indian Ocean. However, this allowed local Arab sheikhs to assert their autonomy and create insecurities along the Gulf, especially after Sa'id moved his capital to Zanzibar, more than six thousand miles from Oman off the coast of east Africa, around 1840. It was one of the centers of the trade in cloves, which had recently been brought from Indonesia by the French and grew very well in Zanzibar's climate, contributing to the success of Sa'id bin Sultan's empire and its merchants. The historian Abdalla Saleh Farsi described the atmosphere of the court at Mtoni Palace, which Sa'id had built on Stone Town's port, and its long procession of peoples of diverse creeds and cultures who supported his far-flung trading network:

> You would see a stream of people arriving, dressed in white spotless kanzuz [long robes], black johos [shorter robes] with gold braid or degles or bushtis [types of robes], with red or white turbans, daggers of gold or silver, swords or scimiters of gold in their hands, sandals of different sort on their feet. Each lord had a crowd of followers, bond and free, behind him. . . .
>
> The hall was spread with valuable carpets and mats to sit on. Chairs were not yet brought unless Europeans came or foreigners of some other race. As 9 [AM] or 4 [PM] struck the ruler descended, surrounded by his children, and entered the court hall. . . . There was complete freedom of speech and all could speak with the same freedom.[14]

Throughout that cosmopolitan network, however, was a structure of Ibadi law, custom, practice, and history, maintained as it was in nearly inaccessible mountains thousands of miles to the north even of Zanzibar.

As prosperous as it was, the Oman trading system was not all powerful. The sultan had to wage war against Oman's rivals, and there were divisions even between Omanis. However, Oman still dominated, and the cities along Africa's eastern shore identified themselves with the commercially minded Sayyid Sa'id bin Sultan.

This success would not have been possible without support from Banian traders, who provided goods from India and even managed the customhouse, a main source of revenue for the sultan and his dependents. In the same years that Saʿid moved most of his operations to Zanzibar, the southern limit of the Omani trading empire was formalized when his agent signed a favorable treaty with the Portuguese governor of Mozambique: it gave free access to Mozambique to hundreds of Omani ships even as only a couple of Portuguese ships still alighted in Muscat or Zanzibar annually. This led to complaints by bureaucrats in Lisbon, which was then in the midst of turmoil as the kings of Brazil and Portugal vied for authority and political and constitutional crises swept through Europe.[15]

Back in Oman, the sultanate's trading empire influenced interior design in everything from households and mosques to fortresses. While images of sentient beings are often banned in Islam, merchants settling on Jabal Akhdar or in the Dakhaliyya (Oman's inner lands) hung Ming-style blue-and-white pottery, supposedly from distant China and sometimes depicting a phoenix or other creature, around the mihrab, the prayer niche showing the direction of Mecca, in Ibadi sanctuaries such as Masjid al ʿAyn. In fortresses far from the sea, such as those in Nizwa and Rustaq, archaeologists have preserved sketches of ships such as dhows (traditional but usually somewhat smaller wooden boats) and *baghlahs* (traditional large teakwood boats, called "mules" and used for luxury items) etched into the walls by soldiers who must also have been sailors, pining for the open water even as they remained cooped up on land duty.[16] The sea did not leave the Ibadis, even when they went into their inner heartlands, and the heartlands did not leave them when they went out to sea. They retained a distinctive manner and style of dress, including the *kuma*, a rounded cap with colorful designs.

The Omani Empire engaged in subtle conflict and competition with British interests under Saʿid, sometimes through his marriages.

FIGURE 11. Saʻid bin Sultan's Omani-Persian baths, built on Zanzibar in 1832. Photo by author.

For instance, in seeking to diversify his alliances, he wed a Persian princess, for whom he built a bathhouse that still stands on Zanzibar (see figure 11). He also proposed to the queen of Madagascar, although the offer was rebuffed. He had more success with the French and the Americans, to whom he gave favored trading status, as they were happy for an ally in their struggles to decrease British maritime dominion. At the time, the United States was a rising power in the sale of textiles to east Africa, where ships from Salem, Massachusetts, regularly arrived with "Mercani" cotton fabrics, which were used in some of the most popular clothing for women. The reach of the "empire of cotton" spanned the Indian Ocean,[17] as reflected in the Indo-African-Arab style of Saʻid's finely woven, intricate choga coat (see figure 12). In 1840, Saʻid sent Ambassador Ahmad bin Naʻaman al-Kaabi to the United States on the *Sultana*, causing a spectacle in New York City and political outrage at the luxuriousness

FIGURE 12. Sa'id bin Sultan's choga, likely from Kashmir, with Kanni weave pattern, date unknown. Metropolitan Museum of Art, New York.

of the gifts presented to President Martin Van Buren, some of which became part of the collections of the Smithsonian Institution.[18] In the end, however, the British overtook Oman in one of its main sources of economic supremacy: shipping. Steamships really turned the tide, although traditional shipping existed in parallel well into the twentieth century.[19] The British did promise to share the technology, but it remained undelivered except for a dysfunctional old engine that was lying unused in the godowns of Zanzibar's port when Sa'id died in 1856. The succession crisis that followed was negotiated by the British under Lord Canning and led to a split of Sa'id's empire into the separate realms of Oman and Zanzibar, each ruled by one of his sons.[20]

Although divided from Zanzibar, Oman maintained its international trade and even entered the dried fruit, date, and coffee market with some success, but California date production eventually ended its mini date boom.[21] Local commerce continued as well, and unofficial and underground exchanges increased in the 1860s. As steamships linked south Asia with the Gulf and east Africa at a faster pace than ever before, "smugglers" and "traffickers" directed flows of weapons, slaves, and other banned trade.[22] Commerce in contraband firearms emerged, despite British attempts to control it, between the Euphrates, the Gulf, and the Indus. These arms were often smuggled on small, light traditional ships. While teak dhows still plied the waters, major business interests shifted to steam. Instead of needing muscle power and favorable winds and currents to move, steamship technology pushed itself through the water, making the Indian Ocean and the Gulf more accessible, less dependent on traditional knowledge of the monsoon, and similar to any other sea under British control. But although they were able to marginalize the Omanis, displacing them from their historic role as a regional powerhouse, especially when it came to politics outside the sultanate's margins, the British did not themselves rule directly in the Gulf. By the 1820s, they had forged a hands-off treaty system, the protectorate, that solidified the strength of most Gulf rulers in order to secure British interests.

Forts Made of Paper

The British East India Company (EIC), a joint-stock company with an army of its own, had defeated its European rivals and the Mughals of India by the end of the eighteenth century and gained supremacy over much of the subcontinent with the defeat of the Hindu Maratha confederation in the first two decades of the nineteenth century. Desiring a good link with Basra, the EIC faced a publicity issue: many people, especially unaccompanied European women, were afraid to take the regular route to India through the Gulf because of its reputation for "piracy." The British needed to tamp down on the threat of raiding and kidnapping to allow relative freedom of movement, but they did not want to invest in security in the Gulf or to control it directly. So they invented a new defense system: they built paper forts out of treaties and words. Instead of viewing all Arab mariners as a "menace" or picking fights with surrounding imperial powers, the British instead signed a series of treaties with Arab sheikhs that held them responsible for keeping the peace in the Gulf: as long as British shipping was not attacked, they could do what they wanted. Over time, this created a bureaucratic paper trail that defined Gulf tribes, peoples, and places, prefiguring the creation of modern borders and national histories.

For their treaty system to work, the British had to identify signatories who could prevent "piracy" along their section of the coastline. They turned to the Bedouin chiefs who were then in control of the various *khors,* or shallow harbors, on the sandy shores of the Arabian Gulf. The Bedouin began arriving there in the eighteenth century seeking food and water for their camels after a series of devastating droughts reduced the productivity of pastoral herding. These poor, migratory groups who knew little if anything of maritime commerce changed their land-based nomadic lifestyle in favor of the pearl and fishing economy. The 'Utubi, for instance, who moved from the interior deserts of Arabia to the shores of the Gulf in what are now Kuwait and Qatar, with the patronage of the local Bani Khalid became Khalijis over just a few generations, fluent in the ways of migrant merchant communities, able to trade in foreign lands and languages and even willing to submit to the protection of a Western power—in this case, the British. The Tamim and al-Thani also settled in what is now Qatar. The Qawasim, another confederation of tribes, went to what is now the United Arab Emirates and to Lingeh on the Gulf's Persian side. With the British recognition of their sovereignty, these Arabs asserted autonomy against Oman and grew politically dominant.

By the end of the eighteenth century, the British had one of the few navies able to exert much influence on the waters of the Gulf. A plague had killed much of the commerce coming out of Ottoman Basra, which the Banu Ka'b had then attacked and ransomed. After the death in the second half of the eighteenth century of Karim Khan Zand, who founded the Zand dynasty, restored relations with Britain, and even controlled Basra for a time, political turmoil reigned in Persia, which turned inward and inland. Gallivats, Persian ships built for yet another attempt at creating a navy, turned to piracy, not the establishment of a *Pax Persica* in the Gulf. Centers of trade and population shifted from Hormuz and Bandar 'Abbas, a city under the command of a *shahbandar* (Persian port governor) and known for its high customs, to Muscat, and from Basra to Bushehr, the new center of a much reduced EIC presence in the Gulf, where often only one agent was stationed. Oman, although maintaining its claims and alliances and still intervening in the Gulf, was more focused on expansion along the east African coast. Both Britain and the Netherlands, one of its important rivals at the time, realized that the Gulf was not particularly profitable, especially given the necessary maintenance for far-flung European empires.[23] But the power vacuum meant that competition, raiding, and outright conflict became regular occurrences.

Insecurity in all three Gulf realms of marsh, desert, and mountain challenged the prestige of the British and their EIC, which had an army and navy twice as large as the Crown's military. Although not originally a part of the government, the EIC often served official British interests, as wars for supremacy in Europe influenced the distant ports of the Gulf and India, and vice versa. After their conquest of Egypt in 1798, the French increased their presence in the Indian Ocean, expanding their claims in India and trying to form alliances with Gulf rulers. A letter from Napoleon to Tippo Sultan, the ruler of Mysore, about French plans for an invasion of British India and the choking of British trade included a special codicil inviting the ruler of of Oman to ally with France.[24] Napoleon's defeat and withdrawal from Egypt in 1801 decreased British concerns over French inroads into the Gulf. Other worries arose, however, regarding the raiding of shipping, particularly on what the British called the Pirate Coast, the Gulf's Arabian side, between India and Basra, then controlled by the Ottomans, a British ally in the fight against Napoleon in Egypt. In 1808, the *Shannon* and the *Minerva,* two ships carrying the British flag, were captured by the Qawasim and their crews put to death. EIC leaders in Bombay called the Qawasim "barbarians" and "fanatical pirates" and began a mission to transform the Gulf from a region of instability into a buffer zone, a pacified space that would "protect the western flank of an evolving, and anxiety-ridden, Indian Empire."[25] In fact, this project helped create the idea of the "Middle East" itself. The term did not really exist until the nineteenth century, when it became necessary as a category for those lands between the Indian east and the European west where calm was required to ensure imperial commerce. The Gulf was a key component of this new strategic category.[26]

Even if the British had wanted to control the Gulf directly, their navy and merchants could not match the local maritime knowledge of the Qawasim and other "migrant Arabs," such as the 'Utubi and Huwala, who had settled along both sides of the Gulf and had an intimate understanding of its shifting sandbanks, shallows, pearl fisheries, and other hazards.[27] In dealing with raiders from these groups, the British at first used a hands-off approach, ordering their warships not to fire until fired upon. They also formed an alliance with the sultan of Oman, hoping that he would end the threat. Several spectacular attacks, however, including one in 1816 on the EIC's *Deriah Dowlat*, to which the response was embarrassingly ineffective, compelled the British to send more ships to resist and to solidify their grasp on the trade route through the Gulf.

Captain Francis Loch thus sailed from Plymouth, England, in command of the HMS *Eden* with orders to pursue and destroy. He soon discovered why previous British warships had such a difficult time against coastal raiders. Local Gulf boats were simply faster and better at maneuvering around shallow sandbanks. As Loch noted in his log, "The superior manner in which the sails were cut and set, as well as the rig of the masts and the form of the hulls, bespoke them at once to be pirate vessels. All was now crowded in chase, they using every exertion to run across our bow, and get before the wind." It was clear to Loch that the Arab boats

> had many advantages over the heavier, slower European-built men-of-war and merchant ships. They were faster and more easily handled, and there was nothing about the weather or the sea which the men who sailed them did not know. The Arab-built ships were shallower, drawing less water, and their captains were familiar with all the uncharted islands and innumerable shoals and reefs which made navigation on both coasts of the Gulf so difficult and dangerous. Even when she was several miles from the shore, the *Eden* could only proceed slowly, constantly swinging the lead, and sometimes sending a boat ahead to take soundings.[28]

Eventually, the *Eden* was close enough to fire and the wind died down. But the ship was stuck in the muck. The Arab vessels, with light sails made of local cloth, moved out of range just in time to evade capture or destruction. Loch gave up trying to approach them in the *Eden* and instead sent small boats in pursuit. His failure meant that the British would turn from force to diplomatic solutions. They also realized that they needed more information about the Gulf's geography if there was to be any hope of providing secure passage through it.

The British did try force one more time. In 1819, fresh from their victory over the Marathas in India, they decided to tamp down on raiding in the Gulf with a punitive raid of their own. Major-General William Keir headed an expedition of over three thousand men, brought on ships including the *Eden* and the *Liverpool* and joined by men sent by Britain's ally Sayyid Sa'id of Oman, with a mission to pacify the Qawasim at their port of Ras Al-Khaimah. Having burned the Qawasim's ships and destroyed their fort, the fleet sailed back to Bombay. The British realized, however, that it would be too costly to send a large fleet to the Gulf every pearl season, the time when attacks were most likely to occur. So when Major-General Keir returned in 1820, it was with a new mandate: not to destroy the sheikhs and their towns but to get their signatures on the first General Treaty with the Arab Tribes of the Persian Gulf.[29]

The language of the treaty, which is written in Arabic and English, shows some sensitivity to Islam: it begins with the general bismillah that opens every official Muslim document and says, "In the name of God, the merciful, the compassionate . . ., who hath ordained peace to be a blessing to his creatures." After this religious appeal, article 1 calls for "a cessation of plunder and piracy by land and sea on the part of the Arabs, who are parties to this contract, for ever." Per the second article, "If any individual of the people of the Arabs contracting shall attack any that pass by land or sea of any nation, whatsoever, in the way of plunder and piracy and not of acknowledged war, he shall be accounted an enemy of all mankind, and shall be held to have forfeited both life and goods." The treaty then states that "friendly . . . Arabs shall carry by land and sea a red flag . . . and this shall be in a border of white."[30] This color combination, white and red (or maroon), is the basis for the current national flags of Qatar and Bahrain. Signatories included Major-General Keir; Hassun bin Rahmah, the sheikh of Ras Al-Khaimah; "Shakbout," the sheikh of Abu Dhabi; and the sheikhs of several other towns along the coast.

Soon, more chiefs were added, and the treaty of 1820 was, for the most part, a success for British interests. Raids decreased. But the loophole allowing "acknowledged war" meant that conflicts kept erupting, especially during pearl season. In 1835, many sheikhs were obligated to accept a treaty of maritime truce ceasing all sea war, acknowledged or not, for a period of six months, which was renewed annually during pearl season until 1843, when a ten-year treaty was signed. In 1853, another general treaty, this time of "perpetual" peace and without the exceptions of earlier agreements, was ratified by Arab rulers including the Qawasim. In opening this era of formalized protection and guarantees, the British did not simply choose passive partners without agency. Instead, Gulf rulers were able to maintain the typical autonomous status afforded to Gulf ports and polities and played both sides of the imperial chessboard.

Prominent Arab leaders who did not sign accords with the British, such as Rahman ibn Jabr al-Jalhami (d. 1826), appear on the wrong side, if at all, in official accounts. Unlike those of treaty signatories, their descendants would not be able to claim sovereignty and power in the Gulf. Labeled a pirate for not agreeing to the general treaties, Rahman, who ruled from various ports including Qatif and Khor Hassan in the north of Qatar, nonetheless scrupulously avoided British shipping and even allied with the Omanis against Saudi Wahhabi influence. Together with his son, he died in battle against the Khalifa, the rulers of Bahrain, dramatically exploding his own ship full of gunpowder to escape capture. While characters like Rahman still operated well into the 1820s, violating the spirit of the first general treaty, they were an increasingly endangered species.

Beginning in the nineteenth century, Britain solidified not only alliances but also information and designations in the Gulf. By bringing particular sheikhs, such as those of the Khalifa in Bahrain and the al-Thani of Qatar, onto their ships to sign agreements, the British identified them and their descendants as the rulers of the Gulf. The observation, in effect, created the reality it described. In the same way, many things social, political, tribal, and even geological that were once "both" or "multiple" in the world of the Gulf suddenly became one or the other in that of the British: either allied sheikh or pirate, either legitimate or illegitimate claimant to land or pearl banks, either a supporter or a detractor of British imperial interests. All of this is laid out in a handy guide: J. G. Lorimer's once secret *Gazetteer of the Persian Gulf, Oman and Central Arabia,* used today by modern Gulf families and official histories to identify the "historic roots" of various claims to power, land, and prestige, contains a dominant narrative, not simply because of his original research but because of the monumental efforts of British residents and staff who produced the sources he used for his work. For instance, in 1820, the same year as the first general treaty, three British ships, the *Discovery,* the *Psyche,* and the *Benares,* began their mission to map the Gulf. Wanting to find routes through its hazardous sandy shoals, they made detailed soundings of what was often called the Pirate Coast, stretching from Ras Musandam to Kuwait, charting the currents and labyrinthine shore. The element of surprise—the ability to attack without warning and disappear to regroup—which produced the aura of invincibility that had served to keep Gulf Arabs free from outside rule for centuries, was slowly being chipped away with this new scientific understanding of the region.[31] The survey of the Arabian coast was complete by 1825, and the first accurate general chart of the entire Gulf appeared in two sheets in 1860.[32] This detailed map was imperative, especially as the British extended official control over India: the Gulf was a vital link in exchanges between the colony and the metropole. The Indian Mutiny of 1857–59 revealed the necessity for rapid communication with Britain and led to the passage of the Government of India Act 1858, under which the British Crown assumed direct control of the subcontinent, a form of rule called the British Raj, and absorbed the large armies of the EIC. In the 1860s, a new technology, the telegraph, began crisscrossing the world, and in 1864 the British laid the Indo-European submarine cable through the Gulf.³³

While the British were signing treaties at sea, the Ottomans were exerting influence on the lands surrounding the Gulf from Kuwait to Qatar. For the Ottomans, the tribe became a bureaucratic category, and several Bedouin, as well as more settled Gulf tribes, were engaged in their administration.³⁴ The Ottomans gave some sheikhs honorific titles, such as *qaim*, a type of governor, even as they were also signatories with the British for all things maritime. Sheikh Qassim al-Thani in Qatar and Sheikh Mubarak al-Sabah in Kuwait, for instance, played the British and Ottoman Empires off each other.³⁵ While British records give an impression of squabbling and ineffectiveness, however, Ottoman records tell a different story: the Gulf rulers were "astute politicians" who "realized the opportunities opened up by great power rivalry."³⁶ For instance, they could connect to traditional trade within the Ottoman Empire while maintaining accords with the British and enjoying the protection afforded by the latter's growing power at sea. By allying with both the British and the Ottomans, therefore, Gulf ports and their rulers supported the diversification of their society: Indians, as subjects of the Crown when the British government took over from the EIC, had special protections that encouraged them to set up shop in the Gulf, and Ottoman subjects could bring in traders from around the Turkish Empire. Even though Ottoman power in the Gulf was often weak and indirect, "inclusion in the Ottoman realm drew an assortment of traders and tradesmen to Hasa [the eastern province of Arabia] and Qatar." Military expeditions to secure Arabia against the Sa'udis were supplied and accompanied by Jewish, Christian, Hindu, Zoroastrian, Shi'a, and Sunni traders. The town of Kuwait went from being a sleepy village to the "Marseilles of the Gulf" as the Ottomans facilitated north-south movement from Anatolia to Arabia during the war.³⁷ The British, who signed formalized treaties with Kuwait in 1899 and

Qatar in 1916, steadily pushed the Ottomans out of the Gulf, sometimes in concert with locals who rebelled against Ottoman attempts to consolidate their power in the region. The Ottomans' influence waned still further after their catastrophic losses during World War I, which ended in 1918. Their territory was carved up between France and Britain, and the last Ottoman sultan was forced to abdicate in 1922. The Republic of Turkey, founded in 1923, remained largely distant from Gulf affairs until major commercial and diplomatic interests arose there in the twenty-first century.

While the Ottomans were still a world power, however, they engaged in a struggle against the Wahhabis and the Sa'ud family that fundamentally influenced the Gulf's religious and political destiny. Wahhabism emerged in the middle of the eighteenth century when Muhammad ibn 'Abd al-Wahhab, a theologian who preached absolute adherence to the doctrine of tawhid, the unity of God, formed a pact with Muhammad ibn Sa'ud, the ruler of the Diriyah oasis in the Najd, Arabia's central region.[38] This was the birth of an extraordinarily successful movement that combined political, tribal, and religious power and threatened to take over the entire Gulf. The joint rise of Wahhabism and founding of the Emirate of Diriyah, called the First Saudi State and based near the present-day capital of Riyadh, was one of the most important events in the modern history of the Middle East, not just Arabia.[39] Despite being in the backyard of the emirate, though, the Gulf held out against complete Wahhabi rule. The Qawasim on the coast of what is now the United Arab Emirates became Wahhabi and relied on assistance from Diriyah but also maintained a level of independence from it. Bahrain refused to embrace the message of the Wahhabis. They considered the Ibadi sultan of Oman an unbeliever, and he was one of their strongest enemies in the south of Arabia, fighting vigorously against Wahhabi conquest, sometimes with British support. The Wahhabis impacted the Gulf in major ways. First, in resisting them and allying with the British to do so, Oman was able to justify its rise as a significant regional force. Second, because Wahhabism and the Saudis presented themselves as an alternative to the Ottomans, sheikhs in the Gulf's ports could keep their options open on land even as the British grew dominant at sea. The sacking of Hussein's tomb at Karbala, assaults on pilgrimage caravans, cutting down of sacred trees, and destruction of saint's shrines and other domed buildings by Wahhabis eventually induced the pasha of Egypt Mehemet 'Ali, at the behest of the Ottoman sultan, to send a force to invade Arabia. Challenges with supply lines in the desert and the Wahhabis' superior knowledge of their homeland made it impossible for Ali's troops to gain a decisive victory, so in 1816 he sent his son Ibrahim Pasha, who, through wit and diplomacy with the Bedouin as much as force of arms, won the Wahhabi War of 1811–18, overthrowing the First Saudi State. This removed an ally of the Qawasim, who had been raiding British ships and now had a good reason to sign the General Maritime Treaty of 1820. In 1818 the Ottomans executed Abdullah ibn Sa'ud, the leader of the Saudi Wahhabis, in Istanbul. While the Wahhabi War and its aftermath seriously weakened the Sa'udis, a new branch of the family emerged a century later. Pushed into the wings for almost a hundred years, the theology of Muhammad ibn 'Abd al-Wahhab remained, waiting to regain center stage.

In the early twentieth century, the Saudis were reborn as the most significant players in the Gulf. Once again, the British contemplated ways to protect the Trucial States from Saudi ambitions. Once again, Wahhabi doctrine arose and spread: Qatar voluntarily adopted Wahhabism to preempt invasion. 'Abd al-'Aziz ibn Abdulrahman al Sa'ud took Hasa from the Ottomans in 1913. In 1930 he established the unified Kingdom of Saudi Arabia, the Third Saudi State. In a historic snub of the British, he granted the Saudi oil concession to the American Standard Oil Company in 1933, leading to the founding of the Arabian American Oil Company (Aramco), to which the kingdom acquired full rights in 1976. Reigning over Saudi Arabia from 1932 to

1953, Ibn Saʻud produced forty-five sons, including all of the nation's kings and most of its ministers.

Despite the threat of Wahhabi expansion at the beginning of the twentieth century, the British had many reasons to feel secure about their Gulf treaty system, which had achieved their main objectives. In November 1904, they celebrated the success of the Trucial States with a durbar. Lord Curzon, the viceroy of India, hosted this gathering of the sheikhs of the Gulf on board the *Argonaut,* which was anchored at Sharjah, the emirate that neighbors Dubai. After proclaiming the greatness of Britain's authority and its policy of "guardianship and protection which has given you peace and guaranteed your rights," he summed up his view of the British role in the Gulf.[40] He also made a remarkable assertion about the independent Arab states period of Gulf history, which was characterized by frequent and dramatic changes in political, religious, and tribal claims to land, power, and pearls.

In his durbar speech, Curzon split the Gulf's past into two eras, one of primeval chaos before the British formalized their treaties in the 1820s–1850s and one of order afterward. The Union Jack formed the curtain between worlds, securing commerce and peace. In justifying British efforts, Curzon painted a brutal picture of the pre-protectorate Gulf, before the Crown's benevolent "pacification": "You know that a hundred years ago there were constant trouble and fighting in the Gulf; almost every man was a marauder or a pirate; kidnapping and slave-trading flourished; fighting and bloodshed went on without stint or respite; no ship could put out to sea without fear of attack; the pearl fishery was a scene of annual conflict; and security of trade or peace there was none." What a relief, he said, that "then it was that the British Government intervened. . . . British forces occupied the forts and towns on the coast that we see from this deck."[41] They handed those same towns and forts over to those rulers who signed treaties. Curzon was fond of comparing the British policy in the Gulf to that of the Portuguese: "'The Sword of the Lord and of Gideon' had served the Portuguese very well as a motto for acquisition; but in the contemptuous neglect by them of the arts of peace, and in the absence of any genius for colonisation, it did not facilitate retention."[42]

To what extent was Curzon correct in his glowing assessment of British presence in the Gulf in the nineteenth century? Is it true that they really practiced the "arts of peace" far better than their imperial predecessors? The current ruler of Sharjah, Sultan bin Muhammad al-Qasimi, is a descendant of the Qawasim whom the British labeled "pirates." Their city, Ras Al-Khaimah, was attacked and destroyed by Major-General Keir, his Indian troops, and his Omani allies in 1819, the year before he returned to compel Gulf sheikhs to sign a treaty with the British. He could have said, as the leader of Scotland described the Romans, "to . . . plunder they give the lying name of empire: they made a solitude and call it peace."[43] They overstated the risk of piracy to control trade and travel between Basra and Bombay. Indeed, far more profit came from Bombay, and the British in the nineteenth century were primarily using the Gulf as a means of getting to India, not as an independent source of revenue. In the end, the British used treaties and the threat of overwhelming force as a means of influencing the ancestors of al-Qasimi and other families but not completely controlling or colonizing them.

The British also had a mixed record when it came to fighting the slave trade, especially in the Gulf, in India, and along Africa's east coast. Article 9 of the 1820 treaty explicitly bans "the carrying off of slaves, men, women, or children, from the coasts of Africa or elsewhere."[44] In the following decades, however, slavery still flourished. The abolitionist movement in England was gaining traction, though, and ending slavery, although not necessarily in Britain's economic interests, became a priority to help justify its presence in the Indian Ocean. A series of agreements and acts of Parliament resulted in British ships going out on missions to stop the slave trade. British negotiators were also dispatched to convince various rulers, such as the sultan of Oman and other Gulf sheikhs, to sign treaties that made the trafficking, if not the owning, of slaves illegal. Just as the British had used sheikhs and sultans as partners in maintaining peace, so they hoped to use them in suppressing the slave trade. The greater interest, however, was almost always maintaining peaceful commerce, not unduly upsetting allies. Although British captains sometimes attempted to intercept and raid slave ships, the British government was sometimes unwilling to exert the full pressure of its navy to enforce treaties against slavery. It was public pressure and the reports of slave suffering in widely read newspapers such as the *Times of India* and the *London Times* that compelled action. The HMS *Vulture,* for instance, sent to catch slaving ships off Ras al-Hadd, the promontory that makes up Oman's southeastern tip, caught a large dhow with 169 slaves packed inside, many of whom were suffering from smallpox and other diseases.[45] The fear of seizure by the British caused slavers to crowd people on deck, showing that they were not locked away below. News of such atrocities spread to London, where the 1871 Select Committee on the Slave Trade demanded more action, including more seizing of slavers.[46] Yet more ships were sent to east Africa on a mission of humanitarian intervention. However, slave dealers were often able to hide their trade, especially after an epidemic of famine hit the center of Africa, leading people to sell themselves into servitude for the mere offer of nourishment and without the need for visible shackles. According to the British, some slave ships flew the French flag as a means of dodging British anti-slavery patrols—and the British may have used it as an excuse, in some instances, to look the other way. As late as the 1920s, in fact, some prominent Gulf families still practiced domestic slavery and used descendants of slaves in pearl fishing and date farming, and British officials chose not to confront them. Writing at that time, the British diplomat Arnold Wilson declared that the British had become "almost blind" to slavery, and he called for missionaries and other groups to cause a "revolution in public opinion." [47]

With their purpose being to ensure peace and safety for their own ships, the British did not necessarily determine or shape many aspects of the Gulf's society or economy. With a series of treaties, they established a durable system by creating allies from within the pre-existing Gulf society and requiring only maritime security. As the next chapter shows, this arrangement, if not the form of the protectorate system, was later inherited by the United States. In 1980, after the British had withdrawn from the Gulf, President James Carter announced the Carter Doctrine, the explicit guarantee that the US would keep foreign powers from controlling the Gulf, which has been a pillar of US foreign policy for decades. The impetus was to protect US access to Gulf oil, which the Soviet Union was then threatening. This was just the latest example of the Gulf's internal economy being well connected to global trends. In fact, many elements of the Gulf's current petroleum-based export economy and society can be found in its predecessor: the Gulf's pearl-based economy.

From Pearls to Petroleum

World historians have increasingly remarked the ability of certain commodities, such as cotton and silk in the ancient and medieval periods, to create and support commercial empires: forces and institutions emerge in unexpected and interconnected ways around the world because of these commodities' influence on global trade. The global price and distribution of pearls in the nineteenth century had major impacts on the Gulf, where a pearl-based economy and society emerged. While it could be argued that oil connects the Gulf to the current largest and most valuable commodity empire, single-resource dependency is not new to the region. The Gulf was a realm of the global empire of the pearl from about the middle of the nineteenth century until the 1920s, when cultured Mikimoto pearls replaced natural fished ones.

Lord Curzon, in his 1904 durbar address, claimed that "the [Gulf] pearl fishery was a scene of annual conflict." The British, according to him, had secured this vital resource for the benefit of the people of the Gulf, but also for the security of India. (In a similar way but on a different scale, the United States has acted to secure the Gulf for oil transport through the Strait of Hormuz.) Pearl profits grew fast. By 1820, the industrial revolution and a growing middle class throughout Europe and the United States had made owning pearls "one of the surest symbols of bourgeois wealth and dignity."[48] The booming Western market for pearls and mother-of-pearl, used in everything from men's tie clips to women's jewelry, transformed the Gulf's regional pearl market, which had previously primarily supplied the rulers of south Asia. Now Gulf pearls were thrust to the forefront of a global market in luxury goods. In 1906 the Gulf provided up to half of the world's pearls. The market often went boom and then bust, creating an economy of debt and of runaway debtors. Merchants, boat captains, and crews bet on successful pearling seasons but often came away without the catch they needed. The British resident in Bushehr became an umpire, negotiating, settling disputes, and demanding that debtors not be allowed to move from one sheikhdom to another. In 1879, he convinced the relevant parties to sign the Mutual Agreement Entered into by the Trucial Coast Rulers about Absconding Debtors, in which they agreed, among other things, to be fined up to fifty Maria Theresa thalers (trade coins used as currency at the time) for harboring a debtor. The British, who supported keeping the pearl banks open to all locals, also prevented foreign companies and prospectors, usually French, from coming into the pearl banks and destroying their fragile ecosystems with modern equipment and methods, such as collecting too close to shore.[49] But while international harvesters were banned, international brokers were allowed to spend their cash in the Gulf. The famous French jeweler Jacques Cartier, for instance, visited in 1912, hoping to win the race among jewelry firms that would be outdone in the Gulf only by the race for oil concessions a few decades later.

Pearl mania in the West did not necessarily change the fundamental trading patterns of Gulf merchants, however. Unlike the oil boom, during which Gulf travel to Europe increased dramatically, the pearling boom did not see many Khalijis in London or Paris. Instead, Gulf merchants continued taking their pearls to India via traditional means. From the 1860s to the 1920s, money was made not from the land but from the sea. In fact, the economy of trade propelled Gulf merchants outward. For many who sold pearls, Indian Ocean ports were more important than the Middle East. As Fahad Bishara and colleagues write, "For them, it was Basra, [Bushehr] and Bombay they knew, not Beirut; Calicut and Cochin, not Cairo; Muhammarah, Mombasa and Mangalore, not Mosul; and Zanzibar, not Suez."[50] From the United Arab Emirates and Qatar to the southern coast of Iran and Kuwait, the pearl was king. As Shaikh Muhammad al-Thani of Qatar famously said to the British traveler William Palgrave, "We are all from the highest to the lowest slaves of one master, Pearl."[51] The industry employed up to 12,890 people in Qatar, 48 percent of its population; ; on the Trucial Coast (around what is now the United Arab Emirates), 31 percent; and in Kuwait, 25 percent. Bahrain, with its established agricultural and merchant classes, was less dependent but still highly involved, with 18 percent of its population working in pearls. Only 0.3 percent of the Iranian population, in contrast, was employed in pearling.[52] Oman was the exception: lacking pearls, it engaged in the international date and coffee trades instead.[53]

Unlike the later maritime oil concessions, the pearl banks at some distance from shore were a common, and no country could claim exclusive sovereignty over them, although there were some informal understandings about the traditional pearling areas of certain towns and their sheikhs. The Qur'an describes the sea as an open realm, often shared between tribes, owned by no king, provided as a blessing from God:

"He it is who subdued the sea, that you might eat moist flesh from it and bring jewelry to wear, and see ships cleaving it, that you may seek His bounty and mayhap be thankful" (Qur'an 16:14–15). In the Gulf, which was divided by imaginary border lines in the latter half of the twentieth century, only recently has national sovereignty trumped traditional law, especially on the Arabian side—and even now, many disputes are still resolved within extended families and do not see official courts. Maritime boundaries, therefore, modern fictions dependent on international legal conventions, have extended the politics of power, petroleum, and possession into what the Qur'an declares is a realm of God.[54]

The pre-oil pearl-based Gulf economy involved layers of loans and payments and a division of labor on the boats that created a society at sea. The captain was called *nakhoda*. This word is still used in local dialects today to designate a person of particular leadership ability. Although often in debt to the local pearl merchant, once at sea he was considered all powerful. The divers were poor tribesmen or sometimes slaves or free descendants of slaves from east Africa. They were paid depending on the number of pearls they fished and often took on debt before the voyage. While men were at sea pearling, often for long stretches during the big season of May to September and the lesser, cold season from October to April, Gulf women remained either in town or in oases, running affairs and making ends meet on their own. On land, the trade's economy was run by a hierarchy of merchants: retail merchants, pearl dealers, and wholesale merchants, who were often sheikhs and their families. The retail merchants, who sold goods to pearl divers and local customers, had the least wealth and power. Next was the pearl dealer, called *tawwash,* who specialized in classifying and valuing pearls by using various formulas based on weight and quality. They sold pearls in Bombay and other Indian Ocean markets. The *tujjar,* the wholesale merchant, was at the top of the system. Although many were sheikhs and other Arab rulers, there were also many from non-Arab and non-Muslim backgrounds. Merchant groups of various religious backgrounds were part of global networks: in Arabia, which had most of the Gulf's pearl banks, there were Shi'as from Bahrain, Twelver Shi'as from Iraq, and Jews from Baghdad and elsewhere, while on the Persian side, Shi'a Muslims worked in the pearl trade in Hormuz and Bushehr. Merchant-princes allowed other merchants to move from one port to another, avoid taxes, experience relative freedom of trade, and check religious fanaticism and other abuses. When necessary, they would simply leave a particular port and go to another, leaving the ruler with little revenue and his tribe with little confidence in him. This happened in Bahrain and later in Qatif on the eastern Arabian shore.[55] These merchants could therefore have a significant impact not just on economic relationships but on power structures in various ports. In Kuwait, for example, merchants continued to play an important role well into the twentieth century and may be one explanation for the significant role of the Kuwaiti parliament today, since merchants had long extracted concessions from the Sheikh.

The pearl market amplified both the cosmopolitan and the local sides of Gulf culture. On the one hand, when the bottom fell out, the downturn both created and enforced distinctions that still shape current systems of power and patronage in the Gulf. On the other hand, however, is a legacy of international commerce, cosmopolitanism, and relative autonomy. While steamships may have devastated the Omani Empire and the primacy of local shipping, they also provided new opportunities, combining with new forms of communication to spur the growth of a European and American market for Gulf pearls: the new industrial elite, depicted with pearl necklaces by artists such as John Singer Sargent, demanded them. In 1900, the value of pearls had tripled from 1877 and seemed to be on an upward path. World War I and the invention of the cultured Mikimoto pearl in Japan in 1916, however, devastated the market, leading to the "years of hunger," especially in the highly pearl-dependent Trucial States and Qatar, where trading settlements were hollowed out and many merchant houses closed. With many merchants gone or under crushing debt, Gulf governments turned to oil concessions for revenue. The people who remained, who did not leave during these lean times, became the core group of citizens who make up the Gulf states today.

The pearl also has a powerful cultural legacy in the Gulf, as reflected in popular Arabic poetry and songs. In the 1930s, just as oil was emerging as a commodity in Bahrain, the poet 'Atiyyah ibn 'Ali (d. 1981) personified it and pearls as lovers, debating with each other and finally driving off together in a gas-powered car.[56] From road junctions, such as the Pearl Roundabout in Manama, to heritage villages and museums, pearls are everywhere, and Khalijis still know their many names and varieties, even though it has been a century since the industry collapsed. Remembering the era of pearls, especially while leaving out the debt and labor issues, implicitly legitimizes that pre-oil period and the bonds between Gulf rulers and citizens.

Just as the pearl market was declining, the Gulf oil market was beginning to rise. In June 1932, much to the chagrin of the British, an American company, Standard Oil of California (Socal; later called Chevron), struck oil in the first major commercial quantities in Bahrain. Some years prior, oil companies had signed exclusive agreements and sent prospectors deep into eastern Arabia. These early prospectors, primarily English but some also American, took great risks on hunches and rumors. Ignoring several naysayers, the swashbuckling visionary Frank Jones, known affectionately from Kuwait to Qatar as Abu Naft ("Father of oil" in Arabic), created the Eastern and General Syndicate, having heard stories of oil seeping out of the ground while an officer during World War I in what was then called Mesopotamia. In 1923, he signed an early agreement with Bahrain's sheikh, Isa bin Ali al-Khalifa, which gave him "the entire concession of all the oil, petroleum and kindred deposits, whether in a discovered or undiscovered state existing in that portion of land known as the Bahrein Islands situated in the Persian Gulf, Arabia."[57] Soon, relatively barren lands and islands, formerly valuable mainly as pasture or stops for pearling vessels and inhabited by tribes who might have loyalties to different sheikhs, became a matter of major concern. Qatar, Kuwait, Bahrain, and rulers all along the Arabian coast signed concessions and received royalties from oil companies. The British ones, however, did not drill successfully in Bahrain, leaving Socal to be the first to strike it rich in the Gulf.

Even as the oil really began to flow, the economy was not instantly transformed. Khaliji oil workers needed both education and training. The shifting of the entire Gulf society from herding and pearl diving to oil prospecting and refining took decades. Sheikhs found it difficult to invest their concession monies because of the lack of infrastructure and developed markets in the Gulf. It was the building of some rudimentary public works that allowed for more advanced systems to follow. Some concessions had terms that helped to move their societies forward. In the 1923 concession, Isa bin Khalifa deftly negotiated the use of exclusively "native labor" (Bahrainis), to be paid a "fair wage" (clause 15). Socal also agreed to dig water wells for use by the Bahraini population, in addition to funding port facilities and other developments. The sheikh, who required Socal to agree not to interfere with Bahrain's interior politics, was given payments at different stages of oil discovery, one-fifth of company shares, and the right to use the company's telegraphs, instantly improving communication. Soon, Bahrain's neighbors sold their own lucrative oil concessions. Sheikh Abdullah al-Thani and the representative of the Anglo-Persian Oil Company (APOC; an antecedent of BP) signed the Qatari oil concession in 1935, more than a decade after the 1923 Bahrain concession. It designated cemeteries and lands deemed by the sheikh to be of religious significance as ineligible for drilling.[58] Qatar seems to have learned from Bahrain's experience and asked for even better terms.

Because Bahrain started the oil race ahead of its neighbors, it was able to take advantage of infrastructure and training paid for by oil companies in the 1930s, and it wasn't hit as hard by the serious depression that the rest of the Gulf experienced during World War II, which led to the shrinking of the population. Those families and tribes that remained behind were usually tied in some way to their ruler, who could provide at least some support with oil concession payments and reserves of previous revenue. In some years, pearling captains returned with their catch only to find no merchants, even in significant ports such as Dubai. Captains and fishermen, many of whom were from Africa, fell into considerable debt. In Dubai alone, the pearl trade was worth more than three million pounds annually in the 1920s but by 1946 had dropped almost to zero.[59] These were the years of hunger, from 1929 to the end of World War II. During the war, the Gulf was a strategic theater, where the US Persian Gulf Command supplied the USSR with matériel through the Lend-Lease program to fight against Germany.[60] For the parts of the Gulf that did not see similar investment, however, World War II was when time stood still: the development of the Arab states was put on hold, and rationing made it difficult to support the population of the pearling days. From Kuwait and Doha to Dubai and Sharjah, towns that once thrived on the natural pearl trade were devastated. The war choked off many exports and stopped the burgeoning of petroleum infrastructure.

After the Second World War, oil fully replaced the pearl as the Gulf's main economic driver. In Bahrain, for example, pearling still employed more than five hundred ships and fifteen thousand men in the late 1920s. But the invention of cultured pearls, two world wars, the Great Depression, and finally an embargo on the import of pearls by the newly independent India extinguished it as a major commercial activity.[61] The oil concessions, rather than suddenly disrupting the Gulf economy, created an incentive for rulers, who were usually offered a certain portion of the oil revenue, to maintain alliances with tribes that claimed parts of the lands that were being explored. Well practiced in diplomacy and treaties after about a century of British influence, the Gulf rulers quickly realized that they could play foreign oil companies, especially British and American ones, off each other. Britain's decline after World War II only further cracked its monopoly on securing and protecting the Gulf, just as American oil companies like Socal rose at its expense.

The Last Decades of the British Protectorate

Britain's history in the Gulf is a paradox. At the height of its influence, in the nineteenth and early twentieth centuries, its power was greater than its interests there, but by the end of its rule, as oil was discovered, its interests in the region outweighed its power.[62] The best example of British favor, as well as the nature of its hands-off empire, is the cannon salute. The display of a monopoly on maritime violence was transformed into a ceremony in which a British naval ship showed the extent of the Crown's pleasure by how many times it shot its cannons: "In 1929, for example, the rulers of Kuwait, Bahrain and Qatar were the recipients of seven-gun salutes; the ruler of Abu Dhabi received a five-gun salute; and the ruler of Dubai, only a humble three. That year, an attempt was made by the family of Shaikh Said of Dubai to depose him. The Political Resident stepped in to uphold the ruler: he warned that any move to depose Shaikh Said would incur the strong disapproval of the British government. To reconfirm this support, . . . he was granted a five-gun salute." The discovery of oil inflated the number of gun salutes to an almost comical degree, showing how much and how suddenly Britain's position in the Gulf had changed. The rulers of Kuwait and Bahrain had their salutes increased to a full eleven "as a mark of approbation after they signed oil concessions a few years later."[63]

Oil changed the balance in favor of the Gulf rulers, who, along with their followers, were already feeling senses of distinction and proto-nationalism thanks to British policies. Britain handled foreign policy for the Gulf as a whole, treating it as a single unit, but its separate relations with each sheikh and the mandate that their ships fly different flags created particular identities, even though there were no great differences between the people of Dubai, Qatar, and Sharjah. These flags became the basis for modern national symbols, which was not the intention of the British. Their main purpose was to safeguard the maritime peace and their access to the Indian market. Therefore, they used a fairly light touch in Gulf affairs, not overthrowing rulers but occasionally enforcing that peace when it became necessary. The coming of the oil era and the rise of the United States and the USSR as global powers after World War II changed everything for the British, whose interests—securing oil in the Gulf, preventing the spread of communism, and containing movements such as Arab nationalism—now outweighed their power. Bureaucratic correspondence and materials dedicated to the last decade of British rule in the Gulf fill volumes. These rich sources provide scholars with insights into the workings of the current Gulf states, which, after independence, became harder to view.

The British endowed the new Gulf states with the bureaucratic machinery and systems that would lead to successful development but left just as these bureaucracies were reaching their maximum size and influence. They were not thrown out of the Gulf by revolution or internal rebellion, protest, or anti-imperial forces. There was no Gandhi of the Gulf to unite this region as Gandhi did the subcontinent. The British did not leave because they no longer had interests in the Gulf. In fact, these were at a peak at the time of withdrawal: British civil servants had made themselves indispensable to Gulf rulers, increasing in the last decades of the British protectorate from just a handful to enough to populate most of the offices and ministries established in each emirate and kingdom in the 1950s and 1960s, and some even called them the "neo-Raj."[64] Instead, it was larger forces, many centered far from the Gulf—such as pressure from leftist political groups in London and the global move away from imperialism—

that finally pushed the British out. In an era of anticolonialism and independence movements, the continued British presence in the Gulf, however beneficial it may have been to some rulers, just did not fit with the times. Moreover, the end of the British Raj in India in 1947 made the route to India through the Gulf less essential, although airports and naval bases there remained important.

Sometimes using Royal Air Force helicopters, British diplomats created a legacy in the very boundaries of the Gulf's modern states.[65] These borders, while providing a level of stability, ended the largely fluid nature of population flows that had existed before the 1960s. Potential oil resources made this mapping process a high-stakes endeavor. This was especially true in al-Buraimi, an oasis with several villages that is not too far from Saudi Arabia and is now split by a border between the United Arab Emirates and Oman. In 1949, just four years after the Second World War, which saw a decisive rebalancing of power in favor of the United States—benefiting, among others, its corporate oil interests—Saudi Arabia claimed the Buraimi territory, and much more of the territory of the Trucial States. Negotiations failed to convince the Saudis to leave, but the British helped to expel them, allowing the United Arab Emirates and Oman to divide this oil-rich region between them.[66]

Despite this example, oil was not always the most important factor in establishing national borders, and it was not the whims of British cartographers or rivalries between oil companies that produced certain geographic peculiarities. In the past, a Gulf tribe might have felt some affiliation with the sultan of Oman and with the emir of Fujairah and shifted its allegiance between them at times. When the maps were being drawn, however, a choice had to made, which set the fate of that tribe and changed its pocket of claimed land into the sovereign territory of a single nation. Asking highly autonomous mountain tribes—such as the Shihuh, who were often the most dominant in the upper regions and wore distinctive decorated axes instead of knives on their belts—to declare a sultan or an emir as their protector resulted in exclaves and even enclaves within exclaves. One of the most extraordinary examples of this is the small territory of Madha, which lies on Musandam, the mountainous peninsula that forms the Arabian side of the Strait of Hormuz. For centuries, its people lived in relative autonomy, often playing powerful emirs off each other in that dynamic process of give-and-take that often occurred between port cities and hinterlands. Compelled to pick a country, the people of Madha believed Oman to be the most developed and its sultan the most likely to invest in their territory. Nahwa, a village surrounded by Madha, however, disagreed and allied with Sharjah. Lines were then drafted between these areas of local tribal control. Today, to enter Madha from the Emirate of Fujairah or the Sharjah port of Khor Fakkan (itself an enclave in Fujairah) there is no passport control, no formal indication that you have entered an entirely new sovereign state. But the streetscape and other outward signs that this is Omani space make the change obvious. The ornamental lampposts are almost exactly the same as those used in Muscat. A Royal Oman Police Office maintains official ties to the mainland. There are images of Sultan Qaboos (the ruler of Oman from 1970 to 2020) and his successor, Sultan Haitham, throughout the enclave, whose infrastructure Oman has invested in as a reward for choosing to join it. The Madha Museum, which highlights local culture, opened its doors in 2018, having been built with donations collected from all over Oman.[67] Although its population stands at only three thousand, Madha has a distinct Omani character. Moving farther inland, into the mountains, you suddenly cross over into the United Arab Emirates—the Emirate of Sharjah, to be precise—and the second-order enclave of Nahwa.

While the British political residents of the Gulf were mapping out the boundaries and constructing the bureaucratic foundations of the modern Gulf states in consultation with tribal sheikhs and other rulers, global forces were eating away at the British Empire's ability to maintain its prewar presence in the region. One such force was a growing movement for the overthrow not only of British colonizers but also of the Gulf monarchs. These rulers, along with the shah of Persia and the president of the United States, were united in their fear of the spread of communism in the Gulf from its base in Yemen, which neighbors Oman. The Popular Front for the Liberation of the Occupied Arabian Gulf (PFLOAG), a Yemeni communist organization, with support from China and Russia, sought to expel the British and what it called "monarchical clients from Dhofar to Kuwait."[68] The plan was to build a unified Arab communist state, spread oil wealth, and supply the group's allies in China and the USSR with cheaper petroleum. The British, realizing the strategic importance of ending the PFLOAG movement, helped to install a new generation of rulers, including Sultan Qaboos in Oman and Sheikh Zayed in Abu Dhabi, who were dedicated to rapid development, education, and the sharing of oil wealth with their subjects. Both in their administrative capacity and through diplomatic pressure, the British were always keen to encourage Gulf rulers to abandon their conservative approach to finance and invest the wealth provided by oil concessions in their countries. Because of their connections to Qaboos and Zayed, when the British left the Gulf, those monarchs became less of a target for anti-Western ideologies and ideologues. By then, the British public had lost the appetite for keeping up the empire's sprawling and declining system of international possessions and protectorates. The United States partially took Britain's place, continuing its triple containment of Saudi Arabia, Iraq, and Iran, maintaining the free flow of shipping through the Gulf, and enforcing the Carter Doctrine, which viewed any outside interference in the Gulf as against US interests, particularly in oil. The British withdrawal was nonetheless seen as the start of a new era, requiring the nascent Gulf states to chart new relationships with one another and with other global powers.

The British were successful players in the Gulf precisely because they did not insist on direct rule or even have much of a presence.

Their policy, until the oil boom at least, was not to extract wealth from the Gulf but merely to secure the far more lucrative route from Basra to Bombay. Instead of patrolling from forts, they used treaties signed on ships. Instead of setting up extensive colonial institutions or forcing the Gulf's people to become culturally or politically British, they largely left the Gulf's rulers to their own devices, as long as they did not engage in war and as long as British ships going to or from Bombay remained undisturbed. This hands-off approach allowed the Gulf to emerge from the era of colonialism with its culture, identity, and institutions largely intact and without the need to react against Westernization as occurred in India, Egypt, and especially Iran. Instead of adopting an anticolonial, anti-Western ideology in the wake of independence, the Arab Gulf states embraced Westernization and development in a way that did not necessarily contradict identity and culture. Today, local Gulf identity exists below the surface of hypermodern skylines and is a crucial element even in the world's most cosmopolitan city: Dubai.

In 1948, Wilfred Thesiger, the British traveler arrived in the city, clustered on the banks of the short Dubai Creek:

> ... rowing-boats patrolled the creek to pick up passengers from the mouths of alleys between high coral houses, surmounted with square wind turrets and pleasingly decorated with plaster moulding. Behind the diversity of houses which lined the waterfront were the suqs, covered passageways, where merchants sat in the gloom, cross-legged in narrow alcoves among their piled merchandise. The suqs were crowded with many races. . . . [Arabs, Bedu], Baluchis, Persians and Indians. Among them I noticed a group of Kashgai tribesmen. . . . and some Somalis off a sambuk [ship].[69]

Dubai was already a cosmopolitan marketplace before the building of a modern mall or skyscraper.

6 Dubai

The Global Gulf in a Global Age (1945–Present)

In the second half of the twentieth century, Dubai's glistening sky-scrapers, turquoise waters, supermalls, and relative safety made the city not just a model of successful development but a paragon and byword of the modern, globalized world order. Instead of trying modest and incremental investments, Dubai's rulers took major strategic risks, which paid off spectacularly. In hindsight, these bold moves seem obvious. That was not the case in the early 1960s, when peak oil—the maximum production rate, which would decline irreversibly afterward, due to resource depletion—seemed like an ever-present cliff. It appeared prudent to be cautious, to save rather than spend. Many older Gulf rulers, such as Sheikh Shakhbut bin Sultan of Abu Dhabi and the sultan of Oman Sa'id bin Taimur, were concerned about having enough money in the future and about the impact of development on cultural identity. They reacted conservatively to the rise of oil revenue, keeping it in their coffers and resisting putting it into the local economy, which made the mass importation of foreign labor a necessity.

Taking a big risk and ignoring both peak-oil warnings and the fears of traditionalists, Sheikh Rashid bin Sa'id Al-Maktoum, who became the ruler of Dubai in the late 1950s, plowed money into a massive modernization project, building far more than what histori-

FIGURE 13. A street in Dubai with skyscrapers and part of the metro system (*right*), 2016. Photo by author.

cal demand suggested would be needed. Before coming to power, he had spent years planning his future transformative policies, attracting talented individuals to his inner circle. Under Rashid, Dubai soon imported massive numbers of laborers and engineers from around the world to manage and implement the construction of hundreds of shining glass skyscrapers, making what is now a quintessential global city (see figure 13).

Dubai was the first out of the gate in the modernization race. This allowed it to overtake similarly situated potential rivals. Rashid was the first development-minded ruler in the later twentieth-century Gulf, but there were others who also embraced economic openness, ties to the West, and investment in local development and infrastructure: Sheikh Zayed bin Sultan al-Nahyan of Abu Dhabi and Sultan Qaboos of Oman, for example, although they came to power in the

1960s and 1970s, after Rashid and after the reigns of more conservative fathers. Their rhetoric of progress and opportunity was beamed into the gleaming new television sets made possible by the rapid expansion of communications and infrastructure. For them, modernization was not a departure from tradition but a renaissance, the past reborn: openness and international connectivity have always been part of Gulf culture. By establishing free-trade zones and reducing barriers to outside investment, Gulf rulers simply updated and extended the policies pursued by their autonomous merchant-prince predecessors. The identity of the people of the Gulf, seemingly threatened by modernization, has in fact been supported, celebrated, and leveraged by the states that have emerged there, allowing the citizen elite to preserve their heritage. Tensions between the citizen minority and the expatriate majority erupt on occasion, but rarely with the violence between identity groups found even in developed democracies such as France or the United States.

Remarkably, in the midst of all these changes, the development-minded rulers did not cut their ties with the coalitions of tribes and families that had brought them to power and to which they were responsible. Instead, traditional means of communication and power sharing remain important formal and informal institutions in the seemingly hypermodern Gulf. The granting of government posts, opportunities in education, investment in health care, and outright subsidies to various tribes and regions became an expectation. Sometimes, however, families and tribes have been split in their loyalties to the rulers and states that emerged in the wake of British withdrawal in the 1960s and 1970s. The previous chapter discusses the relatively recent creation of nation-states and boundaries in the Gulf, traced upon the desert and the water, areas that were once treated as commons but are now enclosed. This has slowly encouraged national citizenship to become the paramount identity: increasingly, being Saudi, Qatari, or Emirati means more than being part of a tribe or family with traditional grazing lands that may cross national borders.

At the beginning of the twentieth century, Dubai was already working to attract foreign tradespeople and their money. Its ruler invited the merchants of Lingeh in Persia, which was then a center of the pearl trade but beset with high duties and other taxes, to come across the Gulf. He promised them a port with no import or export fees, free land, protection, toleration of ethnic and religious differences, and pro-business administration.[1] All of these policies, or variations on them, had been implemented before in the Gulf, from Siraf through Hormuz to Muscat, as means of attracting commerce. Dubai, however, was also ideally positioned to profit from the explosion of oil wealth and rents provided by Britain in the form of payments for landing rights and oil concessions. Even if the proceeds were modest when compared to those of Saudi Arabia or Abu Dhabi, Dubai invested them strategically, helping to develop a preexisting model and pro-business culture.

Instead of only sending its money abroad to invest in developed economies, Dubai plowed its revenues into building world-class ports. This decision transformed a small settlement on Dubai Creek that was focused on local trade, in the shadow of pearling into the world's most exciting metropolis, a buzzing hub of globalization. Since the days of ancient Dilmun in Bahrain, the Gulf's main port had not been on the Arabian desert side. This was because of the sandbanks, shallows, and lack of deep-water moorings for the ever larger vessels needed to keep up with the container shipping revolution, with cargo put into interlocking containers on ships of maximum size and efficiency, a process that changed international trade in the decades after World War II at least as much as the steamship had in the nineteenth century. Starting with Port Rashid and continuing with the much larger Jabal Ali port, both capable of handling the increase in demand after the revolution in Iran cut off some traffic to its ports, Dubai's rulers changed its geographic destiny. They were able to create a social model singularly focused on business, not only because they could embrace free-market ideas that were already part of the functioning and history of Gulf ports but also because they were unencumbered by the postcolonial struggles of oil-producing states outside the Gulf. Dubai became so concentrated on commerce that one scholar calls it "the city as corporation."[2] From the beginning, its political leader and chief executive has been the head of the merchant-prince Al-Maktoum family.

In 1975, just a few years after the British withdrew from the Gulf, Sheikh Rashid sponsored the expansion of Port Rashid and the building of Jabal Ali, the world's largest artificial harbor, forty miles south of Dubai, which Queen Elizabeth II opened in 1979. At the time, Jabal Ali seemed like an overreach to many, as much of the port was unused at first. But this changed quickly, and what started as a potential boondoggle turned into one of the most successful infrastructure investments in the modern world. In 2014, to meet increased demand, Jabal Ali opened new terminals. Dubai Ports (DP) World, a state-owned Emirati company formed in 2005 from the merger of Dubai Ports Authority and Dubai Ports International, runs these ports and more around the world, even in the Americas. In 2006, however, under Muhammad bin Rashid Al-Maktoum, the son of Sheikh Rashid, it dropped a bid to take over the management of multiple US ports because of pressure from Congress.[3] Nonetheless, the global expansion of DP World shows its influence as a leader in the operation of port traffic and trade. It has exported the Dubai model through a collection of ports and terminals stretching from Karachi and Perth to Vancouver and Río de la Plata, with many more under development. Another crucial transportation hub in Dubai is its international airport, which started as a stop for flying boats just four times a week, became a land terminal in 1965, and is now the busiest airport in the Middle East and the world's busiest in international passenger traffic, connecting all of Australasia with Europe and the Americas. Terminal 3, inaugurated in 2008, is the second-largest building in the world by floor space. Thanks to the vision and investments of its rulers, the city's population has exploded from 344,000 in 1985 to around 3,600,000 today. Moreover, Dubai has become a byword for luxury, globe trekkers, and "the Starbucks class."[4]

The Dubai Model

Other parts of the Gulf and the world have tried to replicate the so-called Dubai model. The analyst Martin Hvidt lists its basic elements:

- Government-led development (ruler-led)
- Fast decision-making and "fast track" development
- Flexible labor force
- Bypass of industrialization—creation of a service economy
- Internationalization of service provision
- Creation of investment opportunities
- Supply-generated demand . . .
- Market positioning via branding
- Development in cooperation with international partners[5]

At the heart of the Dubai model is the embrace of internationalism and globalism to benefit a relatively small number of citizens. Some may appreciate the opportunities provided by economic expansion in the Gulf, but not all residents of Dubai see it as the happiest place on earth. The city's citizens, who receive support and dividends from the state, are almost like shareholders. They also make up less than 10 percent of the population. The noncitizen population is mainly male, single, and without any familial attachment to Dubai. Although long-standing expatriate families do live there, most of the noncitizen population is attracted to Dubai, and other parts of the Gulf, by the promise of income far greater than what they could make in their home countries. A majority are first generation, but some have come in the wake of uncles or other relatives who arrived in decades past. They take on many of the physical tasks, especially in the booming construction industry, and most of the service jobs, from working in restaurants and hospitals to teaching in universities, needed for modernization.

In Dubai, there are two main groups of noncitizens. The first and largest comprises the usually single male laborers, mostly from south Asia, who live in worker villages outside town. They come from the same Indian Ocean world where the people of the Gulf have been trading, living, and making connections for millennia. The second group consists of service workers—ranging from baristas through university faculty and administrators to chief financial officers—from around the world who live in the city and constantly interact directly with Dubai citizens and other Emiratis. The imbalance between these two groups and local citizens creates inevitable tensions, but despite international outcry over the lack of rights for noncitizens and internal calls for Emiratization (opportunities for Emiratis over expatriates), Dubai society and culture remain largely intact and Dubai's Emirati minority largely supportive of the ruler.

Dubai's path of development, Westernization, relative tolerance, and openness to capital and investment has brought it global success, but this has not been the outcome everywhere. Just across the Gulf, in Iran, Shah Reza Pahlavi's modernization policies, which included forced economic centralization and brutal tactics, led to the fall of his regime in 1979. The overthrow of this development-minded ruler, who was also allied with Britain and the United States, was a wake-up call and a warning: not all Westernization and development are without a cost. Within Arab Gulf culture too there were voices of dissent and unease with such rapid cultural shifts. In his controversial *Cities of Salt,* the novelist Abderahman Munif communicated an underlying malaise, describing the transformation of an idyllic oasis into an oil facility and the rise of "cities of salt," places without a distinct identity or substance beyond the oil trade.[6] The enormous urban centers built and staffed by migrant labor have provoked a sense of alienation in some citizens. There have been protests and calls for Qatarization, Saudization, Omanization, and Emiratization as Gulf citizen populations have grown, although not as quickly as the foreign populations, whom some Gulf citizens see as taking their jobs and other opportunities.

Reacting to these pressures, Gulf rulers have promised their subjects job training, world-class education at institutions such as New York University Abu Dhabi and Education City in Doha, and other benefits. They have also embraced traditionalism and the preservation of the heritage and history of Gulf nationals, presenting a state-sanctioned narrative that often focuses on the role of Emiratis more than expatriates in the building of modern infrastructure. Saudi Arabia used state control over history and historical representation to help defang Islamist dissidents even as it reordered historical spaces around the country.[7] Several shrines and memorials were destroyed around Mecca in 1998, including the supposed grave of Muhammad's mother, Aminah bint Wahb, just as other sites, especially those associated with the rise of the Sa'ud family in the Diriyah oasis, were being restored. This mollified the Ikhwan, Wahhabi clerics who, while promoting a Saudi-sponsored identity in Diriyah, demanded the destruction of shrines, which they believed distracted from true belief in Islam.

Despite promises to provide more good jobs to citizens and to limit the scale of imported workers, the Gulf is dependent on the labor and expertise of immigrants from the rest of the world—and each wave of modernization seems to lead to the next great plan or massive infrastructure project. Some of these workers have been able to stay in the Gulf for a long time, even starting families that remain there over generations, which often become just as much a part of the fabric of Gulf history as those with Arab backgrounds. Dubai, for instance, has long been dependent on Indians, whom the scholar Neha Vora, claiming a deep cosmopolitan history of the city, one that has been officially embraced but also erased, calls "impossible citizens," since they have been living in the Gulf for multiple generations but often cannot claim citizenship status. Ruling families, expatriates, and nationals all negotiate different ways of portraying Dubai as home.[8] In addition to long-term residents, there is a more transient group of immigrants, the so-called airport society, made up of laborers and members of the upper middle and middle classes who stay for only a short while, gaining some skills and income and then returning home.[9] This phenomenon is far from new to the Gulf: the airport society is similar to the sailor and merchant societies of past centuries, assemblies of seasonal and more temporary residents of medieval Siraf or early modern Hormuz who were waiting, as on a layover, for the next monsoon.

Often it is citizens of the Gulf states, and not the states themselves, who bring in guest workers, through the controversial *kafala,* "sponsorship," system. Although international bodies such as Human Rights Watch have criticized this prerogative, many Gulf citizens would see its abolition not as a progressive or liberal measure but as a significant power grab by the government or the ruling family, which could then monopolize immigration. Nonetheless, some countries have recently banned guest-worker passports—but in many instances this new rule is not enforced. The precarity of their position has led to worker exploitation. At the same time, studies have shown that Gulf nationals are rarely "employed in positions that directly supervise and manage low-income migrants," and some have laid the blame for abuses largely on "a truly transnational migration industry."[10]

The Gulf has a long history of importing labor from abroad, encouraged by its far-ranging contacts and connections throughout the Indian Ocean. Historically, merchant-princes and other rulers who wished to avoid being overly dependent on their kin in inland tribes, who might challenge them through rebellion, instead turned to foreigners. The king of Hormuz assembled a nonnative army against Afonso de Albuquerque, for instance, and a multitudinous group of Baluchis (from what is now Pakistan), Hadramis (from Yemen), south Asians, and Africans made up the navy and the guard of Sayyid Sa'id bin Sultan, the nineteenth-century ruler of Oman and Zanzibar. Slaves from Africa were often put in important posts, but most were set to manual labor in the pre-oil Gulf's two main industries: date farming and pearl fishing. Many of those brought to the Gulf in that era were adopted into tribes and given citizenship rights, especially if they had offspring with Arabs, as many did.

From the Zanj, whose rebellion almost overthrew the caliph in Baghdad in the ninth century, to the slaves who acted as governors and guards of homelands and oasis forts while merchant rulers were away, there is a long history of Black Africans in the Gulf, and their descendants are a large part of its current citizen population. The traveler Freya Stark described African cultural traditions that she saw being practiced in Kuwait in 1937:

> The [Black people] of Kuwait have a club where they dance once a week, on Thursdays. It is a religious sort of a dance, and visitors—who are welcomed in a friendly manner—are expected to take their shoes off as they step into the small mud-walled courtyard where the proceedings take place. . . .
>
> They are Nubians, they tell me, whose grandfathers or great-grandfathers have been carried across Arabia. . . . New slaves are no longer brought to Kuwait, and more already there to-day are free. . . . .

[They play] the *tanbura,* a venerated object like a shallow drum, two feet or so across, with two holes for resonance. . . . Little triangular things like pin-cushions, of many colours, hang in streamers all about it, evidently sacred, for when, in the ardour of the dance, one or other of the men feel that they are becoming "possessed," they stretch out their hand and touch the little cushions, and stroke their head with the same hand, and obviously feel better; or drag themselves prostrate and waggle their heads under the swaying streamers. . . .

I am surprised to see a few Persians among the dancers, poor people possessed by Jinn or by disease, whom the *tanbura* has cured. . . . Haila, my maid, . . . tells me that the *tanbura* "calls the Jinns and can command them. . . . And sometimes . . . a man, or even a woman, gets seized by the Jinn and they will throw off their clothes, and we do not laugh but (putting her fingers to her lips) we say 'thanks be to God . . .'"[11]

The survival of *tanbura* dancing and musical customs in the Gulf into at least the beginning of the oil era and their adoption by locals reveal the influence of Africans on the region's religious and cultural scene: perhaps a visit to the dance club cured psychic ailments that prayer could not fix, or simply provided a way of letting off steam. Despite the history of slavery and large population of Black Africans in the Gulf, however, an awareness of Blackness has not emerged there in a forceful way. Indeed, most expressions of support in the Gulf for Black communities are in reference to ones outside the region.[12] For some historians, this lack of a visible and outspoken African diaspora identity is surprising.[13] There are still racist cultural attitudes and beliefs that have yet to be fully acknowledged or wrestled with in the open: for example, many misconceptions about skin color and prejudicial ideals of beauty continue to be perpetuated, and those with noticeably darker complexions can face discrimination. In the end, though, the lack of a large-scale Black Lives Matter movement in the Gulf may be the result of fear of self-marginalization. Revealing and concentrating on a history of slavery might inadvertently open up rifts within the community of citizens and cause those identified as different to lose the many benefits provided by citizenship. There are also, at times, traditional limitations to marriage between those who claim "pure" Arab ancestry and those who may have Baluchi or African grandparents.[14] A widespread Gulf Black identity movement, however, may yet arise.

Transformations and Continuities

So rarely has so much seemed to change so fast as in the Gulf from the mid-twentieth century to today: The members of autonomous tribes became citizens. Borders were drawn across water and land. Even the geography of the Gulf, so crucial to understanding this region's history, was altered: with the rise of modern communications, oil and natural gas extraction, and air conditioning, it no longer repelled centralization and control. Before the 1960s, there had been relatively free movement around the Gulf and resources, such as pearls, that were shared—or claimed with immediate displays of force. But then there was a rush to claim land and marine areas for oil and gas prospecting. International tribunals fixed local borders, freezing in time the *diyars* (tribal grazing and roaming lands) that had once shifted as quickly and freely as the desert rains.

The birth of the modern Gulf states divided and disrupted old alliance and affiliations but created new ones as well. In 1971, the United Arab Emirates (UAE), a federation of six previously autonomous monarchies, arrived—with the help of British advisers—seemingly fully formed, like a stage set that appears as a curtain is lifted. (It now comprises seven semi-autonomous states: Abu Dhabi, Ajman, Dubai, Fujairah, Ras Al-Khaimah, Sharjah, and Umm al-Quwain.) Before then, other emirates, whose rulers were called emirs and who demanded the same respect as the leaders of port cities, had gained and lost recognition from the British. Said bin Hamad, the emir of Kalba, a city with a Portuguese fort on a bay south of the Emirate of Fujairah in what is now the UAE and on the border with Oman, became a trucial leader in the 1930s. After his sudden death, however, the principality was ruled by various regents, including a servant named Barut, and it was absorbed by the Emirate of Sharjah in the 1950s, becoming an exclave.[15] Bahrain and Qatar, originally supposed to be founding members of the UAE, instead became independent states.

While there was existing infrastructure in some places, such as Bahrain, where oil was first exploited, institutions had to be built from scratch in many others. Construction was financed by massive state investment far greater, at least per capita, than the World War II spending of the United States, almost exponentially boosting the growth of economies and businesses. A whole people went from "rags to riches," as Mohammad Fahim, a successful Abu Dhabi businessman, titled his memoir.[16] From bare feet and the threat of starvation, deprivation, and cholera outbreaks to access to almost every imaginable luxury, Fahim's generation, roughly equivalent to the baby boomers in the United States, has experienced a transformation in living standards that outpaced almost anything seen before. The UN Human Development Index, which tracks life expectancy, education, and average income, regularly ranks the Gulf states near the top.[17] At the beginning of Fahim's life, these indicators were near the bottom. Because of its role in this monumental evolution, the nation has become a primary focus of loyalty for many Gulf citizens, especially in the past twenty years. Western models of development suggest that Khalijis will finally become like people elsewhere, subject to the same notions of nationhood, citizenry, and exclusion that plague the rest of the world. Under the pressures of modernization and the resulting extreme changes, nonstate, nonnational communities like the ones examined in this book should collapse into near irrelevance and submission to the current global model of the nation-state. Many people have also predicted the inevitable fall of the sheikhs, just as Europe saw its monarchies lose power to democratization in the wake of industrialization. In fact, the distinctiveness of Gulf communities is still very much alive, and the way that they, particularly the citizens, interact with their governments, especially the rulers, explains its resilience. Instead of breaking from tradition and the past, leaders such as Sultan Qaboos (ruler of Oman, 1970–2020) and Sheikh Zayed bin Sultan al-Nahyan (president of the UAE, 1971–2004) aimed, in the words of Sultan Qaboos in his second National Day address, "to restore the past glories" and the "past civilization" of their countries.[18] When he came to the throne, Sultan Qaboos consolidated his power and started development projects throughout his country, even in the remotest parts, places that were once under the control of the Ibadi imam, whom the sultan's father had defeated. By offering a unifying message, building necessary infrastructure—modern hospitals, free-trade ports, a postal service, and roads—and fostering national symbols and heritage, Qaboos created a new national narrative and an Omani national identity. In less just a decade, from 1970 to 1980, Oman was transformed from a region of troubling instability into a success story.[19]

In Saudi Arabia, in contrast, there was less rapid change, and Wahhabi groups such as the Committee for the Promotion of Virtue and the Prevention of Vice, a type of morality police, have been empowered to enforce strict Islamic norms and practices in public places.[20] The transfer of some state authority to bodies like these is motivated by the desire to placate religious conservatives, who often prevent the Saudi state from moving forward with reforms. Recently, Muhammad bin Salman, the crown prince, has clamped down on the authority of the religious police and even changed some of the kingdom's most controversial laws, such as the one forbidding women to drive. He also dramatically opened the country up to tourism, revealing and preserving rather than hiding some pre-Islamic archaeological sites. Saudi Arabia's more conservative religious groups have based their dissent on ideals and interpretations of Islam going back to the preaching of Muhammad ibn 'Abd al-Wahhab, including the notion of an apocalyptic triumph of true faith outside history. One revolutionary, inspired by this eschatological vision, attempted to bring about the end of days: in 1979, Muhammad al-Qahtani, the self-proclaimed Mahdi, the awaited one, seized Mecca. He was ousted only after three weeks of battle with Saudi and French special forces, who supplied the Saudis with tear gas.[21] Al-Qaida and other extremist groups, objecting to the alliance between the United States and the house of Sa'ud, have attacked US bases in Saudi Arabia and called for the end of the monarchy. None of these actions, however, have seriously challenged the role or the rule of the Saudi royals.

Despite threats and predictions that they would fall like houses of cards after the British left, most of the ruling groups on the majority-Arabic-speaking side of the Gulf have remained steady, although some faced internal coups and other crises through the early 1990s. The Gulf states have had the support of the United States and Britain, as well as, increasingly, the growing number of their citizens who benefit from their development plans and distribution of oil wealth. In Qatar, Kuwait, the UAE, and Oman, successions have happened in a relatively peaceful manner. To secure their position, ruling families have dispensed benefits including resources to their citizens and worked to project a cosmopolitan, moderate image of Islam.

By the end of the 1970s, the transition from British to American influence seemed to be going smoothly in the Gulf, where the most successful rulers were following a path of Westernization and development. The most important modernizer was the shah of Iran. His dramatic fall in 1979 had global and local repercussions, ending James Carter's presidency and provoking great fear throughout the Gulf, causing sheikhs to reconsider heavy-handed policies and find ways to secure the foundations of their legitimacy and internal allegiances. Throughout the 1980s and 1990s, therefore, the Gulf states poured money into subsidies and other benefits for citizen nationals. They also concentrated on creating national identities while establishing a transnational organization and trade bloc, the Gulf Cooperation Council, founded in 1981 by Qatar, Kuwait, the UAE, Saudi Arabia, Bahrain, and Oman to present a united front against revolutionary Iran.

The Iranian Revolution was the most important threat to the Gulf status quo in the twentieth century, as it embraced both government based on Islamic law and overt hostility to the West, especially the United States, which had sponsored the shah. Revolutionaries both secular and clerical latched on to the issue of Western influence and labeled the process of modernization *gharbzadegi,* "Westoxification": the idea that Western culture inherently corrupts and weakens a country's moral fabric, leading to decline and turpitude. Iran's Guardianship of the Islamic Jurist, the system of religious rule meant to hold off this "Westoxification," has remained surprisingly resilient, despite problems driven by sanctions, such as major economic crises, and the protests of the country's youth in the 2020s. Many of these protests were sparked by the death in police custody of Mahsa Amini, who was arrested for not properly wearing her head covering, and the brutal reaction by Iran's security forces, including the killing of more civilians, has led to a breakdown of basic trust between the urban population and the government. This is similar to the situation under the shah in 1979, when he was accused of detaining rivals and violently suppressing dissent. The breaking point was when he lost the support of the *bazaaris,* the middle-class merchants in the cities.[22] Although the clerical establishment and the military, especially the elite Revolutionary Guard, have survived mass protests before, it is possible that Iran is heading in the same direction today and their overthrow is coming. Arbitrary actions such as the trial, conviction, and sentencing to ten years in prison of two young engaged Iranians for dancing happily in front of the Freedom Monument instill fear but may ultimately be counterproductive. Although intended as promises of security, these acts seem to indicate desperation and an inflated fear of the populace on the part of the Iranian government, which is losing the battle of messaging, isolating itself internally as it chooses allies, such as Russia, that have been isolated by much of the international community.

Despite the still ongoing protests there, Iran was on a path of increased power in the Gulf, what Vali Nasr called "the Shia revival." In 2003, the fall of Saddam Hussein left a major opening for influence in the region, especially in Iraq. In the face of constant rebellion there, neoconservative dreams of a stable Iraqi government that would support US interests failed to materialize. As the United States faltered and eventually withdrew most of its forces in 2011, Iran celebrated: "By pulling out of Iraq in December 2011 after more than eight years of military occupation, the United States allowed Iran to reap all the desired benefits from the new geopolitical order. . . . The American administration had . . . put in place an Iraqi state that was weak, divided, and dominated by the Shiite community, three major objectives that the Iranian regime had vainly attempted to accomplish. . . . The Islamic Republic of Iran could now celebrate its victory."[23] Fearful of Iranian expansion, the Arab states did not stand idly by. Saudi Arabia, for one, realizing it would have to take matters into its own hands and not rely completely on the US presence in the region, invested heavily in weapons and defense, often to the delight of US arms dealers and companies. They might, however, be leery of the kingdom's homegrown defense industry programs.[24] The Iran-Saudi rivalry is, at heart, the reason for the recent failed campaign against the Houthis of Yemen and the 2017 blockade of Qatar, which other Arab Gulf states accused of supporting Iran.

The Gulf has always been subject to global trends, and those of the twenty-first century have been no exception. In 2008, the Gulf was the very embodiment of free trade and free communication, success writ large. Al Jazeera, established by the emir of Qatar Sheikh Hamad bin Khalifa in 1996, was in its heyday. Worldwide globalization and the flow of money and goods reached their peak that year—but then what economists call "the great trade collapse" occurred.[25] The world economy fell much more sharply in 2008 than during the Great Depression and has yet to regain its pre-crash level. COVID-19 threw another large wrench into the machine of global commerce. While the hyper-successful cities of the Gulf, such as Doha and Dubai, have since recovered, in the first years of the crisis the dramatic sight of abandoned rows of Mercedes-Benzes and unfinished towers lining their horizons showed some of the vulnerabilities of economic success.

Visitors and scholars often want to put the Gulf into a category determined by Western social, economic, and political models, but these can be misleading in this context. For one thing, the importance of the extended family persists and continues to shape the culture. From marriage and business to a sense of value and belonging, the currency of success is not (or not just) riyals but relationships. This is true for rulers as well as nonroyal citizens, whose perspective is often missing from the full story of the Gulf's modernization, even though they are the beneficiaries of much of the economic expansion of the past decades.

Elements of Gulf Society

In the West, industrialization pulled families and communities apart as people moved to the city, often living in tenements and slum conditions, to provide labor for factories and industrialists, who frequently monopolized the benefits. This provoked an intellectual and social backlash, forming the basis for communism. Income inequality remains one of the core political issues in the West. The Gulf, however, had a fundamentally different experience, buffered by foreign labor and the desire of its Arab leaders to secure the tribal allegiances that would legitimate their control of oil-rich lands. In the very first decades of oil, there was a mini industrial revolution in the Gulf. Many Gulf citizens, most without an advanced education, worked on the oil fields. They occasionally went on strike and demanded more support from their leaders in a collective way. However, as opportunities for more education and other jobs arose, those who could leave the fields did, and much of the hard labor began to be supplied by people brought in from south Asia and elsewhere around the Indian Ocean. Instead of breaking them up, many rulers settled formerly nomadic families and tribes together in new homes and neighborhoods, subsidizing the building of villas and other accommodations in exchange for their loyalty and allegiance. Gulf tribes and families were also encouraged to set up their own businesses and to buy into the development game. The *kafala* system was instituted to make this easier for them.

Under the surface of hyperglobalization, the distinctiveness of Gulf communities and Gulf citizens remains. A focus on lineage and identity has been a means of resisting homogenization among the Baluchi and Arabic speakers who are a plurality of the 5.5 million residents of the Iranian Gulf shore. On the Arabian side, where extended tribal and family genealogy is even more important, the majlis—a regular assembly, council, or tribunal—is still the glue that holds together the minority citizen populations of the Gulf states, one of the primary forums of social, cultural, and even political expression from the neighborhood all the way to the legislature, to which it gives the name in many Islamic states.

While formal democratization has often met with resistance and delays in the Gulf, tribal networks and the tribal majlis (called *diwaniyya* in Kuwait) offer informal ways of expressing concerns even to members of ruling families, who are expected to visit from time to time. This is often faster than going through the bureaucracy. Although some issues may be settled at a family majlis, those that cross family or tribal lines often require the help of persons of importance or other outsiders, who will therefore be invited to attend. As one report from Qatar notes, more than half of Qataris attend or host a majlis regularly and almost half on a daily basis. If going to one of these conferences is a semipolitical or civil act, then this is an extraordinary level of civic participation, far outpacing the rates of US and European civil groups. Although both men and women can be part of official diwans and advisory councils, only men can attend the traditional tribal majlis, so women host parallel majlises themselves, but at a lower reported rate.[26] These are often surprisingly powerful: if, for instance, a sheikh had to deny a male subject's request, he would not dishonor the man by saying so in the tribal majlis, which often includes invited guests and other outsiders, but would instead tell his wife, who would communicate the bad news to the subject's wife in the female majlis—a less public forum.

Fluidity, informality, and the ability to cross hierarchies and transform from a place of banality into a center of importance are the main factors in the majlis's success. These are the grassroots assemblies that keep the Gulf moving. The ones that sheikhs host happen regularly, normally once a week or more, in the *sablah*, or long room, and often include coffee and treats piled high for display. The most important invitee is usually a relative of the emir or the emir himself, who makes his circuit among the tribal councils, arranging marriages, hearing complaints, learning about issues of medical or governmental concern, and discussing daily topics of importance. In almost every instance, the rules of etiquette and modest politeness prevail, especially in the higher, more formal council chambers, such as the diwans of the ruling families, to which tribal chiefs are invited for regular conversation. When George W. Bush attended the Qatari diwan during a visit to expand the number of bases used for the Second Gulf War (2003–11), he caused disruption with his Texas manner, entering loudly and informally, shaking the hands of the assembled chiefs, and shattering this type of meeting's usual staid decorum.

An earlier outsider made himself more welcome as a guest at an informal majlis. Intrepid and independent, the British explorer Wilfred Thesiger, in his *Arabian Sands,* wrote about how in the 1930s he went on vacation from the rigors of desert travel in the oasis of al-Buraimi, where he was hosted by Sheikh Zayed, later the president of the UAE. In the village of Muwaiqih, now in the border region of al-Ain in the UAE and Buraimi in Oman, Thesiger found Sheikh Zayed's fort, the walls half covered by drifting sands and the palm grove ragged. Jabal Hafit was in the distance. Thesiger remained for almost a month with Sheikh Zayed (whose name he spelled "Zayid"), who created powerful human networks of obligation while mediating among various tribes and local inhabitants:

> In the mornings, after we had breakfasted on tea and bread, a servant would come in and tell us that the Sheikh was 'sitting' [holding his regular informal majlis]. We would go out and join him. Sometimes Zayid would be on the bench in the porch, but more often under a tree outside the fort. He would call for coffee and we would sit there chatting till lunch-time, though we were frequently interrupted. Visitors would arrive, Bedu from the Sands [Rub' al Khali] or from Saudi Arabia, tribesmen from Oman, or perhaps a messenger from Shakhbut [Zayed's brother, the ruler of Abu Dhabi until overthrown in a bloodless coup in 1966 with the help of a confederation of the Trucial Oman Scouts and tribes loyal to Zayed]. . . .

Perhaps an Arab would get up from the circle, sit down immediately in front of Zayid, hit the ground a wallop with his stick to attract attention, and interrupting us as we spoke together, would say: 'Now Zayid, what about those camels which were taken from me?' Zayid, who might be in the middle of a sentence, would stop and listen to the man's complaint. Most of the complaints were about camels. Frequently the complainant averred that some notorious outlaw, who might well be sitting with us, had taken his animals. Zayid had many of these outlaws in his entourage, since it suited him better to have them with him than in some rival sheikh's fort. . . . Zayid had no desire to offend the outlaw, nor to lose his reputation for justice. It was a proof of his skill that he usually satisfied both sides by his judgement.[27]

Like Sheikh Zayed, ʿAbd al-ʿAziz Ibn Saʿud, who ruled Saudi Arabia from 1932 to 1953, used cunning and mediation skills to keep his people and realm together, as well as to make claims to lucrative oil contracts and land in Buraimi. It was in Sheikh Zayed's interest to prevent tribal chiefs from defecting to him—and they were happy to play both sides, as Thesiger recalled: "Some of the Rashid [tribe] on the southern coast thought it worth while to ride fourteen hundred miles to Riyadh and back in the expectation of getting something from Ibn Saʿud."[28]

Rather than an absolute sovereign, the Gulf ruler is often much more constrained, a mediator who must form loose alliances, as was the case with Sheikh Zayed. The way the guest interrupted Zayed and hit the ground with his stick to get the sheikh's attention shows the importance of the client-patron relationship and the extent to which it did not rest on decorum. While Zayed was using deft negotiation and judgments to maintain his authority in the oasis, oil company representatives were collecting information in the area. The sheikh and others pressed the claims of the UAE and Oman over Buraimi on the basis of the loyalty and allegiance of the local tribes, prevailing in the Treaty of Jeddah, much to the chagrin of the Saudis. The UAE now has the sixth-largest proven oil reserves in the world, including a large field near Buraimi.

The contours and architecture of tribal mediation and power in the Gulf are far more complex even than Thesiger's story suggests. Frauke Heard-Bey, one of the first Westerners to work in the Abu Dhabi archives, noted the importance of tribal networks at every level of society, helping the state to run: "In most villages, hamlets, or quarters of a town, each tribal group had its own leaders, and they would be the channels of communication between heads of families and the *wāli* [governor] or the Ruler himself. Such a person would lead a delegation of his people to the local *wāli* in case of a grievance, and he would also pass on the *wāli*'s instructions to them. Usually there was no formal appointment nor a regular salary."[29] Recently, however, some states, such as the Sultanate of Oman, have bureaucratized the leaders of tribes, making them part of the government and giving them salaries. Oman's Interior Ministry produced *A General Guide to the Provinces and Tribes in the Sultanate of Oman*, which highlights the importance of traditional ties there.[30] But while the overall tribal chief, the *tamima* (a kind of sheikh of sheikhs), is sometimes a government-sponsored position, the way that consensus functions in the majlis means that it is still often outside the control of the central state. Before the tamima was salaried, he (and other sheikhs) would sometimes receive gifts from the ruler. In the 1930s and 1940s, this may have included money from oil concessions.[31]

Instead of imposing their will and taking what they wanted by force, as the British East India Company had done, oil companies had to woo the rulers of the Gulf. World War I and World War II were fought, at least in part, over the right of self-determination, and colonization was no longer in vogue. Although the British still had some advantages in the Gulf, thanks to their treaties with its rulers, there would have been a backlash had they attempted to take over the region's newly valuable oil resources. Britain also did not want to alienate its main ally, the United States, now active in the Gulf, but it still very much wanted as large a piece of the pie as possible. British and American oil companies became proxies for the competition, sometimes cutthroat, between the two countries. While these companies could not directly control the concessions they were granted, the contracts they signed with emirs gave them significant leeway in how they extracted oil. These rulers, in turn, based their claims to their lands, now potentially full of untold wealth, on loyalty from tribal groups, which still got to decide whether to give homage to one or another. In the twenty-first century, the borders that were set by this process are not necessarily complete or static: they could change again. Indeed, in just the past few years, boundaries have been flash points, their fate decided not by force but by formal arbitration, often involving the United Nations or other outside powers.

Especially in times of crisis, transborder affiliations matter. When Saddam Hussein invaded Kuwait during the First Gulf War (August 1990–February 1991), Qatar took in thousands of Kuwaiti refugees, including women who had been threatened with sexual violence by Iraqi troops. The Qataris, including the royal al-Thanis, treated their Kuwaiti guests, who had been dispossessed of their wealth, status, and lands, like close family members, and both sided reminded themselves of ties going back centuries. Although Qatar was part of the coalition that pushed Saddam Hussein out of Kuwait in Operation Desert Storm, its earlier welcome may be a bigger reason for why Kuwait remained fairly neutral during the blockade of Qatar that began in 2017.

In other cases, tribal lineages and claims have led to cross-border conflicts or made whole tribes stateless. Some groups, such as the Murrah Bedouin, who traditionally served as the border guard for

Saudi Arabia, traditionally existed as nomadic herders who traveled between states. This has caused a whole host of contentious issues, such as what to do about those left without citizenship. Caught outside the borders, *Bidoon jinsiyya* (Without nationality), those lacking official ties to any state or nation, have no citizenship. Sometimes they had citizenship but were stripped of it for not supporting a particular ruler. In Kuwait, there are around one hundred thousand people, about 10 percent of the population, with this status.[32] A Bidoon protest in 2011, during the Arab Spring, highlighted their situation. Kuwait continues to struggle with this category of illegal residents even as it has set out to maintain a list of "Bidoon rights" and given them scholarships.[33] In the UAE and Qatar, citizenship laws often require proof of a family's residency before 1925—that is, before the oil boom and toward the end of the pearling era. This has excluded tribal nonelites and people who cannot establish a clear lineage. At the same time, there are minorities who manage to hold positions of influence. Members of the Lawati Khoja tribe, a small Shi'a Isma'ili minority known for financial and commercial acumen throughout the Gulf, have gained citizenship by working not only with Omanis as traders and businesspeople but also with Kuwait's ruling al-Sabah family as high-level advisers. They also have families in India.[34]

Tribal identities are, in fact, far more fluid and flexible in the Gulf than current official categorizations recognize. Unlike in the West, where tribes have been seen as "backward," "elementary," or "primitive" and fragmented, marginalized, dispersed, and confined to reservations and other particular places, sometimes far from their original lands, in the Gulf, tribalism has always been an active and living part of the sociopolitical system. Informal tribal ways remain as important as formal government structures. It is the Gulf's unique geographic conditions, which promote adaptation and alliance shifting, that govern its identities, practices, and customs. Rather than a petrified category, tribal identity is often used as a means for including, not excluding, groups in modern Gulf states, and claims of patrilineal and matrilineal descent have allowed for associations and even whole tribes to form, dissolve, and re-form again. The current "royal" or "ruling" tribes are relatively set, having been established often through the intervention of the British, who selected particular leaders to keep the peace in their parts of the Gulf. Also, some major tribes, prominent merchant or Bedouin families, especially those that can be traced through Lorimer's *Gazetteer of the Persian Gulf*, once a secret British government document and now a well-known source for Gulf tribal ancestries, are fairly well accepted, since their lineages are written down and printed.[35] But not all tribal categories are stable, and "the groupings and nomenclature of lineages and other groups, as well as of subordinate groups associated with major tribes, are often blurred and in flux."[36] As Ibn Khaldun noted of people and families that change tribal affiliations, "when the things resulting from common descent are there, it is as if (common descent) itself were there."[37] In the Gulf, the adoption of outsiders, including non-Arabs, into tribes has always been common. People who provided particular services to the tribe in ports of call around the Indian Ocean, for example, or whose ancestors were enslaved east Africans or clients of a major tribe might be taken in, sometimes through marriage and sometimes just through a rewriting of the oral and genealogical past. During the Zanzibar Revolution in 1964, which overthrew the island's Arab ruling class, for instance, Swahili-speaking Arabs and Africans fled to Oman, which welcomed them with open arms. Many were middle-class professionals, including teachers, who then helped to drive the Omani renaissance, the country's rapid modernization. In three years, from 1970 to 1972, Oman went from three schools and nine hundred students to forty-five schools and fifteen thousand students.[38]

While some formal democratization, such as elections for municipal posts and members of parliament, has been instituted in the

Gulf, it has not led to the decline of tribal loyalties and affiliations. Instead, tribes have voted in blocs for their own and their preferred candidates, across generational and other divides. In most elections, lineage and affiliation matter a great deal, even if they are often reimagined and realigned for political purposes. One example of the alignment of tribes and political parties is found in the UAE. Political scientists consider its Federal National Council fairly weak, but members such as Mona Al Bahar, Noura Al Kaabi, and Hamad Al Rahoumi have used it to express the concerns of UAE nationals. In trying to keep these assemblies from being seen as replacing the traditional majlis, representatives attempt to replicate the type of personal access and intervention provided by patrons and prominent guests at informal majlises on a wider scale, using modern technology and new media to hold regular meetings with constituents: Al Kaabi had sixty-two thousand followers on Twitter, and Al Rahoumi gave the public his private cell phone number.[39]

In other Gulf states, legislative councils have taken some effective power from rulers, who nonetheless still often control national budgets. Kuwaitis remember 1938 as "the Year of the Majlis," when prominent merchants and members of the ruling family worked together to resolve conflicts and promote commerce. In 1963, the British ambassador to Kuwait described the National Assembly and its nineteen-thousand-member electorate as Hellenic, because they represented only a small percentage of the population, as was the case in ancient Athens, where only citizens of demes (the city's official clans), and especially members of aristocratic families, could vote. Today, however, as one of the strongest and most developed of the parliamentary bodies in the Gulf, the National Assembly, which has power over ministerial conduct, has evolved into a check on Kuwait's emirs, often at the prompting of the United States, which expelled Saddam Hussein from Kuwait. According to Freedom House, in 2017, "opposition lawmakers in the National Assembly grilled senior ministers summoned for questioning about austerity measures implemented to reduce budget deficits, as well as corruption."[40] Right before a no-confidence vote on the acting information minister was taken, the cabinet resigned.[41] Dubai also experienced a reform movement in 1938, when Sheikh Sa'id bin Maktoum reluctantly agreed to a more formal legislative and executive council, run by his cousin. The principle of *shura*, consultation, is enshrined in the teachings of Muhammad and the Qur'an. In 1991, when he opened the first session of a Majlis Ashura (Consultation council) in Oman, Sultan Qaboos declared that it was "inspired by the principles of Your [God's] Noble Law."[42]

No matter how much power they have given to legislative councils, the Gulf's ruling families still retain control over succession. Primogeniture, and even general father-to-son succession, is not a regular custom or guarantee. In Saudi Arabia, rule usually transfers from brother to brother, which has sometimes happened in other Gulf states as well. Royal grandees would meet in a family majlis to determine the next monarch in Qatar and in the former Trucial States, the UAE. Women could have also their say: powerful mothers and wives in particular have often had an outsize role in the ruling families of the Gulf. After several instances of fratricide threatened their hold on power, Salamah bint Butti, the mother of Abu Dhabi's Sheikh Shakhbut, gathered her sons and made them swear not to use violence to resolve their differences with one another.[43] In Dubai, Sheikha Hussa bint Murr, called Umm Rashid (Mother of [Sheikh] Rashid), was involved in business, landownership, and state affairs.[44] Nonelite women have been unusually important parts of their families and communities as well, even before the rise of modern, highly educated women professionals, as Rosemarie Said Zahlan remarked: "Gulf women traditionally enjoy considerably more involvement in day-to-day activity than many of their sisters elsewhere in the Arab world. The mobility of Bedouin [and pearling] life has always been such that women have had a direct and active role to play in community affairs. . . . Since the pearling boats stayed at sea for up to four months at a stretch during the season, the women who remained behind inevitably moved forward to assume greater responsibility. Many of their daughters and granddaughters today continue in the same tradition." [45] Women, in fact, are often the glue that holds informal tribal networks together.

As long as there is a sense of the "inside" being tribal majlis-style consultations and alliances, what goes on in "outside," or nontribal, institutions such as advisory councils and assemblies matters less than it may seem. The hidden geography of Gulf ports illustrates this well. In some instances, the rise of modern infrastructure and the need to demolish old and decaying buildings and other structures has appeared to erase the past in cities such as Doha and Kuwait. In fact, new shops and neighborhoods often retain the names of their original tribal residents, who have grown wealthy off their property holdings. The presence of a modern glass building does not negate the imagined space dominated by much older and traditional ties. Similarly, new Gulf villas and other houses are usually far larger than needed for the families who live in them—this is so they can host the council meetings that will bring them prestige. Even offshore construction reflects the notion of onshore space identified by tribe. The artificial islands and free-trade zones throughout much of the Gulf aren't about a need just for more land. In fact, there is a surfeit of land. Rather, the need is for land that is not claimed by any lineage group or family, which can serve as a space for unaffiliated activities and inhabitants, or "nontribals," as long-term residents without a tribal connection are sometimes called in colloquial Gulf Arabic. While anybody can buy a ninety-nine-year lease on the Pearl, an artificial island off Doha, for instance, a noncitizen cannot purchase land in a poor oasis or even a sand dune in the middle of nowhere, and all businesses must have a citizen control at least a 51 percent stake. This majority-ownership policy is explained in part by the pressure and influence that citizens have brought to bear on their more technocratic governments. Some scholars, used to Western definitions of power based on formalized institutions and focused on economic output, have declared that the "desert democracy" of the Arabian Gulf has been co-opted by ruling families and regimes in a process that has created "neotraditional" states.[46] The increase in clout-enhancing oil rents and their consolidation in the hands of leading families are important developments, but economics is not the sole driver of power in many of these states. Culture, symbolism, and history matter: the effectiveness of traditional and informal systems is not diminished simply because they do not follow a Western model of democratic engagement. In the end, the tribe and the majlis, which offer informal means of communicating between rulers and citizens, are integral parts of how the Gulf works, both formally, in that the state recognizes tribal identity as a basis for citizenship, and behind the scenes.[47]

When the state acquired land from tribes, whether for oil exploitation or other forms of development, it involved a major transfer of wealth. The Gulf does not have the typical eminent domain process seen in Europe and the United States. Instead of the fair-market value of the large tracts owned and claimed by various tribes and families, the state, in many instances, has paid much higher sums, effectively transferring ruling family and state wealth to nonruling tribes.[48] Similar transfers have occurred throughout the Gulf, often explicitly cast as signs of the bonds between monarchs and citizens. In Kuwait, speculators in the Suq al-Manakh stock market lost everything, sometimes millions of dollars, in a 1982 crash following a decline in oil prices. The al-Sabah ruling family, led by Sheikh Jabir al-Ahmad al-Sabah, stepped in with a bailout, despite protests from the National Assembly and many Kuwaitis. Although this action was unpopular, it prevented unlucky investors from falling into destitution.

The scale of the problem was enormous. Just one Kuwaiti, a former immigration clerk, personally owed ten and a half billion dollars. While some of the "Magnificent Nine"—the innermost group of traders, thought to account for two-thirds of the market's ninety-four-billion-dollar debt—were held responsible, many were given bridge payments that did not need to be reimbursed, a few in the millions of dollars.[49]

The Gulf's ruling families have been wise to invest so much in their societies and to stay connected to the tribal and less formal networks there. The shah of Iran was deposed in 1979 in large part because he isolated himself from the rest of his country, and some observers keep expecting the same thing to happen elsewhere in the Gulf, eagerly awaiting the fall of the current Gulf system and the rise of brittle and unsustainable authoritarianism. The economic argument for keeping the political status quo seems quite easy to make: the collapse of oil prices—because of cycles of falling demand, increases in production in the United States, and the growth of alternative energy—is always a threat on the horizon. In fact, however, the oil monarchs have weathered many price collapses and business cycles, and most take a measured approach to rule. They have learned that with increased concentration of power comes increased international scrutiny, often from the main oil consumers, Europe and the United States. Indeed, while the decade from 2010 to 2020 was especially turbulent, with the 2017 Qatar embargo and a new generation of leaders taking the helm in Saudi Arabia (Muhammad bin Salman as heir apparent), Qatar (Tamim bin Hamad, r. 2013–present), and Oman (Haitham bin Tariq al-Saʻid, r. 2020–present), loyalty to ruling families in many cases seems as strong as ever, as has been typical during times of crisis in the past. The spread of the Middle East respiratory syndrome (MERS) coronavirus, associated with camel hosts, and then COVID-19 exposed the dangers of the Gulf's global links but also the related importance of the heavy investments in health infrastructure and the welfare state by Gulf rulers, although rising case numbers have strained the system.

Many political scientists presume that state and nation formation inevitably leads to the "decline of intermediary elites"—in the Gulf's case, tribal sheikhs—thereby giving monarchs even more power.[50] Bureaucracy, in this theory, formally replaces informal links: walloping a stick on the floor of the majlis, as described by Thesiger, is not common anymore, and instead one must go through ministerial channels, all of which are controlled, it is assumed, by the ruling family. One interesting tendency that began the 2010s, however, was the opening of ministerial positions to people outside the ruling family, as happened in Qatar after the accession of Sheikh Tamim.[51] Certainly, however, there are some signs of vulnerability in informal tribal networks.

Some scholars believe the that history of the Gulf since 1971 is largely one of erasure and appropriation by the state and ruling families.[52] While it is true that the state shapes many aspects of social life, civil society, and the media and has tried to foster a sense of belonging in its citizens by nationalizing and folklorizing pre-oil tribal traditions and ways of life, this does not mean that Gulf society and history have somehow been consumed by a homogenous "distributional state" that orients "interests . . . to the center."[53] As much as they are heavy hitters in international commerce and finance and as much as their sovereign wealth funds have risen to astronomical heights and their buildings reach far into the sky, the Gulf states are relatively small, with small citizen populations, so their large numbers of expatriates keep them quite heterogenous. As we have seen, such an international component, mainly made up of Asians, not Arabic speakers, is not new to the Gulf or to Gulf culture. Rather than being radically different from the past, Gulf society today still rests on long-term continuities such as informal institutions and practices that link citizens, foreigners, and rulers. The region has also experienced state formation, rapid urbanization, and the growth of new identities and alliances before—during the pearl boom, for instance.

Although Arab Gulf rulers have been promoting a sense of national ethnic culture, they have simultaneously embraced cosmopolitanism. This dual commitment—to an exclusive notion of heritage and an inclusive tolerance of difference—is seen not as a contradiction but as a continuation of the millennia-long openness of Gulf society, which they have tried to nationalize and institutionalize. Indeed, cosmopolitanism and attracting trade are almost part of a ruler's legitimacy, and today's distinctive cosmopolitanism, while still coming from a culture of commerce, is actively promoted and claimed by the state, which encourages celebrations of the Gulf's noncitizens as well. As part of this trend, the UAE created a Ministry of Tolerance in 2016 and declared 2019 "the Year of Tolerance." Coordinated by the minister of state for tolerance, it included the branding of a Tolerance Bridge in Dubai, the decorating of Christmas trees, the Pope's first visit to the UAE, and the building of a Hindu temple. Sheikh Muhammad bin Zayed Mosque, near Abu Dhabi International Airport, was renamed to Mariam, Umm Eisa Mosque, after Mary, the mother of Jesus.[54] Surely such displays of state-sponsored cosmopolitanism and moderate Islam are meant primarily for an outside audience? In fact, the narrative of openness and hospitality is important to Khaliji identity, not only acknowledging long-standing traditions and morals, going back to the obligation of a good tribal sheikh to be good to his guests, but also tempering concerns about the role of culture in modern life and the new built environment. Because of this, the UAE also celebrates the distinctiveness of Emirati culture. Featuring Saluki dogs, horse exhibits, and booths with traditional foods and crafts, the Sheikh Zayed Heritage Festival shows off unique features of the UAE, alongside world heritage in the same venue. I had the opportunity to visit in 2016, part of a trip to several heritage villages and fairs throughout the Gulf, from Oman through Bahrain to Kuwait. While also enjoyed by tourists and non-nationals, these are mainly meant for consumption by Gulf citizens. Despite being sponsored by the state, cosmopolitanism mixed with distinctive heritage, sometimes awkwardly, remains popular. As scholars like Karen Exell and Trinidad Rico have revealed in their important work, it would be a mistake to assume that all attempts at emphasizing national heritage are somehow set in stone and top down. Although heritage projects are often managed by Western consultancies, nationals can have direct oversight and input. These are not just external shows: there is buy-in from regular Gulf citizens.[55] Often, in fact, local groups demand more heritage villages.

In Iran, heritage, along with what it means to be a citizen of the state, is often a much more contentious issue, not as convincingly managed as elsewhere in the Gulf. As part of a continuing "Green Wave," which began in 2011 and challenges the legitimacy of clerical rule, protesters have called for the embrace of diversity and the revival of historical cosmopolitan identities in Iran. In 2016, Kurds and Iranian Arabs as well as Persians in traditional clothing celebrated the unofficial Cyrus the Great Day, praising his tolerant rule in the sixth century BCE. The commemoration became a demonstration against the restrictions of the state's Guardianship of the Islamic Jurist. On the other side, many ruling Shi'a clerics have dismissed Iran's pre-Islamic period, which was embraced by the overthrown shah, who tied his legitimacy to Persia's universal kings.[56] The "global port" model of cosmopolitanism and the centralized, "universal" cosmopolitanism of Cyrus, with its imperial mission, now have somewhat opposite, competing roles in the Gulf: Baluchi, Sunni, and other identities are subsumed and even forcefully repressed in Iran, while in Dubai and Doha, in contrast, the state supports both tolerance and local-identity heritage.

Since the 1990s, Gulf states from Oman to Kuwait have focused on preserving heritage, both tangible and intangible, as a way to make the argument that modernization, business, and the city as corporation need not mean the destruction of the past, whose conservation will in fact ensure the future and lessen the social costs of rapid development. Perhaps no event represents the challenges of identity in the Gulf today better than the heritage festival. These are major, sometimes multiday affairs, such as the Qasr al-Hosn Festival in Abu Dhabi, which occurs outside in the cooler winter months each year. Qasr al-Hosn, built in the late eighteenth century as a watchtower, guarded one of the very few freshwater sources on Abu Dhabi Island and became a base of the ruling family. In the first decade of the 2000s, this fortress, which was abandoned for a series of more modern royal residences and is now almost completely surrounded by asphalt and glass buildings, became a symbol of Abu Dhabi identity.

"A person who does not know their past cannot make the best of their present or future": these words are featured during the Qasr al-Hosn Festival, even projected on the building's historic walls. Sheikh Zayed bin Sultan al-Nahyan, celebrated as the Founder of the United Arab Emirates and often called simply Baba Zayed, "Papa Zayed," by longtime residents of Abu Dhabi, said this as he reviewed the master plans of that capital city, which became extremely modern and international in a short matter of decades. This phrase and images of Sheikh Zayed are seen throughout the Qasr al-Hosn Exhibition, where the ruler is encountered multiple times and in several contexts: video projections, still photographs, and quotes in large letters, written in both Arabic and English. Even as he funded and oversaw Abu Dhabi's planning and development, he was also a conscious preservationist, seeming to foresee what challenges Emiratis would face in the midst of change and how best to overcome them. Thus, unlike the European or American experience, modernization in Abu Dhabi was begun with the end and the consequences of that end in sight: a city of hypermodern complexity and globalization in which Emiratis, already from diverse backgrounds, would become a minority and so would need to protect their identity as they entered the world stage.

From its first occurrence, in 2013, the festival has aimed to let "the Qasr al-Hosn breathe again," as I read on a sign there, not to create some stale living museum. While it is happening, tents and booths with camels, Saluki dogs, traditional crafts, local food, and storytellers appear around the fort, which is usually empty of these activities.[57] The festival's motto is "Take part in history," and it begins with a march of thousands, soldiers and royals and citizens all together. Instead of confining historic traditions to the past or paving them over in the name of development, events like this link the Gulf's history to today's cosmopolitan trade, maritime activities, and dynamic markets. As Sheikh Mohammed bin Zayed remarked of the Qasr al-Hosn Festival, making the link between distinctive identity and future growth, "The UAE is proud of its cultural heritage, which we'll preserve and transfer to future generations to safeguard our authentic Emirati identity. We will be loyal to the values of our forefathers, finding inspiration in their glorious history to continue our approach for development. What we live today is a continuation of our past efforts which we are determined to sustain and enhance."[58]

Abu Dhabi is the political capital of the UAE, and the Qasr al-Hosn is at the center of Abu Dhabi. The emirate, which also shares its name with the island on which the capital city is built, is the biggest and wealthiest of the UAE's seven, stretching well into the desert bordering Saudi Arabia and Oman, almost to Qatar. It has its own flag, a red rectangle with a white box in the left corner, from the period of the Trucial States. This banner is rarely displayed—but it flies on the reconstructed officers' quarters in the Qasr al-Hosn during the festival. According to the festival guide, an exhibition at the fort is dedicated to "the story of Abu Dhabi and its people." It quotes Sheikh Zayed as saying, "People are the foundation of any urban development.... No matter how many buildings, schools and hospitals we build or how many bridges we lay or beautiful things we create, all of this remains an empty shell, devoid of spirit, and without a future. The spirit is the people, people enabled by their ideas, creativity and skills to shape these institutions and develop and grow with them." Similarly, in a famous TV interview, he said it was the people living in and around the Qasr al-Hosn who made it what it was, not the building itself. By focusing on the people and their actions as generators of spirit, Sheikh Zayed made a classic, almost instinctual case for the importance of intangible heritage.

It is people, after all, not texts or buildings, who possess collective memory and use it to make decisions about who they are both for the present and in preparation for the future. Many Gulf states recognize this and are increasingly celebrating the intangible component of their heritage, both royal and nonroyal. The memory of Sheikh Zayed, including the symbols he promoted, such as a distinctive pattern used in fabrics, is preserved as a core part of Abu Dhabi's national heritage. In 2016, a booth in the People's Market at the camel festival near Abu Dhabi focused on photographs and other images of him (see figure 14). Next to pictures of Sheikh Zayed performing various traditional activities, however, was a poster of Emirati pilots and other recent martyrs of the war in Yemen. Their faces are arranged on a tree of the type usually reserved for family charts, not national ones (see figure 15). This image replaces the typical tribal ancestors with martyrs, who thus become the new heroic precedents—for the whole nation, not just for one family. Similarly, in Kuwait, the annual Liberation Day, celebrating the end of Saddam's occupation, includes water balloon fights and a poetry contest in the Mubarakiya Market, where the same traditional forms that used to be employed to glorify the tribe now glorify the nation and the memory of those who defeated the Iraqi enemy (see figure 16). In Saudi Arabia too, "kinship has taken on a new resonance as a key idiom of modern Gulf nationalism," and more tribes there have embraced traditional ways of showing their loyalty to the ruling family and the state.[59] In a multi-

FIGURE 14. A photographer and pictures of the sheikh in Sheikh Zayed Photography, People's Market, Al Dhafra camel festival, outside Abu Dhabi, 2016. Photo by author.

billion-dollar museum in Qatar, one exhibit re-creates the exact Bedouin campsite, with all the detail of its textiles and other fabrics, photographed by a Danish anthropological expedition in 1959.[60]

Even in comparison to the UAE, Oman was ahead of the curve when it came to heritage preservation. Sultan Qaboos was one of the earliest proponents, and other Gulf rulers and states have followed his example of approaching development and modernization deliberately—for instance, respecting the traditional height of buildings in the old parts of towns. The Sultan Qaboos Grand Mosque, which is open to non-Muslim visitors and tours, celebrates, in its many beautiful mihrabs, or prayer niches, the styles and patterns of mosques found throughout the Islamic world, thereby weaving Gulf and Omani heritage into the larger tapestry of Islamic heritage as a whole (see figure 17). Heritage can be seen as a reminder of the bond

FIGURE 15. Emirati martyr tree for recent campaigns in Yemen, 2016. Photo by author.

FIGURE 16. Poetry contest on Kuwait Liberation Day, Mubarakiya Market, Kuwait City, February 26, 2016. Photo by author.

FIGURE 17. American visitors in front of a Persianate mihrab in the Sultan Qaboos Grand Mosque, Muscat, Oman, 2013. Photo by author.

between rulers and their citizen populations, reaching far back into the past. Identity, after all, is not something that can be created by the state alone—it involves all social groups and constituencies. It was no small sign of Sultan Qaboos's focus that he named Haitham bin Tariq al-Sa'id, Oman's minister of heritage, as his successor.

Many scholars have studied the use of heritage in the Gulf through the lens of a Western critical model influentially posited by the historians Eric Hobsbawm and Terence Ranger as "the invention of tradition." Gulf modernization, however, is not the same as European modernization, and the narrative of heritage is read differently by today's Gulf citizens than by the industrializing English or the Scots of the nineteenth century. For the former, maintaining the traditions of the past implicitly means maintaining a tradition of consultation, making the link between rulers and citizens the very basis of state legitimacy and cohesiveness: that informal governance, often hidden from outside view and therefore frustratingly obscure to the Western observer, is important to all parties. The rulers of the Gulf seem to be as interested as their citizens in understanding—and even performing—many of the traditions of of the past, so rather than separating the people from the royals, festivals and other celebrations of the Gulf's history might strengthen those distinctive elements of its modern society.

Gulf culture has always favored informal networks over formal institutions: distinctive cosmopolitans have built global connections while basing the success of their trade on maintaining local ties and identities. Even if the Gulf monarchies were to fall and its ports to lose preeminence, they would most likely be replaced not by one large imperial power or interest but by a new set of autonomous polities. There seems little appetite, and still less ability, to control the Gulf as a whole. If an antagonistic empire were to conquer it, however, the merchants, ships, and wealth would simply shift to different ports, as has happened multiple times before. From Basra of the ninth century and Siraf of the tenth through Hormuz of the fifteenth to Muscat of the nineteenth and Dubai of the twentieth and twenty-first, the Gulf's future has been based on its history as a trade and commercial hub open to all. Over five thousand years, the Gulf has been the world's most important transit zone. Adapting well to modern globalization, it is still a global success—and a final destination, not just a stop on the way to someplace else.

Conclusion

The Future of the Global Gulf

During the 2022 men's World Cup, global media attention was on the host, Qatar. Some in the Western press criticized FIFA's decision to hold the soccer tournament there. Migrant labor and the rights of LGBT fans were put under a magnifying glass. Argentina won the trophy, with Lionel Messi as the celebrated champion. Qatar's team, nicknamed the Maroons after one of the colors of the Qatari flag, was eliminated early, despite the investment of more than a billion dollars in Aspire Academy to develop a winning team.[1] Despite these disappointments, the whole Gulf region, with Qatar as the striker, still scored a huge victory.

Part of the win was the spotlight on Qatar and the Gulf as the host of a major international sporting event. Emir Tamim bin Hamad, the ruler of Qatar, presented Messi with a *bisht*, a typical Gulf-style robe traditionally given for heroic acts, embroidered with golden thread. Even more important, however, the World Cup accelerated the healing of divisions between Qatar and its neighbors on many levels. It was the beginning of a new period of cooperation, of repaired feelings. The surprising success of the Saudi team allowed its country, which had blockaded and threatened Qatar during the Gulf crisis of 2017–21, to shine, though it was not the host. The World Cup was framed as a Gulf success, not just a Qatari one. Qatar offered special visas and easy travel for Gulf citizens, just a couple of years after Saudi airspace was forbidden to its airline. Soon the Saudis and the Iranians, once archenemies, also agreed to talks brokered by the Gulf's great peacemaker, Oman. A successful World Cup and an era of good relations among Gulf powers would have been very difficult to foresee just five years earlier.

In 2017, there were fears of bullets flying across borders, not soccer balls across goalie boxes. Troops were amassing at the boundary between Qatar and Saudi Arabia. Bedouin who used to cross fairly freely between them were now blocked along with their camel herds, a large number of animals.[2] Saudi Arabia banned Qatar Airways from flying through its airspace and stopped sending food to Qatar, prompting Iran to supply blockaded Doha with provisions by using traditional dhows. A dangerous conflict seemed to be in the offing as Qatar did not agree to the thirteen extraordinary, sovereignty-limiting demands of its neighbors, including that it pay reparations for years of perceived wrongs, seek permission to naturalize citizens of other Gulf countries, shut down Al Jazeera, and submit to monitoring for ten years.[3] Moreover, this situation arose after the United States had announced its intention, a few years before under the Obama administration, to pivot its focus from the Middle East to China. In 2017, the Gulf got a taste of a world in which the United States no longer supported the triple containment of Iraq, Saudi Arabia, and Iran or the sovereignty of the Gulf states. Instead of encouraging the parties to back away from conflict and reasserting US interests in maintaining the Gulf's status quo, President Donald Trump tweeted to encourage the blockade.[4] Adding to the confusion, Secretary of State Rex Tillerson went to reassure the Qataris and worked feverishly against his own president to restore confidence in the old architecture of triple containment and peace in the Gulf, which, he knew as a former Exxon CEO, was crucial to the flow of inexpensive oil through the Strait of Hormuz. How did the relationship between the

United States and the Gulf get to this point? What does the future hold for the Gulf as the United States continues its withdrawal from the Middle East?

As with much US strategic policy, the Cold War was a starting point, the root of decisions whose consequences continued well after the fall of the USSR. During that era, the United States viewed the Gulf as vulnerable to exploitation, a potential arena for Soviet expansion. In 1979, the fall of the shah, a longtime US ally, the takeover of the US embassy and the hostage crisis that followed, and chants of "Death to America" made Iran an example of what could go wrong with United States–supported modernization. Moreover, the resurgent Iran went to war with Iraq after finishing its revolution, potentially upsetting the triple-containment calculus and creating an opening for the USSR to intervene and capture the Gulf's oil wealth. Instead of favoring Iraq, which could have overrun Iran with US aid, the Reagan administration supported both sides in the devastating Iran-Iraq War and the tanker wars in the Gulf, preventing either one from gaining the upper hand. The Iran-Contra hearings revealed the extent to which the United States was dealing directly with and helping its supposed enemy Iran when it seemed that Iraq was winning. But the United States was also backing its future enemy Saddam Hussein as a bulwark against Iranian expansion, as long as he stayed within his box. The balance changed when Iraq decided to upset the territorial boundaries and claims of other Gulf states, particularly Kuwait, which Hussein felt he had a right to invade. He may also have thought that the United States saw the Gulf as less in need of protection when the Berlin Wall fell in 1989, putting his own neighborhood much more on Mikhail Gorbachev's mind and presaging the end of the USSR. While the US ambassador to Iraq April Glaspie may or may not have caused the Gulf War by giving Hussein a green light to invade Kuwait, there was certainly miscommunication between Baghdad and Washington.[5] Hussein did not realize the extent to which the

United States was invested in maintaining free access to the region's oil supply even well after the collapse of the Soviet Union.

The Gulf War proved Saddam wrong. The United States not only remained but also sent troops to defend the oil-rich Gulf states, beginning with Kuwait. One of Hussein's most infamous acts was forcing the Gulf's geography, which had protected the autonomy of those on its shore for so many millennia, to yield to his will. He began, in the summer of 1990, to drain the great moat of the Iraqi marshes and to suppress the Marsh Arabs on his way to laying claim to Kuwait. In trying to expand its territory, Iraq made a major mistake in testing triple containment, and it was quickly and decisively defeated by an international coalition headed by the United States. The number of Arab Gulf allies showed how many were interested in maintaining the status quo, perhaps fearing that Hussein's ambitions included absorbing them as well. The Gulf War was, in part, proof that the independence of the Gulf states was crucial to the United States as an oil-consuming nation: its paramount concern was maintaining price stability in oil markets by preventing the region from falling into the hands of a power that could block trade through the Gulf, possibly the most strategic body of water in Eurasia. The success of the unified front of Arab and Western partners in support of Kuwait, combined with the USSR's collapse not long after the war, ushered in a period of unparalleled US influence in the region. The United States was able to build extensive bases and expand its military presence on the Arabian Peninsula and elsewhere in the Gulf, an arrangement that remains to this day.[6] The small independent Arab states all along the Gulf were especially grateful to the United States for intervening on behalf of Kuwait and guaranteeing their security at a time of existential threat. In many respects, this was the triumph of a highly realist strategy in the United States, one that kept its direct interests in the forefront: a commitment to the free flow of oil and commerce through the Strait of Hormuz, as articulated in the Carter Doctrine.

While the United States had been able to contain regional hegemons, however, it could not stop the spread of powerful and potentially destructive ideologies, unintentionally encouraged by its very presence in Arabia's holy lands: the rise of transnational Islamic terrorism, perhaps best exemplified by al-Qaeda, was about to begin. One of al-Qaeda's main complaints, in fact, was the presence of US troops in Saudi Arabia, the birthplace of Islam. The United States has since moved many of its bases from there to other Gulf states, with the largest one now at Al Udeid in Qatar, alongside "a ground-force base in Kuwait, the Fifth Fleet naval base in Bahrain, . . . Al Dhafra Air Base in the UAE and . . . access arrangements in Oman."[7]

The Gulf War seemed to create an implicit border guarantee for even the smallest of Gulf states, backed by the might of the US military. This may have prepared the ground for eventual conflict, since it allowed those states, especially Qatar and the UAE, to break away from regional powers and assert themselves. Instead of resting under the protection of the Saudis, as was the case in the 1980s, Qatar under Sheikh Hamad, the father of Tamim, became a major force, one with great influence and global reach through the Al Jazeera network and its investment funds. Soon Qatar was brokering peace agreements, hosting US university campuses, and emerging as one of the world's most powerful small countries. With the already global center of Dubai and the ambitious Abu Dhabi, the UAE was also rising, however, and wished to compete with its neighbor, introducing its own global media networks, its own cultural soft power, its own US university campuses. Instead of breaking with Saudi Arabia like Qatar did, the UAE partnered with the kingdom—joining the Saudi-led alliance in the war against the Houthis in Yemen that started in 2015, for instance—while being sure to maintain boundaries between them, a level of autonomy. Dubai–Ahu Dhabi and Doha suddenly became rival world centers of trade and exchange, and the rulers of the UAE and Qatar developed strategic national funds and militaries, with which they intervened abroad to protect a network of holdings in Asia, Africa, and the Americas.

The prominence of the small states along the Gulf runs counter to the expectations of world history, scholars of which have long studied the imperial and economic centers of world-systems, not transit zones like the Gulf.[8] World historians have focused on the metropoles, capitals of empires, on the interactions and ties between centers and peripheries, and on the role of empires in fostering and manipulating cosmopolitan identities.[9] In this view, imperial cities are at the centers of webs of culture, civilization, and economy, and the fall of one, be it Rome, Ctesiphon, Baghdad, Lisbon, London, or Washington DC, heralds the growth of another. The Gulf, however, shows the importance of the autonomous transit zone, that place neither in the core nor completely on the periphery. While Dubai and Doha have foreign interests and investments and have been involved in distant wars, often finding themselves on different sides of conflicts over resources, especially in Africa, they are hardly imperial centers. Although they have increased their military spending and partnered with US arms suppliers, their armies pale in comparison to the largest ones in the world. Instead of trying to compete with metropoles, they have followed a different model, one that has existed in the Gulf since ancient times. Dilmun and Magan avoided being under the direct power of Babylon while benefiting richly from its trade through the Gulf. The Hormuzis used their control of maritime silk to compel the English to help expel the Portuguese. Rather than being a victim of mercantilism, the slave trade, or outright colonization, the Gulf has gained directly and indirectly from a balancing of regional powers and external imperial interests. The discovery and exploitation of oil did not disrupt this pattern but only made the Gulf a far more attractive prize for potential take-over, so the triple-containment policy of the United States, far from causing or seeming to cause submission to American imperium, has been welcomed by the Arab Gulf states, which it has allowed to flourish in relative security. They might host US bases, but they also have true autonomy from their American protectors, being able to chart paths at odds with US interests, such as setting oil prices that may not be the best for the US economy. The important point is that all of their interests align concerning the Gulf status quo.

However, as the world has continued to transition from oil to alternative energy, the United States has repeatedly indicated a desire to pivot its focus from the Middle East to Asia.[10] Long promised and often delayed, the withdrawal of US forces from Afghanistan finally began under President Joseph Biden in 2021, part of a deal brokered in Qatar between the Taliban and the United States, which could at last decrease its presence in the region: the major military bases in the Gulf that had supported its efforts in Afghanistan were no longer necessary. While it remains unlikely that the United States will withdraw from the Gulf entirely, the Iraq War and the Afghanistan pullout have drained much of the goodwill that it gleaned from the Gulf War and have soured its own taste for more adventures in the region, no matter how high oil prices might rise. Neoconservatism and nation building have been largely discredited, and there is little appetite for Middle East wars on either side of the political spectrum. The Qatar crisis, which saw the UAE, Saudi Arabia, and Bahrain try to constrain their local competitor, was a test of the new US doctrine: had their blockade been successful, it could have been the beginning of Saudi hegemony. However, just a year before the World Cup, as Biden assumed the presidency, the parties retreated from brinkmanship and things returned to the status quo ante.

Oil, of course, has been at the heart of this strategic game, and although it has contributed to the success of the modern Gulf, it is far from the only factor. There are many examples of nations where oil development caused major disruption, political disintegration, and economic decline: from Nigeria, Libya, and Sudan to Venezuela and

Iran, it has fueled far more inflation, instability, and despair than progress. In contrast, the Arab countries of the Gulf have not only avoided the "oil curse" but also excelled in a rapid, seemingly spectacular fashion, bringing their citizens out of poverty and showering them with privileges—such as free health care, higher education, and housing—far beyond those offered to their entire populations by even the richest Western nations. Although some has been squandered and exported, put into European and American banks, London real estate, and the New York Stock Exchange, oil revenue has been used locally to a great extent, despite the Gulf economy's relatively small size and low capacity for investment before the twenty-first century. While return on investment abroad might have been higher in the short term, the concerted effort to develop real estate and ports and create a livable environment for an international community of businesses and travelers has reaped greater rewards over a longer period. Gulf rulers have expanded their largess beyond their immediate family or tribe, encouraging other tribes, particularly those important to establishing national borders, to support them and creating a citizen elite. Using the promise of free housing and modernization, rulers were able to convince formerly nomadic populations to settle. To develop modern urban life, they supported business leaders in importing massive amounts of labor, millions of migrants from around the world, whose numbers overtook those of local populations but were also key to the creation of today's skyscraper cities.

Since the 1970s, the Arab Gulf states have used their oil wealth, strategic investments, and maritime culture to become and remain centers of world commerce, diplomacy, media, and culture. To do this, they have relied on the most distant and global connection of all: a guarantee of security from the United States, a country on the other side of the world. This has changed, as Gulf powers, which had almost insignificant armies until the first decade of the 2000s, have increased their weapon supplies and professionalized their military forces. Instead of being transit points for empires, they are exerting their own might, often in distant lands in Africa and Asia, searching for resources opportunities. As political and military power grows, however, so does rivalry, and the Gulf's status as a forum and market for all could be at risk as the region's security becomes an increasingly internal affair. This is why the recent efforts toward peace between the Gulf states are so crucial. There have been some close calls, even with US security guarantees. One major happening with serious consequences for the region is currently ongoing.

When the Abraham Accords, bilateral agreements between Israel and the Arab states of Bahrain and the UAE, were signed in 2020, with Saudi Arabi on the verge of joining, it seemed that the United States might be able to begin withdrawing from the Gulf. The massacre in Israel on October 7, 2023, and the resulting Gaza crisis suddenly brought Palestine and Israel front and center again, leading to attacks on US bases in the region, since the United States is seen as Israel's closest ally. While Israeli and Gulf leaders were willing to deal with each other before, the killing of so many Palestinian civilians and Hamas's unwillingness to release all Israeli hostages have ended that openness. At the same time, however, Saudi Arabia has used the prospect of normalizing relations as an inducement for Israel to cease its campaign against Hamas.[11] Regardless of whether such an arrangement emerges, in the post–October 7 world, it seems unlikely that the United States will withdraw very quickly from the region. For one thing, Iran and its proxies would have to end their attacks on US personnel. Iran says that these are meant to compel the United States to force a cease-fire on Israel and leave the Gulf, but they only make more US troop deployments probable, since they confirm the need to defend the status quo from potential Iranian hegemony.

Iran has long had designs on dominating the Gulf, where it has repeatedly come into conflict with the Arab states over resources and maritime boundaries. Yet while the United States stands in its way,

Iran has little chance of success. Aware of this, Iran avoids direct con-frontation with the massive and dominant battleships of the US Navy, instead harassing them with small gunboats.[12] MARAD, the Maritime Administration of the US Department of Transportation, has warned of "threats to commercial vessels by Iran and its proxies" and advised US-flagged ships to email their Gulf transit plans to the US Fifth Fleet or the United Kingdom Maritime Trade Office. From May to August 2019, there were "six attacks against commercial ves-sels," an "attempted at-sea interdiction of the . . . BRITISH HERIT-AGE," and the "seizure of STENA IMPERO."[13] In the end, though, British and US fleets can easily overpower Iran's small boats and their machine guns. The Arab Gulf states and Iran, perhaps with Oman as mediator, will need to agree on a set of rules about freedom of trade through the Strait of Hormuz and the sharing of oil and gas fields that lie under the water and across maritime boundaries.

In addition to an arrangement among the Gulf states, their main-tenance of internal stability will be crucial to the entire region's con-tinued prosperity. During the first decades of the twenty-first cen-tury, the United States tried to nudge the Gulf monarchies toward democratization, through initiatives such as the Middle East Part-nership Initiative. But the 9/11 attacks had driven a neoconservative ideology forward in the United States, one that did not necessarily reflect a realist understanding of the country's interests and that broke with a long-standing policy of hands-off containment in the Gulf stretching all the way back to the pragmatic approach of the Brit-ish. Unlike the Gulf War, the Iraq War and the overthrow of Saddam Hussein were not supported by a broad range of US allies, Arab or other. Neither were they conducive to the regional balance of power: US-style democracy in Iraq opened the door to Iranian-backed par-ties there and to what some have called "the Shi'a crescent," a region of strong Iranian influence that reaches from the east of Arabia up though Iran and around to the Levant. This presumed expansion of

Iranian power and the realization that the United States would do little to stop it prompted the Sunni Saudis and Emiratis to offer an independent response, building up their military power and exertion of influence around the Gulf.

In 2011, the Arab Spring shook the Arab world. Protests in the Gulf were less dramatic than those elsewhere, but they did reveal a real desire, especially of new generations, for reform, including more voice in governance.[14] The careful, gradual opening and democratization of governments, through elections and the expansion of advisory council and parliamentary power, could be an important part of securing the Gulf's future, since democratic states rarely go to war with each other. The threat and fear of sectarianism silenced some protests, but others led to change.[15] Oman's Sultan Qaboos responded to protests in Sohar, a city famous for its diverse population, with aid and reforms, including more constitutional rights for the Consultative Council. A new emir of Kuwait, Sheikh Meshal al-Ahmad al-Sabah, came to power in December 2023 pledging to work with the influential National Assembly, which pressured him to institute reforms as well. It remains to be seen if this elected body, often mired in gridlock, will be granted more formal authority. Qatar formed an advisory council, which was technically able to dismiss ministers, and had its first ever national elections in 2021. Many Gulf rulers have moved to stabilize succession, instituting the position of crown prince to ensure a smooth transition, as in Oman's 2021 Constitution. While the Arab Spring produced dramatic changes from Tunisia to Egypt, in the Gulf it resulted in incremental progress toward formalized representation.

The 2020s seems to be a time of good feelings among Arab Gulf states. Despite their differences and the decades of fervent competition that led to the Qatar crisis, they know that unless they work together to provide regional security, they all risk inevitable instability and dramatic decline. A Gulf-centered and Gulf-enforced defense architecture will require even more than the cosmopolitan spirit seen in the shared table of Hindus, Muslims, and Zoroastrians in eleventh-century Siraf, however. In a modern world of hard borders and hard disputes over resources, all the Gulf states—especially the three major players, Iran, Iraq, and Saudi Arabia—must agree to transparent rules based on mutual goodwill and respect. The realization of this fact is perhaps behind the rapprochement and honoring of red lines between Qatar and its neighbors before and after the World Cup. It is the motivation for the peace negotiations between the longtime enemies Iran and Saudi Arabia, brokered by Oman and China, which could mark the beginning of a truly extraordinary shift in Gulf and Middle East history in general.[16] If peace holds in the Gulf, especially one that rests on clear agreements upheld by all parties, it could mean a return to a pre-British or even pre-Portuguese set of relationships: regional Gulf powers, without the interference of a distant Western actor, maintaining a tradition of free trade and cooperation oriented toward the Indian Ocean. The deep history is there, as are the economic motivations for long-term peace.

For now, however, the Arab Gulf is still primarily dependent on US naval and military protection. If a peaceful, self-protecting Gulf does emerge, the region will probably focus not on the United States or on the US rival China but on its historical, most natural partner: south Asia. After all, the extraordinary world history of the Gulf cannot be understood without an appreciation of the immense pull of the Indian Ocean. Before the rise of oil led to strategic understandings with distant lands such as the United States, it was contacts and connections with the Indian subcontinent that were most important to the Gulf's merchant-princes. It could be argued that no two noncontiguous regions of the world have been tied to each other longer than south Asia and the Gulf: Dilmun merchants traded with the Indus valley civilization. Siraf sent horses to India. Hormuz linked Portuguese Goa and Africa. The route between Basra and India was crucial to the British and Omani Empires, and Indians helped the Omanis capture Muscat and administer their empire in east Africa. Today, Pakistan, India, and Bangladesh are the geographically rational partners of the Gulf. As their prominence grows, encouraged by the United States to serve as a counterweight to China, the Gulf will benefit from its historical role as a bridge to south Asia. South Asians supply much of the expertise and labor—India's population now exceeds China's—that run the modern Gulf, especially in the wealthy Arab states, and their low cost is the most important control on inflation, one of the possible side effects of rapid investment and development. To be attractive to south Asian powers, with whom it will need to negotiate new trade agreements, convincing them to do away with some of the barriers to entry into their markets, the Gulf will have to build on labor reforms and standards to avoid alienating their leaders and voters. It might start this process with little to no cost, simply by celebrating the many ways that Gulf nationals, south Asians, and other expatriates have cooperated to achieve mutual goals. The surprising support of expats for Qatar during the Qatar crisis, with many putting images of Emir Tamim on their cars in solidarity, shows that foreigners need not be feared and perhaps should be embraced as contributors to a Gulf identity and a new cosmopolitanism that respect and appreciate the many ways in which the region's connections to the Indian Ocean world have enabled it to thrive. For its part, the Gulf has much to offer south Asia. It can prioritize its role as a stable bridge and strategic link between south Asia, west Asia, and Europe. And it can offer collaboration far beyond earth: recently, the UAE sent a spacecraft to Mars, and Gulf astronauts have been on the International Space Station.[17] The Indian Space Research Organisation, which has had three successful moon landings, is already exploring cooperation with the Gulf. The countries there are also investing heavily in the knowledge economy, which requires an enormous amount of labor to establish the necessary campuses and knowledge cities. Even Iran celebrates its scientists as heroes and has set up booming free-trade zones, like the one on the island of Kish. There is a knowledge arms race developing as both Iran and the Arab states try to reform their higher education systems and encourage scientific research and technology. King Abdullah University of Science and Technology, founded in 2009 in Thuwal, Saudi Arabia, and Carnegie Mellon University in Qatar, which opened in Doha in 2004, exemplify this push. Saudi Arabia, wanting to outdo the successful planned cities of its smaller Gulf neighbors, also aspires to build a trillion-dollar city of mirrored skyscrapers that will house up to five million people.[18] Rather than seeing south Asia only as a source of laborers for such megaprojects, partnering long-term with the region and recognizing long-standing links with the Indian Ocean will lead to far better outcomes for the Gulf.

This millennia-deep history, however, may be ignored as it conflicts with another goal of many Gulf states: creating a sense of national identity. In 2019, Qatar University sponsored a National Identity Conference, which highlighted the need to support this sense of belonging in the Gulf and was attended by members of the government.[19] The coronavirus epidemic accelerated an already growing sense of nationalism over other forms of identity, which Gulf states have only encouraged. According to some polls—which are admittedly problematic, since many responders assume that the state security apparatus is listening in to the call—Khaliji identity and tribal ties that cross borders have declined in recent years in favor of loyalty to the nation and its rulers. The UAE's national identity index is particularly high, at almost 98 percent.[20] At the same time, traditional modes of culture and informal networks that cut across national boundaries continue to exist, such as tribes. The challenge of Gulf leaders is to also foster a cosmopolitan national identity that explicitly respects both the contributions of non-Khalijis to life in the Gulf and the cooperation between the people of the Gulf and the people of the Gulf's most important future—and past—partner: an emerging south Asia.

Even if US triple containment draws to an end, the Gulf is still a dynamic global center. Historians must go back several centuries to find a close parallel to what the region has become: perhaps ninth-century Basra or the fourteenth-century Hormuz-Kish rivalry. Port cities on the edge of the world, Dubai, Doha, and Abu Dhabi are chaotically forging a global and cosmopolitan vision of Islam for today. They are also, however, courting danger and interference. Being at the center of the world stage, in charge of its many exits and entries, has its benefits and its risks. In the past, it was possible for the Gulf's port dwellers to cut their losses on the coast and retreat inland to the oases, or simply set up in another protected cove. Rulers, when they grew tired of complaints from their subjects, could threaten to resign, realizing that their positions were as much about mutual obligation as about real benefits for them. Ruling and governing now, though, even in relatively small states, is far more complex, and the corporate-city model has had to shift to recognize and acknowledge the political, social, environmental, and cultural consequences of untrammeled development. The superlative cities of the modern Gulf have forged their own geographic realities, including their own microclimates and ecology, as water is desalinated via artificial means. But the very success of the Gulf states has made them vulnerable, targets of external powers and ideologies.

The Gulf's twenty-first-century status as a world center of possibility is not guaranteed. The observation deck of the mile-high Khalifa Tower can feel like the top of the world. But down below and past the horizon are rumblings of danger. Antiglobal forces are at work. Divisions and rivalries, extremism, sectarianism, nationalism, even conflicts between citizens and noncitizens on the streets could spoil the current spectacular success of the Gulf states. The Gaza crisis that started in 2023 has spread to the Houthis and other armed groups affiliated with Iran, such as Kataib Hezbollah, which attacked a US base in Jordan in 2024, prompting retaliatory strikes. With just one miscalculation by either side, an accidental large-scale war could break out between the United States and Iran, a possibility whose likelihood that has risen greatly.[23] Iran is a major supplier of oil to China, which it sees as a potential ally against the United States, and benefits from a special relationship with Russia, to which it sent drones to use against Ukraine.[21] These three could link into an effective axis against the US-led global order. Although Iran and Saudi Arabia agreed to some normalization of diplomatic ties in a China-brokered deal in 2023, the simple exchange of ambassadors and establishment of lines of communication between the Arabian and Persian sides of the Gulf will not be enough to prevent conflict in the region.[22] Instead, the United States and Iran must resolve their rivalry. This is a far taller order than a Saudi-Iranian detente. If a US-Iran war should occur, the Gulf will inevitably be drawn into the conflict, no matter how many bilateral agreements the Arab states there make with Iran, and faced with the choice of which of these two to back, they must always pick the United States: full alliance with Iran is a nonstarter, as it would end the historic autonomy of the Gulf states. Neutrality would require denying the United States access to Gulf bases, protecting them from being targeted, but could also lead to submission to a victorious Iran—a far more devastating fate than being hit by Iranian strikes for hosting US troops. Turning the Gulf into a battleground would also be an unmitigated disaster by breaking the reputation of cities like Dubai, Abu Dhabi, and Doha as relatively safe, peaceful places to do business, effectively ending the region's prosperity and bringing back the "years of hunger" that characterized its experience during the Second World War, or worse. The Arab Gulf states have every interest in dampening tensions between their main military protector, the United States, and Iran and avoiding a great-power conflict centered in their region. Despite their desire to help the Palestinians, the rise of Iran and the prospect of its pushing the United States out of the Gulf is an existential threat. According to one analyst, "it's looking like the 1930s," with Iran, Russia, and China flouting the US-led world order, similar to the actions of Japan, Germany, and Italy that led to World War II.[24] To continue to thrive, the Gulf states must create a peace architecture that maintains the region's flexible character both internally and externally. Some rulers, such as the sultan of Oman, are already working to decrease conflicts through quiet diplomacy, including fostering talks between Iran and the United States. Qatar is also a potential bridge: it has a solid relationship with Iran, which supported it during the Qatar crisis, even as it is a key US partner, nominated as a major non-NATO ally by President Biden in 2022.[25]

While lowering the temperature of the conflict between the United States and Iran is potentially the most immediate and important task for the Arab Gulf states in the next decade, internal governmental reforms could also help to stabilize the region. Rulers can follow the path set by their ancestors, maintaining the Gulf's historical role as an open, tolerant zone for world commerce. Or they could take a different course, one of blind nationalism, top-down police-state centralization, threats of war, and increasing intolerance. Further democratizing Gulf constitutions would allow Khalijis, who are highly interconnected across the Gulf's recent and rather arbitrary national borders, to be explicitly involved in deciding whether escalation or militarization is really in their best interest. The tensions that led to the Qatar crisis from 2017 to 2021 were caused by disputes between ruling families, not between regular Gulf citizens, whose families are often international. Including more voices in real decision making may slow down development but might also prevent the greatest risk of all, conflict.

An increase in democratic governance and the support of more formal democratic institutions will help bolster security in the Gulf even if the United States has an opportunity to depart. These reforms, however, must occur internally, not through pressure from the United States or its allies. As the old forums of informal tribal consensus, such as those observed by Wilfred Thesiger in Sheikh Zayed's domain, become less practical, the rulers of the Gulf should resist the temptation to consolidate power and isolate themselves from their subjects. In the past, the Gulf's merchant-princes had little control, while today's Gulf princes maintain large militaries and massive investment funds that have allowed them to gain major influence abroad. Were power to be too concentrated in the monarch and the palace, however, the risk of instability would rise and the traditional connection with loyal tribes could break down. Should the Gulf states enjoy political continuity into the long term without US security guarantees, it will be with a new, non-Western model of sustainable governance, something built on local traditions. As the heady days of the Gulf's booming development have waned and its economies matured, the expectations of its increasing number of young citizens have only grown, far beyond the dreams of their mothers and fathers. Although many of the face-to-face interactions of the past are no longer feasible, there is more room for power sharing in written, formal ways. If the United States makes good on its plan to slowly withdraw from the region, it pulls back a two-hundred-year-old curtain, one that was put in place by the British protectorate. As this curtain of containment opens, the ordinary people and rulers of the Gulf will need to choose what will occur on the stage behind it, what boundaries and institutions will disappear, remain, or be put in place.

Commerce, consensus, and cosmopolitanism are not Western concepts imposed on the Gulf. Instead, they exist deep in the veins of Gulf history, often originating there long before they were practiced in the West. With the rise of oil, the extent to which the Gulf was already a globally connected region with a sophisticated past went mostly unnoticed. The region's social and cultural inheritance, not only the economic story of petroleum, however, is extremely valuable. In the Gulf's extraordinarily challenging and rewarding land of marshes, deserts, and mountains, various distinctive societies, various ships of faith, in the imagery of the *Shahnameh,* first set sail toward long-distance trade and a culture of cosmopolitanism and relative tolerance not mediated by the interests of a single emperor or king. Although not without conflict, the Gulf's past has many examples of rivals finding a way forward. During pearling season, for instance, captains from many parts of the Gulf followed an unwritten code of understanding, creating a maritime commons: no ship or port had exclusive use of the region's pearl banks. Instead, the resource was shared—before the drawing of maritime boundaries in the oil age. If the United States withdraws, many of the answers about the Gulf's possible future are to be found in its extraordinary past, including the important lesson that it is possible to have commerce, consensus, and cosmopolitanism without an empire in charge. Increasingly in control of their own destinies and no longer constrained or protected by geographic barriers or the British and US containment doctrines, the diverse, global communities of people living on the Gulf's shores are set to embark on a new adventure. The Persian qanat and Arab falaj aqueduct systems that have made dry lands green for centuries are a perfect analogy: they require shared effort, rely on mutually enforced and respected rules, and result in great benefits to all. If the Gulf today can similarly maintain cooperation and peace among its member states—and between the local potential hegemon Iran and the world's hegemon the United States—it will easily be able to continue in its ancient role as the world's bridge between the Indian Ocean, Persia, Mesopotamia, and the Mediterranean. The Gulf at peace means a greater chance of the Middle East and of the world at peace. After all, the Gulf is at the center of the world.

Notes

Introduction

1. Wilfred Thesiger wrote about and photographed these three realms for his book *Desert, Marsh and Mountain*. He traveled there at a time when all three were about to be changed by Land Rovers, mines, and oil rigs.

2. *Pirate* is favorite word used by empires, and the constant concern with piracy in imperial accounts shows that there have been autonomous agents able to circumvent imperial checkpoints since the beginning of recorded history.

3. Sulayman the Merchant, *Voyage du marchand arabe Sulaymân*, 138–39.

4. See, e.g., Brethren of Purity, *Animals versus Man*.

5. "Bani Adam," in Saadi [Shirazi], *Selections from Saadi's Gulistan*. President Obama quoted this poem in his remarks to the people of Iran celebrating Nowruz on March 20, 2009 (White House, Office of the Press Secretary, "Videotaped Remarks").

6. Translation from the *Book of Kings* in Shani, "Ship of Faith," 35. This epic, called *Shahnameh* in Persian, recounts the creation of the world and the acts of its first kings, an era of justice and harmony that eventually declines into decadence and conflict.

7. "Khalij," in Lane, *Arabic-English Lexicon*, book 1, 783.

8. J. Homann, *Imperium Turcicum in Europa*, Nuremberg, Germany, c. 1720.

9. Potter, "Arabia and Iran," 116.

10. Al-Shahrastani, the twelfth-century scholar, speaks of the region's many religious and philosophical sects in his *Kitab al-milal wa al-nihal*, "Book of sects and creeds."

11. Lancaster and Lancaster, *Honor Is in Contentment*, 490.

12. Matthew 13:45 (New Oxford Annotated Bible).

13. Stavridis, *Sea Power*, 87–105.

14. Sulayman the Merchant, *Voyage du marchand arabe Sulaymân*, 39.

15. BBC, "Iran Seizes British Tanker."

16. Floor, *Rise of the Gulf Arabs*, 1–21.

17. Hokkaido University, "Strong Winter Dust Storms."

18. Ibn Shahriyar, *Wonders of India*, 94.

19. Potts, *Arabian Gulf in Antiquity*, vol. 1, 15.

20. Rose, "New Light on Human Prehistory," 850; Kennett and Kennett, "Early State Formation"; Potts, "Archaeology and Early History," 28; Dalongeville and Sanlaville, "Confrontation des datations isotopiques," 568.

21. Vosmer, "Maritime Trade," 31.

22. Kennett and Kennett, "Early State Formation," 67.

23. Marshall, "Other Cradle of Humanity."

24. Strabo, *Geography* 16.3.3.

25. Bulliet, *Camel and the Wheel*, 93.

26. Al-Mas'udi, *Prairies d'or*, 202–3.

27. Heard-Bey, *From Trucial States*, ch. 1.

28. Appiah, *Lies That Bind*; Fukuyama, *Identity*.

29. Mehta and Onley, "Hindu Community in Muscat."

30. Boustany, "Barrier-Breaking Bahrani."

31. *Sea of Precious Virtues*, 323.

32. Fromherz, *Ibn Khaldun*, 114–48.

33. Jill Crystal's theory about the role of merchants voting with their feet, explained in her *Oil and Politics*, could easily be extended to earlier periods and other parts of the Gulf.

34. Roberts, *Embassy to the Eastern Courts*, 357.

35. Hakluyt, *Principal Navigations*, 344-47, https://www.perseus.tufts.edu/hopper/text?doc=Perseus:text:1999.03.0070:narrative=462.

36. Subrahmanyam, "Iranians Abroad."

37. See chap. 5; for the nineteenth century, see Onley, *Arabian Frontier*.

38. Fuccaro, *Histories of City and State*, 63.

39. Fuccaro, "Pearl Towns"; quote in Potter, *Society in the Persian Gulf*, 13.

40. Al-Nakib, *Kuwait Transformed*, 75.

41. The fact that Bahrain and the United Arab Emirates officially recognized Israel in 2020, despite conflict between Palestinians and Israelis that has entangled the entire Islamic world for decades, may show that a new, economi-

cally based realpolitik is emerging in the Gulf. Bulliet, *End of Middle East History*, 7.

42. Frank and Gills, *World System*.

43. Conrad, *What Is Global History?*, 90.

Chapter 1. Dilmun

1. The towers have since eroded into the famous Dilmun Burial Mounds found on Bahrain today. UNESCO, "Dilmun Burial Mounds."

2. Kraemer, "Enki and Ninhursag," 38.

3. Potts, "Rethinking Some Aspects of Trade."

4. Louvre Museum, "Gudea"; Léon, "Statue complète de Goudéa."

5. McPherson, *Indian Ocean*, 1; Vosmer, "Maritime Trade," 34.

6. King, *Chronicles Concerning Early Babylonian Kings*, 88–89.

7. See, e.g., Howard-Carter, "Dilmun."

8. Bibby, *Looking for Dilmun*.

9. UNESCO, "Cultural Sites of al Ain."

10. So ancient was Ur that archaeologists use the phrase "the Ur city" to refer to the lowest or first settlement in the strata of archaeological sites around the world. The remains of Ur itself, now at the site of Mukayyar, were devastated by the Gulf Wars. Fortunately, enough evidence has been preserved to tell the story of its remarkably early global reach. The independent kings of Sealand ruled from 1730 to 1460 BCE. A recent dig at Tell Khaiber near Nasiriyah revealed settlement debris and a one-acre building that probably acted as a castle keep when invaders came along. See Crawford, *Ur*.

11. Van Seters, *Abraham in History and Tradition*, 5–7.

12. Van Seters, 13.

13. Magee, *Archaeology of Prehistoric Arabia*, 152–96.

14. Woolley, "Excavations at Ur"; Leemans, *Foreign Trade*, 18–23.

15. Edens, "Dynamics of Trade."

16. Magee, *Archaeology of Prehistoric Arabia*, 170.

17. Potts, "Trends and Patterns," 23.

18. Kenoyer and Heuston, *Ancient South Asian World*, 64–72. More than a thousand examples of Harappan script have been discovered around the Gulf and remain unpublished. Magee, *Archaeology of Prehistoric Arabia*, 169.

19. Metropolitan Museum of Art, "Vase with Overlapping Pattern."

20. Magee, *Archaeology of Prehistoric Arabia*, 175.

21. Bibby, *Looking for Dilmun*, 204.

22. Woolley, *Ur of the Chaldees*, 201–4.

23. Woolley, *Ur of the Chaldees*, 205.

24. Nehemiah 2:1–10.

25. Herodotus's fifth-century BCE description of the Persian postal system was the basis of the United States Postal Service's unofficial motto, "Neither snow nor rain nor heat nor gloom of night stays these couriers from the swift completion of their appointed rounds." Bekhrad, "Surprising Origins."

26. Peter Magee and his team have shown how the reliefs at Naqsh e-Rostam display the many ethnic groups deployed by Xerxes I in his army ("Achaemenid Empire in South Asia").

27. *Charax Spasinou: Alexander's Lost City in Iraq* (2016), https://www.charaxspasinou.org/wp-content/uploads/2016/12/CHARAX2016_EN.pdf.

28. The first-century CE Roman author Pliny the Elder noted that when "approaching the border of Charax, there is great danger of the robbers called Attalae, a nation of the Arabians" (*Natural History*, 139).

29. Roller, *World of Juba II*, 217.

30. D'Ancona, "Indian Statuette from Pompeii."

31. Pollard, "Indian Spices and Roman 'Magic.'"

32. Swan, "Archaeology of Glass."

33. Isidore of Charax, *Parthian Stations*.

34. Strabo, *Geography* 16.15.

35. Strabo, *Geography* 16.19.

36. Polybius 13.9, quoted in Wilson, *Persian Gulf*, 46.

37. Strabo, *Geography* 16.3.

38. Potts, *Arabian Gulf in Antiquity*, vol. 2, 158.

39. Payne, *State of Mixture*.

40. Sirhan bin Sirhan, *Kashf al-Ghumma*, translated by E. C. Ross as *Annals of Oman*, 4–9.

41. Marcellinus, *Roman History* 23.6.11.

42. Daryaee, "Persian Gulf Trade," 14.

43. Rodinson, *Mohammed*, 33.

44. Daryaee, "Persian Gulf Trade," 5.

45. Daryaee, *Sasanian Persia*, 137.

46. See, e.g., al-Jahiz, *Kitab al-taj*.

47. Qureshi, *Letters of the Holy Prophet*, 49ff. For a facsimile and translation of this letter, see https://en.m.wikipedia.org/wiki/File:Muhammad_Bahrain_letter_facsimile.png.

48. Reynolds, *Emergence of Islam*, 49.

49. These Azd had migrated to Oman after the famous bursting of the Ma'rib dam in Yemen in 120 CE. The name *Oman* comes from the dry riverbed, or wadi, near Ma'rib. Al-Salimi, *Tuhfat*, 29.

50. Al-Baladhuri, *Origins of the Islamic State*, 116–17.

51. Wilkinson, *Ibadism*.

52. Chap. 5 tells more of this story.

53. Al-Baladhuri, *Origins of the Islamic State*, 120–24.

54. Eickelman, "Musaylima."

55. El Cheikh, *Women, Islam, and Abbasid Identity*, 75–76.

56. Kennedy, "Desert and the Sown."

57. Al-Kalbi, *Book of Idols*, 23.

58. Insoll, *Land of Enki*, 10.

59. Khusraw, *Book of Travels*, 111.

60. Khusraw, *Book of Travels*, 111–15.

61. Insoll, *Land of Enki*, 10.

62. Insoll, "Changing Identities." A Fatimid gold dinar suggests that the Qarmatians probably maintained contacts with the Fatimids, the Isma'ilis in distant Tunisia and Egypt with whom they shared origin stories and other ties. Coins from their enemies the 'Abbasids have also been found in Bahrain, indicating continued trade links with Baghdad.

63. Lewental, "Qādesiya, Battle of."

64. Daryaee, "Persian Gulf Trade," 16.

65. Miles, *Countries and Tribes*, 45.

66. Christides, "Arab-Byzantine Struggle."

67. The great inscription and relief of Darius at Behistun is a prime example of the almost geological scale of ancient Persia's imprint on the landscape. See Olmstead, "Darius and His Behistun Inscription."

68. Bates, "Arab-Sasanian Coins."

69. Bulliet, *Cotton, Climate, and Camels*, 137.

Chapter 2. Basra

1. Mez, *Renaissance of Islam*, 56, 93, 408, 448, 457.

2. There are several versions of Muhammad's last sermon. This quotation is from one that is based on the sayings of the Prophet as recorded by Imam Ahmad and favored by the famed ninth-century Basra scholar of African descent al-Jahiz (see his *Al-bayan*, 31). The translation here is edited from a version provided by Nuh Keller at http://www.masud.co.uk/ISLAM/nuh/adab_of_islam.htm.

3. Donner, "Tribal Settlement in Basra."

4. A. Peterson and Northedge, "Archaeology of Early Islamic Basra," 53.

5. A. Peterson and Northedge, "Archaeology of Early Islamic Basra," 53.

6. Basra was once known for its superior Zahidi dates, whose quality was among the highest, but war and pollution have devastated their production. See Al-Rubaie, "Date Growing Crisis."

7. Bennison, *Great Caliphs*, 145.

8. Crone, "'Barefoot and Naked.'"

9. Firdawsi, *Shahnama*, 119, quoted in Crone, "'Barefoot and Naked,'" 1.

10. For more on the complexities of Basra's role in the establishment and disintegration of Umayyad power and the first Arab Caliphate, see Hawting, *First Dynasty of Islam*; Kennedy, *Age of the Caliphates*.

11. Al-Sirafi, *Accounts of China and India*.

12. Ottwill-Soulsby, *Emperor and the Elephant*.

13. Akhtar, *Philosophers, Sufis and Caliphs*, 20.

14. Cooperson, *Al-Ma'mun*, 115–18.

15. Abdulrahman al Salimi, "Wajihids of Oman," 5.

16. Metropolitan Museum of Art, "Cup with a Poem."

17. Ibn al-Balkhi, *Province of Fars in Persia*, 17 (brackets in the original). Kufa was an important city in what is now southern Iraq.

18. Zarrinkub, "The Arab Conquest of Iran."

19. Shaffer, "Southernization."

20. Ball, "Some Rock-Cut Monuments."

21. In Oman, Chinese bowls were plastered into merchant houses, especially the public majlis, or meeting room, to show off wealth. They were also placed in the mihrab, or prayer niche, of Ibadi mosques. Fromherz, "Ibadism in World History."

22. Metropolitan Museum of Art, "Bowl Emulating Chinese Stoneware."

23. Ziaii-Bigdeli, "Medieval Globalism."

24. Ibn Khurdadhbih, *Livre des routes*, 227.

25. Al-Muqaddasi, *Ahsan al-taqāsīm*, 128, quoted in Naji and Ali, "Suqs of Basrah," 301–2.

26. Naji and Ali, "Suqs of Basrah," 305.

27. Valeri, *Oman*, 14.

28. Al-Tabari, *History of al-Ṭabarī*, 30.

29. Gordon, *Breaking of a Thousand Swords*, 47–55.

30. Al-Tabari, *History of al-Ṭabarī*, 37.

31. Al-Tabari, *History of al-Ṭabarī*, 46.

32. Pellat, "Al-Jāḥiẓ," 81.

33. Benjamin of Tudela, *Itinerary*, 63. Bdellium is related to myrrh.

34. Benjamin of Tudela, *Itinerary*, 51.

35. Benjamin of Tudela, *Itinerary*, 53.

36. Donner, "Arabic Language."

37. Stewart, "Structure of the *Fihrist*." Ibn Khallikan, who claimed descent from the Barmakids, wrote a famous biographical dictionary in the thirteenth century.

38. Blachère, "Bashshar b. Burd," 1080.

39. Others say the name *Sufi* comes from the sobriquet "the people of the Bench [*suffa*]," who gathered near the home and mosque of Muhammad. Or it may be related to the word for purity (*safa*). Schimmel, *Mystical Dimensions of Islam*, 14.

40. Schimmel, *Mystical Dimensions of Islam*, 31.

41. Rabi'a, quoted in Smith, *Rabi'a the Mystic*, 98. See also Cornell, *Rabia from Narrative to Myth*.

42. Schimmel, *Mystical Dimensions of Islam*, 84.

43. Schimmel, *Mystical Dimensions of Islam*, 67.

44. Eilers, "Iran and Mesopotamia," 486.

45. Brethren of Purity, *Epistles*, 135.

46. Daftary, foreword to Brethren of Purity, *Epistles*.

47. Netton, *Muslim Neoplatonists*, 2.

48. Brethren of Purity, *Epistles*, 344–45.

49. Brethren of Purity, *Animals versus Man*, 313–14.

50. Al-Hariri, *Assemblies of al-Hariri*, 13.

51. Massignon, *Passion of al-Hallāj*, 66.

52. Abdullah, *Merchants, Mamluks, and Murder*.

53. Ibn Battuta, *Travels in Asia and Africa*, 86–87.

54. Le Strange, *Baghdad during the Abbasid Caliphate*, 344.

55. Bembo, *Travels and Journal*, 136.

56. Gibbon, *Decline and Fall*, 336.

57. Fattah, "Patterns of Intra-Gulf Relations," 87.

Chapter 3. Siraf

1. Hodgson, *The Venture of Islam*.

2. Al-Shahrastani, *Kitab al-milal wa al-nihal*. For an English translation of the section on Islam, see al-Shahrastani, *Muslim Sects and Divisions*.

3. Al-Istakhri, quoted in Daryaee, "Persian Gulf Trade," 8.

4. Al-Sirafi, *Accounts of China and India*, 7.

5. Ben-Dor Benite, foreword to al-Sirafi, *Accounts of China and India*.

6. Ibn al-Balkhi, *Province of Fars in Persia*, 42.

7. Morier, *Journey through Persia*, 51.

8. Wilson, *Persian Gulf*, 92–94.

9. Whitehouse, *Siraf*.

10. Hourani, *Arab Seafaring in the Indian Ocean*, 70.

11. Al-Istakhri, quoted in Wilson, *Persian Gulf*, 94.

12. Ibn Khaldun, *Livre des exemples*, 582.

13. The name of the island of Kish, today a free-trade zone with many malls, is often spelled *Qeys* in earlier sources.

14. Ibn al-Balkhi, *Province of Fars in Persia*, 42–43.

15. Polo, *Description of the World*, 20.

16. Piacentini and Maestri, "Sāhil ʿUmān al-Shamāl."

17. Polo, *Description of the World*, 30.

18. Carter, *Sea of Pearls*, ch. 2.

19. Bulliet, *Cotton, Climate, and Camels*.

20. Wilkinson, *Ibâḍism*, 403–6.

21. Ibn al-Mujawir, *Traveller in Thirteenth-Century Arabia*, 289.

22. See, e.g., Prange, *Monsoon Islam*.

23. Horton, "New Thalassology."

24. Chakravarti, "Early Medieval Bengal."

25. Chakravarti, "Nakhudas and Nauvittakas," 53.

26. Ashtor, "Kārimī Merchants."

27. Chakravarti, "Nakhudas and Nauvittakas," 53.

28. Cresques, *Atlas de cartes marines*.

29. Polo, *Travels of Marco Polo*, 43. The first sentence in this quotation does not appear in *Description of the World*.

30. Williamson, "Trade of the Gulf."

31. Ibn Khaldun, *Livre des exemples*, 693.

32. Sharon Kinoshita, in her translation of Polo's *Description of the World*, 21n21, informs us that at least two versions of this story appeared in French in the medieval period: one by Hayton, an Armenian prince, who presented his *La flor des estoires d'Orient* to Pope Clement V in 1307, and the second by Jean de Joinville in *Vie de Saint Louis,* completed in 1309.

33. Polo, *Description of the World*, 20.

34. Carter, *Sea of Pearls*, 59.

35. Kelly, *Britain and the Persian Gulf*, 18.

36. Ibn al-Balkhi, *Province of Fars in Persia*, 48–49.

37. Fernández, "Ormuz pendant l'únion dynastique."

Chapter 4. Hormuz

1. Afonso de Albuquerque did enslave some of the residents of Gulf ports during the Portuguese conquest, but it was soon determined that enslaving merchants in large numbers could be counterproductive.

2. Campos, "Portuguese Military Architecture," 153.

3. Campos, "Portuguese Military Architecture," 153.

4. Polo, *Description of the World*, 31.

5. Agius, *Classic Ships of Islam*.

6. Wilson, *Persian Gulf*, 117.

7. Campos, "Portuguese Military Architecture," 151.

8. Portugal's taking of Hormuz angered the Persians, who were natural allies against the Ottomans. To mollify them, Albuquerque sent a treasury of gifts of combined Portuguese and Indian Ocean origin and style, including "two gold bracelets, one featuring seven rubies, of which the middle one was 'very large', and twenty-nine diamonds; . . . a pear made of amber, decorated with gold; . . . a gold chain; and a black velvet cowl decorated with seventy-four gold *cruzados*. . . . There were also two pieces of artillery" (Vassalo e Silva, "Diplomatic Embassies," 219).

9. Floor, *Hula Arabs of the Sibukh Coast*.

10. Faria e Sousa, *Portugues Asia*, vol. 3, pt. 1, ch. 4, 30. Text slightly modernized.

11. Kauz and Ptak, "Hormuz," 27.

12. Varthema, *Travels*, 94–95.

13. Varthema, *Travels*, 95, 99.

14. "A world-economy (Braudel's *économie-monde*) is a large geographic zone within which there is a division of labor and hence significant internal exchange of basic or essential goods as well as flows of capital and labor. A defining feature of a world-economy is that it is *not* bounded by a unitary political structure." Wallerstein, *World-Systems Analysis*, 23 (italics in the original).

15. Alvares, *Prester John of the Indies*, 369–76.

16. Casale, *Ottoman Age of Exploration*, 30.

17. Curtin, *Cross-cultural Trade*, 139.

18. Powers, *Society Organized for War*, 1–5.

19. Albuquerque, *Commentaries*, 71. Albuquerque died in 1515, and this work was compiled from his notes by his son around 1557.

20. Albuquerque, *Commentaries*, 118.

21. Albuquerque, *Commentaries*, 130–31.

22. Camões, *Lusiads*, 376, canto 10, stanza 40.

23. Faria e Sousa, *Portugues Asia*, vol. 2, pt. 3, ch. 2, 249. Text slightly modernized.

24. Stephen Dale, who mentions the weakness of Safavid artillery in particular, prefers not to use the term "gunpowder empires," even though it has stuck in the literature (*Muslim Empires*, 6).

25. Cunha, *Inquisição no Estado da Índia*.

26. Faria e Sousa, *Portugues Asia*, vol. 1, pt. 3, ch. 1, 210.

27. Wicki, *Documenta Indica*, 104.

28. Piacentini, "Hormuz."

29. Silva y Figueroa, *Comentarios*, 253–54.

30. Floor, *Political and Economic History*, 18.

31. Diamond, *Guns, Germs and Steel*.

32. Teixeira, *Travels*, 266.

33. Boxer, *Portuguese Seaborne Empire*.

34. Floor, *Political and Economic History*, 29.

35. Della Valle, *Pilgrim*, 134.

36. Della Valle, *Pilgrim*, 135.

37. Della Valle, *Pilgrim*, 133.

38. I experienced this danger myself in 2016 on a small ship touring Musandam. Large numbers of dolphins and sharks were patrolling the shallow, transparent waters, and when I jumped overboard, rocks immediately scraped my feet, leading to significant blood loss. Fortunately, I was able to swim to land without any sharks noticing and extracted myself from the water.

39. Godinho, *Relação*, 79, quoted in Floor, *Political and Economic History*, 270–71.

40. An inner courtyard exhibit at the Khasab Fort Museum in Musandam provided this information in 2016.

41. Gaspar Barzeu, quoted in Floor, *Political and Economic History*, 29.

42. Floor, *Political and Economic History*, 30.

43. Floor, *Political and Economic History*, 193.

44. Floor, *Political and Economic History*, 600.

45. Steensgaard, *Carracks, Caravans and Companies*, 81.

46. Couto, Bacqué-Grammont, and Taleghani, *Historical Atlas*, 146.

47. Ibn Majid, *Arab Navigation*.

48. Albuquerque, *Commentaries*, 67.

49. See Braudel, *Civilization and Capitalism*, vol. 3.

50. Curtin, *Cross-cultural Trade*, 150–51.

51. Della Valle, *Pilgrim*, 182.

52. Della Valle, *Pilgrim*, 198.

53. Khachikian, "Merchant Hovannes Joughayetsi."

54. M. Crawford, "Religion and Religious Movements."

55. Axworthy, *Sword of Persia*; Lockhart, "Navy of Nadir Shah," 15–18.

56. Wilson, *Persian Gulf*, 260.

57. Faria e Sousa, *Portugues Asia*, vol. 2, pt. 4, ch. 20, 514.

58. Alpers, "Maritime History, World History," 19.

Chapter 5. Muscat

Parts of this chapter are taken from Fromherz, "Persian Gulf."

1. Pomeranz, *Great Divergence*.

2. "None of the modern amenities—such as electricity, air-conditioning, refrigerators—were then available, and daily life was fairly difficult for these Europeans who were not accustomed to the heat and humidity" (Zahlan, *Modern Gulf States*, 22).

3. Onley, "Britain's Native Agents."

4. Ptolemy, *Sixth Map of Asia*. Sixteenth-century versions of this map still used the words *Cryptus Portus* for Muscat.

5. Niebuhr, *Travels through Arabia*, 115–16. Italics in the original.

6. Al Salimi, "Banians of Muscat," 107.

7. Al Salimi, "Banians of Muscat," 109.

8. Niebuhr, *Travels through Arabia*, 116.

9. Irfan, "Merchant Communities."

10. Allen, "Indian Merchant Community of Masqat."

11. Risso, *Merchants and Faith*, 55–72.

12. Alpers, *Ivory and Slaves*.

13. Curtin, *Cross-cultural Trade*, 36.

14. Farsi, *Seyyid Said bin Sultan*, 59–60.

15. Al Salimi and Jansen, *Portugal in the Sea of Oman*, 103; for the full treaty, see 157–61; for complaints from Lisbon, 222. See also Arquivo Histórico Ultramarino, Moçambique, Caixa 206, N.º 48//102 Mozambique, 22/02/1826.

16. Fromherz, "Ibadism in World History."

17. Beckert, *Empire of Cotton*.

18. Eilts, *Ahmad bin Na'aman's Mission*.

19. Landen, *Oman since 1856*, 29–76.

20. R. Burton, *Zanzibar*, vol. 2, 405–16.

21. Hopper, "Globalization of Dried Fruit."

22. Mathew, *Margins of the Market*.

23. Floor, *Rise of the Gulf Arabs*, xvii.

24. Nicolini, "History of Muscat and Zanzibar."

25. Crouzet, "British Empire in India," 867.

26. Crouzet, "British Empire in India," 864.

27. Abdullah, *Merchants, Mamluks, and Murder*, 1–10.

28. Captain Francis Loch, quoted in Belgrave, *Pirate Coast*, 56.

29. Woodbridge, "'Cessation of Plunder and Piracy.'"

30. British Library: India Office Records and Private Papers, IOR/L/PS/10/606.

31. Peszko, "Important Work."

32. Wilson, *Persian Gulf*, 263.

33. J. Peterson, "Britain and the Gulf."

34. Barakat, *Bedouin Bureaucrats*.

35. Al-Sabah, *Mubarak al-Sabah*.

36. Anscombe, "Ottoman Role in the Gulf," 273.

37. Anscombe, "Ottoman Role in the Gulf," 272.

38. Wahhabis preferred and still prefer the name Unitarians, indicating that they are believers in the absolute unity of God.

39. Al-Rasheed, *History of Saudi Arabia*, 13–35.

40. Curzon, *Lord Curzon in India*, 500.

41. Curzon, *Lord Curzon in India,* 500–501.

42. Curzon, *Persia and the Persian Question*, 218.

43. Tacitus, Agricola, 30. https://www.perseus.tufts.edu/hopper/text?doc=Perseus%3Atext%3A1999.02.0081%3Achapter%3D30. Accessed, March, 2024.

44. British Library, "Treaties and Engagements."

45. Wilson, *Persian Gulf*, 224.

46. Various parliamentary committees and investigations focused on slavery in the Gulf, Arabia, and the Indian Ocean, creating a vast paper trail of correspondence and official documentation. These are organized in the nine-volume *Slave Trade into Arabia,* ed. Burdett.

47. Wilson, *Persian Gulf*, 224.

48. Rosenthal, *Pearl Hunter*, 6.

49. Hightower, "Pearls."

50. Bishara et al., "Economic Transformation of the Gulf," 191.

51. Palgrave, *Narrative of a Year's Journey*, 232.

52. Carter, "Pearling in the Persian Gulf," 199.

53. Hopper, *Slaves of One Master*, 51–80.

54. See, e.g., Maritime Delimitation and Territorial Questions between Qatar and Bahrain (Qatar v. Bahr.), Jurisdiction and Admissibility, 1994 I.C.J. Rep. 112 (July 1); Jurisdiction and Admissibility, 1995 I.C.J. Rep. 6 (Feb. 15); Judgment, 2001 I.C.J. Rep. 40 (Mar. 16).

55. Bishara et al., "Economic Transformation of the Gulf," 194.

56. Holes, "Language, Culture and Identity," 274.

57. British Library: India Office Records and Private Papers, IOR/R/15/1/664.

58. British Library: India Office Records and Private Papers, IOR/R/15/2/416.

59. That is, "a mere £250,000 pounds per annum" (Davidson, *Dubai*, 31).

60. Jackson, *Persian Gulf Command*, 1–44.

61. Woodward, "Bahrain's Economy."

62. J. Peterson, "Britain and the Gulf."

63. Zahlan, *Modern Gulf States*, 27.

64. Bradshaw, *End of Empire*, 35–69.

65. Langton, "British Diplomat."

66. Morton, *Buraimi*, chap. 14.

67. Times News Service, "Oman's New Private Museum."

68. Takriti, "1970 Coup in Oman," 157.

69. Thesiger, *Arabian Sands*, 276.

Chapter 6. Dubai

1. Hvidt, "Emergence and Spread," 207.

2. Kanna, *Dubai*.

3. David Sanger, "Under Pressure."

4. Hvidt, "Emergence and Spread," 207.

5. Hvidt, "Dubai Model," 401.

6. Munif, *Cities of Salt*.

7. Bsheer, *Archive Wars*, 1–3.

8. Vora, *Impossible Citizens*, 1–35.

9. Wiedmann and Salama, *Building Migrant Communities*.

10. See, e.g., Gardner et al., "Low-Income Migrants," 15.

11. Stark, *Baghdad Sketches*, 121–22.

12. However, there are growing voices of protest online, led by Black Arab and Arabic speakers, and Sheikh Abdullah bin Zayed, the United Arab Emirates foreign minister, recently voiced his support of Black Lives Matter in the United States. *The National* (United Arab Emirates), "Sheikh Abdullah Speaks Out."

13. Hopper, *Slaves of One Master*, 1–51.

14. Valeri, *Oman*, 5–50.

15. Heard-Bey, United Arab Emirates, 91–96.

16. Fahim, *Rags to Riches*.

17. Excepting Iran and Iraq, the Gulf countries have human development index values well above those of the Arab world average, with all of them above 0.8 and the UAE above 0.9. United Nations Development Programme, "Human Development Insights."

18. Qaboos, *Royal Speeches*, 17.

19. Fromherz, "Introduction."

20. In 2002, a segment of the religious morality police was criticized for not letting a group of schoolgirls leave a burning school because they were not wearing head scarfs or *abayat* (Al-Tuwaim and Almotawa, "14 School Girls Die").

21. R. Wright, *Sacred Rage*, 148.

22. Ansari, *Modern Iran since 1797*, chap. 13.

23. Razoux, *Iran-Iraq War*, xiii.

24. *Asharq al-Awsat*, "Saudi Military Industry Flourishes."

25. Martins and Araújo, "Great Synchronization."

26. This may be due to lower self-reporting of informal female gatherings as majlises. Social and Economic Survey Research Institute, Qatar University, *Qataris' Attitudes towards Foreign Workers*, 14.

27. Thesiger, *Arabian Sands*, 270.

28. Thesiger, *Arabian Sands*, 270–71.

29. Heard-Bey, *Trucial States*, 100–101.

30. Ministry of the Interior, Sultanate of Oman, *Al-murshid al-'am*.

31. Heard-Bey, *Trucial States*, 100–101.

32. Beaugrand, *Stateless in the Gulf*, 1–43.

33. Human Rights Watch, "Bedoons of Kuwait."

34. Eickelman, "Tribes and Tribal Identity," 224.

35. British Library: India Office Records and Private Papers, IOR/L/PS/20 /C91/1.

36. Eickelman, "Tribes and Tribal Identity," 225.

37. Ibn Khaldun, *Muqaddimah*, 100.

38. Valeri, "Nation-Building and Communities," 479–80.

39. G. Burton, "Advisory Assemblies."

40. Freedom House, "Kuwait."

41. Clay, "Parliamentary Politics in Kuwait."

42. Qaboos, *Royal Speeches*, 273.

43. Zahlan, *Modern Gulf States*, 109.

44. Zahlan, *Modern Gulf States*, 113.

45. Zahlan, *Modern Gulf States*, 4–5.

46. Nonneman, "Political Reform."

47. Cooke, *Tribal Modern*, 129–38.

48. Al-Najjar, "Decision-Making Process in Kuwait."

49. Lewis, "Kuwait's Market Bailout."

50. Hertog, "Oil-Driven Nation-Building," 343.

51. Fromherz, *Qatar*, xvi.

52. As Lawrence Potter states, "What is often lost in discussions of oil, security threats, and international entanglements is the people themselves—the changes they have undergone, and how they will adjust to the future" (*Society in the Persian Gulf*, 1).

53. Hertog, "Oil-Driven Nation-Building," 347.

54. United Arab Emirates Ministry of Culture, "Tolerance Initiatives."

55. See Exell and Rico, *Cultural Heritage*.

56. Ansari, "Royal Romance."

57. Bedirian, "Al Hosn Festival 2023."

58. Webster, "'Seeing It Like This.'"

59. Alexopoulos et al., "Making Kinship Bigger."

60. See Ferdinand, *Bedouins of Qatar*.

Conclusion

1. Afsal, "Qatar."

2. BBC, "Qatar Camels."

3. Associated Press, "List of Demands."

4. Wintour, "Donald Trump Tweets Support."

5. Walt, "Wikileaks, April Glaspie."

6. S. Wright, *Persian Gulf Security*, 163–203.

7. Gause, "Should We Stay?," 22.

8. See, e.g., Wallerstein, *World-Systems Analysis*.

9. Cooper and Burbank, *Empires in World History*, 1–23.

10. See, e.g., BBC, "'Top US Priority.'"

11. Berman and *Times of Israel* Staff, "Saudi FM Urges Ceasefire."

12. Nadimi, "Iran's Evolving Approach."

13. U.S. Department of Transportation, Maritime Administration, "MSCI Advisory."

14. Minoret, *Joyriding in Riyadh*, 1–19.

15. Matthiesen, *Sectarian Gulf*, 110–30.

16. Farouk, "Riyadh's Motivations."

17. Determann, *Space Science*, 1–35.

18. Al Jazeera, "$1 Trillion Mirrored Skyscraper."

19. *The Peninsula*, "QU Holds National Identity Conference."

20. United Arab Emirates' Government Portal, "Preserving the Emirati National Identity."

21. Harold and Nader, *China and Iran*; De Luce, "Recovered Debris."

22. Jash, "Saudi-Iran Deal."

23. Copp, Zeyad, and Baldor, "US Hits Hard."

24. Cropsey, "It's Looking like the 1930s."

25. Lopez, "'Major Non-NATO Ally.'"

Bibliography

Abdullah, Thabit. *Merchants, Mamluks, and Murder: The Political Economy of Trade in Eighteenth-Century Basra*. Albany: State University of New York Press, 2000.

Afsal, A.P. Muhammed. "Qatar: Fans Pin Hopes on Aspire Academy Despite World Cup Losses." Middle East Eye, December 19, 2022. https://www.middleeasteye.net/news/qatar-aspire-academy-world-cup.

Agius, Dionisius A. *Classic Ships of Islam*. Leiden: Brill, 2007.

Akhtar, Ali. *Philosophers, Sufis and Caliphs: Politics and Authority from Cordoba to Cairo and Baghdad*. Cambridge: Cambridge University Press, 2017.

Albuquerque, Afonso de. *The Commentaries of the Great Afonso Dalboquerque*. Translated by W. Birch. Vol. 1. London: Hakluyt Society, 1875.

Alexopoulos, Golfo, Nadav Samin, David Henig, and Gísli Pálsson. "Making Kinship Bigger: Andrew Shryock in Conversation with Golfo Alexopoulos, Nadav Samin, David Henig, and Gísli Pálsson." Interview by Andrew Shryock. Comparative Studies in Society and History website. April 1, 2018. https://sites.lsa.umich.edu/cssh/2018/04/01/making-kinship-bigger-a-conversation-with-golfo-alexopoulos-nadav-samin-david-henig-and-gisli-palsson-andrew-shryock/.

Allen, Calvin H., Jr. "The Indian Merchant Community of Masqaṭ." *Bulletin of the School of Oriental and African Studies* 44, no. 1 (1981): 39–53.

Alpers, Edward. *Ivory and Slaves in East Central Africa: Changing Patterns in International Trade in the First Half of the Nineteenth Century*. 1975. Reprint, Berkeley: University of California Press, 2022.

———. "Maritime History, World History, Global History: Some Thoughts on Past, Present, and Future." In *Oman: A Maritime History*, edited by

Abdulrahman al-Salimi and Eric Staples, 17–28. Hildesheim: Georg Olms, 2017.

Alvares, Francisco. *The Prester John of the Indies*. Edited by C. F. Beckingham and G. W. B. Huntingford. Translated by Lord Stanley of Alderley. Vol. 1. Cambridge: Hakluyt Society, 1961.

Ansari, Ali. *Modern Iran since 1797: Reform and Revolution*. New York: Routledge, 2019.

———. "A Royal Romance: The Cult of Cyrus the Great in Modern Iran." *Journal of the Royal Asiatic Society* 31, no. 3 (July 2021): 405–19.

Anscombe, Frederick. "The Ottoman Role in the Gulf." In *The Persian Gulf in History*, edited by Lawrence Potter, 261–76. New York: Palgrave Macmillan, 2009.

Appiah, Kwame Anthony. *The Lies That Bind: Rethinking Identity*. New York: Liveright, 2018.

Asharq al-Awsat. "Saudi Military Industry Flourishes: Localization Surge to 13.6%." Accessed February 16, 2024. https://english.aawsat.com /business/4834351-saudi-military-industry-flourishes-localization -surge-136.

Ashtor, E. "The Kārimī Merchants." *Journal of the Royal Asiatic Society* 88, nos. 1–2 (April 1956): 45–56.

Associated Press. "List of Demands on Qatar by Saudi Arabia, Other Arab Nations." June 22, 2017. https://apnews.com/general-news-3a58461737c44a-d58047562e48f46e06.

Aubin, J. "Les princes d'Ormuz du XIIIᵉ au XVᵉ siècle." *Journal Asiatique* 241 (1953): 77–137.

Axworthy, Michael. *The Sword of Persia: Nader Shah, from Tribal Warrior to Conquering Tyrant*. London: I. B. Tauris, 2009.

al-Baladhuri. *The Origins of the Islamic State*. Translated by Philip Hitti. New York: Columbia University Press, 1924.

Ball, Warwick. "Some Rock-Cut Monuments in Southern Iran." *Iran* 24 (1986): 95–115.

Barakat, Nora. *Bedouin Bureaucrats: Mobility and Property in the Ottoman Empire*. Stanford, CA: Stanford University Press, 2023.

Bates, M. "Arab-Sasanian Coins." In *Encyclopaedia Iranica*, online edition. New York, 1996–. Article originally published December 15, 1986; last updated August 10, 2011. https://iranicaonline.org/articles/arab-sasanian-coins.

BBC. "Barack Obama Says Asia-Pacific Is 'Top US Priority.'" November 17, 2011. https://www.bbc.com/news/world-asia-15715446.

———. "Iran Seizes British Tanker in Strait of Hormuz." July 19, 2019. https://www.bbc.com/news/uk-49053383.

———. "Qatar Camels Caught Up in Gulf Crisis." June 20, 2017. https://www.bbc.com/news/world-middle-east-40346329.

Beaugrand, Claire. *Stateless in the Gulf: Migration, Nationality and Society in Kuwait*. London: Bloomsbury, 2019.

Beckert, Sven. *Empire of Cotton: A Global History*. New York: Vintage, 2015.

Bedirian, Razmig. "Al Hosn Festival 2023 Celebrates Abu Dhabi's Past with Contemporary Flair." *The National* (United Arab Emirates), January 13, 2023. https://www.thenationalnews.com/arts-culture/2023/01/14/al-hosn-festival-2023-celebrates-abu-dhabis-past-with-contemporary-flair/.

Bekhrad, Joobin. "The Surprising Origins of the Postal Service." BBC, June 25, 2020. https://www.bbc.com/travel/article/20200624-iran-the-surprising-origins-of-the-postal-service.

Belgrave, Charles. *The Pirate Coast*. New York: Roy, 1966.

Bembo, Ambrosio. *The Travels and Journal of Ambrosio Bembo*. Translated by Carla Bargellini. Edited by Anthony Welch. Berkeley: University of California Press, 2007.

Ben-Dor Benite, Zvi. Foreword to Abu Zayd al-Sirafi, *Accounts of China and India*, translated by Tim Mackintosh-Smith, xi–xiii. New York: New York University Press, 2017.

Benjamin of Tudela. *The Itinerary of Benjamin of Tudela*. Translated by Marcus Adler. London: Henry Frowde, 1907.

Bennison, Amira. *The Great Caliphs: The Golden Age of the ʿAbbasid Caliphate*. New Haven, CT: Yale University Press, 2009.

Berman, Lazar, and *Times of Israel* Staff. "Saudi FM Urges Ceasefire, Says Riyadh Interested in Israel Normalization." *Times of Israel*, January 16, 2024. https://www.timesofisrael.com/saudi-fm-urges-ceasefire-says-riyadh-interested-in-israel-normalization/.

Bibby, Geoffrey. *Looking for Dilmun*. London: Stacey International, 1996.

Bishara, Fahad, Bernard Haykel, Steffen Hertog, Clive Holes, and James Onley. "The Economic Transformation of the Gulf." In *The Emergence of the Gulf States*, edited by J. E. Peterson, 187–222. London: Bloomsbury, 2016.

Blachère, R. "Bashshar b. Burd." In *Encyclopedia of Islam*, new edition, vol. 1, 1080–82. Leiden: Brill, 1960.

Boustany, Noura. "Barrier-Breaking Bahrani Masters Diplomatic Scene." *Washington Post*, December 19, 2008.

Boxer, Charles. *The Portuguese Seaborne Empire, 1415–1825.* London: Penguin, 1973.

Bradshaw, Tancred. *The End of Empire in the Gulf: From Trucial States to United Arab Emirates.* London: I. B. Tauris, 2019.

Braudel, Fernand. *Civilization and Capitalism, 15th–18th Century.* Translated by S. Reynolds. Berkeley: University of California Press, 1992.

Brethren of Purity. *The Case of the Animals versus Man before the King of the Jinn.* Translated by Lenn Goodman and Richard McGregor. Oxford: Oxford University Press, 2009.

———. *Epistles of the Brethren of Purity.* Edited and translated by Carmela Baffioni. Oxford: Oxford University Press, 2013.

British Library: India Office Records and Private Papers. IOR/L/PS/10/606. File 2902/1916, "Treaties and Engagements between the British Government and the Chiefs of the Arabian Coast of the Persian Gulf" [131r] (272/448). In Qatar Digital Library. Accessed November 23, 2023. https://www.qdl.qa/archive/81055/vdc_100038130333.0x000049.

———. IOR/L/PS/20/C91/1. "Gazetteer of the Persian Gulf. Vol I. Historical. Part IA & IB. J G Lorimer. 1915." In Qatar Digital Library. Accessed November 23, 2023. https://www.qdl.qa/en/archive/81055/vdc_100000000884.0x000148.

———. IOR/R/15/1/664. "Annex to File 86/2 Bahrain Concession Duplicate." In Qatar Digital Library. Accessed June 30, 2023. https://www.qdl.qa/en/archive/81055/vdc_100000000193.0x00027e.

———. IOR/R/15/2/416. File 10/3 VII, "Qatar Oil Concession" [16v] (47/536). In Qatar Digital Library. Accessed November 23, 2023. https://www.qdl.qa/archive/81055/vdc_100024084949.0x000030.

Bsheer, Rosie. *Archive Wars: The Politics of History in Saudi Arabia.* Stanford, CA: Stanford University Press, 2021.

Bulliet, Richard. *The Camel and the Wheel.* New York: Columbia University Press, 1990.

———. *Cotton, Climate, and Camels in Early Islamic Iran.* New York: Columbia University Press, 2009.

———. *The End of Middle East History and Other Conjectures.* Boston: Ilex Foundation, 2019.

Burdett, Anita, ed. *The Slave Trade into Arabia, 1820–1973.* 9 vols. Slough, UK: Archive Editions, 2006.

Burton, Guy. "What Influence Do Advisory Assemblies Have?" *Journal of Arabian Studies* 9, no. 1 (April 2019): 13–32.

Burton, Richard. *Zanzibar: City, Island, and Coast.* 2 vols. Cambridge: Cambridge University Press, 2011.

Camões, Luiz de. *Os Lusiads (The Lusiads).* Translated by Richard F. Burton. Edited by Isabel Burton. London: Wyman and Sons, 1880.

Campos, João. "Some Notes on Portuguese Military Architecture in the Persian Gulf: Hormuz, Keshm and Larak." In *Revisiting Hormuz: Portuguese Interactions in the Persian Gulf Region in the Early Modern Period,* edited by D. Couto and R. M. Loureiro, 149–61. Wiesbaden: Harrassowitz, 2008.

Carter, Robert. "The History and Prehistory of Pearling in the Persian Gulf." *Journal of the Economic and Social History of the Orient* 48, no. 2 (2005): 139–209.

———. *Sea of Pearls: Seven Thousand Years of the Industry That Shaped the Gulf.* London: Arabian Publishing, 2012.

Casale, Giancarlo. *The Ottoman Age of Exploration.* Oxford: Oxford University Press, 2010.

Chakravarti, Ranabir. "Early Medieval Bengal and the Trade in Horses: A Note." *Journal of the Economic and Social History of the Orient* 42, no. 2 (1999): 194–211.

———. "Nakhudas and Nauvittakas: Ship-Owning Merchants in the West Coast of India (c. AD 1000–1500)." *Journal of the Economic and Social History of the Orient* 43 (2000): 34–64.

Christides, V. "Arab-Byzantine Struggle in the Sea: Naval Tactics (AD 7th–11th Centuries); Theory and Practice." In *Aspects of Seafaring,* edited by Y. Y. al Hijji and V. Christides, 87–101. Athens: n.p., 2002.

Clay, Clemens. "Parliamentary Politics in Kuwait." In *Routledge Handbook of Persian Gulf Politics,* edited by Mehran Kamrava, 327–45. New York: Routledge, 2020.

Conrad, Sebastian. *What Is Global History?* Princeton, NJ: Princeton University Press, 2016.

Cooke, Miriam. *Tribal Modern: Branding New Nations in the Arab Gulf.* Berkeley: University of California Press, 2014.

Cooper, Frederick, and Jane Burbank. *Empires in World History: Power and the Politics of Difference.* Princeton, NJ: Princeton University Press, 2011.

Cooperson, Michael. *Al-Ma'mun.* London: OneWorld, 2005.

Copp, Tara, Abdulrahman Zeyad, and Lolita C. Baldor. "US Hits Hard at Militias in Iraq and Syria, Retaliating for Fatal Drone Attack." Associated Press, February 6, 2024. https://apnews.com/article/attack-military-iran -iraq-houthis-229a735edbb7759ba9ade543013917df.

Cornell, Rkia E. *Rabiʿa from Narrative to Myth: The Many Faces of Islam's Most Famous Female Saint*. London: Oneworld Academic, 2019.

Couto, D., J. Bacqué-Grammont, and Mahmoud Taleghani, eds. *Historical Atlas of the Persian Gulf*. Turnhout, Belgium: Brepols, 2006.

Couto, D., and R. M. Loureiro, eds. *Revisiting Hormuz: Portuguese Interactions in the Persian Gulf Region in the Early Modern Period*. Wiesbaden: Harrassowitz, 2008.

Crawford, Harriet. *Ur: The City of the Moon God*. London: Bloomsbury, 2015.

Crawford, Michael. "Religion and Religious Movements in the Gulf, 1700–1971." In *The Emergence of the Gulf States*, edited by J. E. Peterson, 43–84. London: Bloomsbury, 2016.

Cresques, Abraham. *Atlas de cartes marines, dit [Atlas catalan]*. Bibliothèque nationale de France website. Accessed May 2020. https://gallica.bnf.fr /ark:/12148/btv1b55002481n/f11.image.

Crone, Patricia. "'Barefoot and Naked': What Did the Bedouin of the Arab Conquest Look Like?" *Muqarnas* 25 (2008): 1–10.

Cropsey, Seth. "It's Looking like the 1930s." *National Review*, November 14, 2023. https://www.nationalreview.com/magazine/2023/12/its-looking-like -the-1930s/.

Crouzet, Guillemette. "The British Empire in India, the Gulf Pearl and the Making of the Middle East." *Middle Eastern Studies* 55, no. 6 (2019): 864–78.

Crossley, Pamela. *What Is Global History?* Boston: Polity, 2008.

Crystal, Jill. *Oil and Politics in the Gulf: Rulers and Merchants in Kuwait and Qatar*. Cambridge: Cambridge University Press, 1990.

Cunha, Ana Cannas da. *A Inquisição no Estado da Índia*. Lisbon: Arquivos Nacionais / Torre do Tombo, 1995.

Curtin, Philip. *Cross-cultural Trade in World History*. Cambridge: Cambridge University Press, 1984.

Curzon, Lord. *Lord Curzon in India: Being a Selection from His Speeches as Viceroy and Governor-General of India, 1898–1905*. London: Macmillan, 1906.

———. *Persia and the Persian Question*. Vol. 2. London: Longmans, 1892.

Daftary, Farhad. Foreword to *Epistles of the Brethren of Purity: The Ikhwān al-Ṣafāʾ and Their Rasāʾil; An Introduction*, edited by Nader El-Bizri, xv–xix. Oxford: Oxford University Press, 2008.

Dalongeville, R., and P. Sanlaville. "Confrontation des datations isotopiques avec les données géomorphologiques et archéologiques: À propos des variations relatives du niveau marin sur la rive arabe du Golfe Persique." In

Chronologies in the Near East, BAR International Series 379, edited by
O. Aurenche, J. Evin, and F. Hours, 568–83. Oxford: Archaeopress, 1987.

Dale, Stephen. *The Muslim Empires of the Ottomans, Safavids, and Mughals.*
Cambridge: Cambridge University Press, 2009.

D'Ancona, Mirella Levi. "An Indian Statuette from Pompeii." *Artibus Asiae* 13,
no. 3 (1950): 166–80.

Daryaee, Touraj. "The Persian Gulf Trade in Late Antiquity." *Journal of World
History* 14, no. 1 (2003): 1–16.

———. *Sasanian Persia: The Rise and Fall of an Empire.* London: I. B. Tauris, 2013.

Davidson, Christopher. *Dubai: The Vulnerability of Success.* New York: Columbia
University Press, 2008.

Della Valle, Pietro. *The Pilgrim: The Travels of Pietro Della Valle.* Translated and
abridged by George Bull. London: Hutchinson, 1989.

De Luce, Dan. "Recovered Debris Offers 'Undeniable' Proof Russia Is Using
Iran-Made One-Way Drones in Ukraine, U.S. Intel Analysts Say." NBC
News, August 4, 2023. https://www.nbcnews.com/news/world/recovered
-debris-proof-russia-using-iran-made-shahed-drones-rcna98245.

Determann, Jörg. *Space Science in the Arab World: Astronauts, Observatories and
Nationalism in the Middle East.* London: I. B. Tauris, 2018.

Diamond, Jared. *Guns, Germs and Steel: The Fate of Human Societies.* New York:
Norton, 1999.

Donner, Fred. "Arabic Language: Arabic Literature in Iran." *Encyclopaedia
Iranica*, vol. 2, fasc. 3, 237–43. Leiden: Brill, 1985–.

———. "Tribal Settlement in Basra during the First Century A. H." In *Land
Tenure and Social Transformation in the Middle East,* edited by T. Khalidi,
97–120. Beirut: American University of Beirut Press, 1984.

Dorsey, James. *The Turbulent World of Middle East Soccer.* Oxford: Oxford
University Press, 2016.

Edens, Christopher. "Dynamics of Trade in the Ancient Mesopotamian 'World
System.'" *American Anthropologist*, n.s., 94, no. 1 (March 1992): 118–39.

Eickelman, Dale. "Musaylima: An Approach to the Social Anthropology of
Seventh Century Arabia." *Journal of the Economic and Social History of the
Orient* 10, no. 1 (July 1967): 17–52.

———. "Tribes and Tribal Identity in the Arab Gulf States." In *The Emergence of
the Gulf States,* edited by J. E. Peterson, 223–40. London: Bloomsbury, 2016.

Eilers, Wilhelm. "Iran and Mesopotamia." In *The Cambridge History of Iran,* vol.
3(1), edited by Ehsan Yarshater, 479–504. Cambridge: Cambridge University
Press, 1983.

Eilts, Hermann. *Ahmad bin Naʿaman's Mission to the United States in 1840: The Voyage of al-Sultanah to New York City.* Salem, MA: Essex Institute, 1962.

El Cheikh, Nadia Maria. *Women, Islam, and Abbasid Identity.* Cambridge, MA: Harvard University Press, 2015.

Exell, Karen, and Trinidad Rico, eds. *Cultural Heritage in the Arabian Peninsula: Debates, Discourses and Practices.* Farnham, UK: Ashgate, 2014.

Fahim, Mohammad. *Rags to Riches: A Story of Abu Dhabi.* Scotts Valley, CA: Createspace Independent Publishing, 2008.

Faria e Souza, Manuel de. *The Portugues Asia.* 3 vols. Translated by John Stevens. London: C. Brome, 1695. Available at https://quod.lib.umich.edu/e/eebogroup/.

Farouk, Yasmine. "Riyadh's Motivations behind the Saudi-Iran Deal." Carnegie Endowment for International Peace. March 30, 2023. https://carnegieendowment.org/2023/03/30/riyadh-s-motivations-behind-saudi-iran-deal-pub-89421.

Farsi, Abdalla Saleh. *Seyyid Said bin Sultan: Joint Ruler of Oman and Zanzibar (1804–1856).* 1942. Reprint, New Delhi: Lancers Books, 1986.

Fattah, Halah. "Patterns of Intra-Gulf Relations: Iraq and the Gulf until 1980." In *The Emergence of the Gulf States,* edited by J. E. Peterson, 85–99. New York: Bloomsbury, 2016.

Ferdinand, Klaus. *Bedouins of Qatar.* London: Thames and Hudson, 1993.

Fernández, Luis G. "Ormuz pendant l'únion dynastique du Portugal et de l'Espagne (1582–1622)." In *Revisiting Hormuz: Portuguese Interactions in the Persian Gulf Region in the Early Modern Period*, edited by D. Couto and R. M. Loureiro, 177–90. Wiesbaden: Harrassowitz, 2008.

Firdawsi. *Shahnama.* Edited by E. E. Bertels. Vol. 9. Moscow: Oriental Institute, 1971.

Floor, Willem. *The Persian Gulf: A Political and Economic History of Five Port Cities, 1500–1730.* Washington DC: Mage, 2006.

———. *The Persian Gulf: The Hula Arabs of the Sibukh Coast of Iran.* Washington DC: Mage, 2014.

———. *The Persian Gulf: The Rise of the Gulf Arabs.* Washington DC: Mage, 2007.

Fuccaro, Nelida. *Histories of City and State in the Persian Gulf: Manama since 1800.* Cambridge: Cambridge University Press, 2009.

———. "Pearl Towns and Early Oil Cities: Migration and Integration in the Arab Coast of the Persian Gulf." In *The City in the Ottoman Empire: Migration and the Making of Urban Modernity,* edited by Ulrike Freitag, Malte Fuhrmann, Nora Lafi, and Florian Riedler, 99–116. Abingdon, UK: Routledge, 2011.

Frank, Andre G., and Barry K. Gills, eds. *The World System: Five Hundred Years or Five Thousand?* New York: Routledge, 1996.

Freedom House. "Kuwait." In "Freedom in the World 2018." Accessed February 17, 2024. https://freedomhouse.org/country/kuwait/freedom-world/2018.

Freer, Courtney. *Rentier Islamism: The Influence of the Muslim Brotherhood in Gulf Monarchies.* Oxford: Oxford University Press, 2018.

Fromherz, Allen James, ed. *The Gulf in World History: Arabia at the Global Crossroads.* Edinburgh: Edinburgh University Press, 2018.

——. "Ibadism in World History: Ming Pottery, Ibadi Mihrabs and Cosmopolitan Paradox." In *Today's Perspectives on Ibadi History,* edited by Reinhard Eisener, 269–78. Hildesheim: Georg Olms, 2017.

——. *Ibn Khaldun: Life and Times.* Edinburgh: Edinburgh University Press, 2011.

——. "Introduction: Sultan Qaboos, Omani Society, and the 'Blessed Renaissance,' 1970–2020." In *Sultan Qaboos and Modern Oman, 1970–2020,* edited by Allen James Fromherz and Abdulrahman al-Salimi, 1–30. Edinburgh: Edinburgh University Press, 2022.

——. "The Persian Gulf in the Pre-protectorate Period, 1790–1853." In *Routledge Handbook of Persian Gulf Politics,* edited by Mehran Kamrava, 17–24. New York: Routledge, 2020.

——. *Qatar: A Modern History.* Washington DC: Georgetown University Press, 2017.

Fukuyama, Francis. *Identity: The Demand for Dignity and the Politics of Resentment.* New York: Farrar, Straus and Giroux, 2018.

Gardner, Adam, Silvia Pessoa, Abdoulaye Diop, Kaltham Al-Ghanim, Kien Le Trung, and Laura Harkness. "A Portrait of Low-Income Migrants in Contemporary Qatar." *Journal of Arabian Studies* 3, no. 1 (June 2013): 1–17.

Garthwaite, Gene. *The Persians.* London: Wiley-Blackwell, 2006.

Gause, F. Gregory. "Should We Stay or Should We Go? The United States in the Middle East." *Survival, Global Politics and Strategy* 61, no. 5 (2019): 7–24.

Gibbon, Edward. *The Decline and Fall of the Roman Empire.* Vol. 5. New York: Everyman's Library, 1994.

Godinho, Manuel. *Relação do novo caminho que fez por terra e mar, vindo da India para Portugal, no anno de 1663, o padre Manuel Godinho.* Lisbon: Agência Geral das Colónias, 1944.

Goodman, Lenn, and Richard McGregor, trans. *The Case of the Animals versus Man before the King of the Jinn.* Oxford: Oxford University Press, 2012.

Gordon, Matthew. *The Breaking of a Thousand Swords: A History of the Turkish Military of Samarra (a.h. 200–275/815–889 c.e.)*. Albany: State University of New York Press, 2001.

Hakluyt, Richard. *The Principal Navigations, Voyages, Traffiques and Discoveries of the English Nation*. 16 vols. London: J. M. Dent, 1927. First published 1589–1600.

al-Hariri. *The Assemblies of al-Hariri*. Translated by F. Steingass. Vol. 2. London: Royal Asiatic Society, 1898.

Harold, Scott, and Alireza Nader. *China and Iran: Economic, Political, and Military Relations*. Santa Monica, CA: RAND Corporation, 2012. https://www.rand.org/pubs/occasional_papers/OP351.html.

Hawting, G. R. *The First Dynasty of Islam: The Umayyad Caliphate, 661–750*. London: Routledge, 2000.

Heard-Bey, Frauke. *From Trucial States to United Arab Emirates: A Society in Transition*. London: Longman, 1982.

Hertog, Steffen. "The Oil-Driven Nation-Building of the Gulf States after the Second World War." In *The Emergence of the Gulf States*, edited by J. E. Peterson, 323–52. London: Bloomsbury, 2016.

Hightower, Victoria. "Pearls and the Southern Persian/Arabian Gulf: A Lesson in Sustainability." *Environmental History* 18, no. 1 (January 2013): 44–59.

Hobsbawm, Eric, and Terence Ranger, eds. *The Invention of Tradition*. Cambridge: Cambridge University Press, 1983.

Hodgson, Marshall. *The Venture of Islam: The Expansion of Islam in the Middle Periods*. Vol. 2. Chicago: University of Chicago Press, 1977.

Hokkaido University. "Strong Winter Dust Storms May Have Caused the Collapse of the Akkadian Empire." Research press release. October 24, 2019. https://www.global.hokudai.ac.jp/blog/strong-winter-dust-storms-may-have-caused-the-collapse-of-the-akkadian-empire/.

Holes, Clive. "Language, Culture and Identity." In *The Emergence of the Gulf States*, edited by J. E. Peterson, 262–88. London: Bloomsbury, 2016.

Hopper, Matthew. "The Globalization of Dried Fruit: Transformations in the Eastern Arabian Economy, 1860s–1920s." In *Global Muslims in the Age of Steam and Print,* edited by James L. Gelvin and Nile Green, 158–82. Berkeley: University of California Press, 2014.

———. *Slaves of One Master: Globalization and Slavery in Arabia in the Age of Empire*. New Haven, CT: Yale University Press, 2015.

Horton, Mark. "East Africa, the Global Gulf and the New Thalassology of the Indian Ocean." In *The Gulf in World History: Arabia at the Global Crossroads,* edited by Allen James Fromherz, 160–84. Edinburgh: Edinburgh University Press, 2018.

Hourani, George. *Arab Seafaring in the Indian Ocean in Ancient and Early Medieval Times*. Princeton, NJ: Princeton University Press, 1995.

Howard-Carter, Theresa. "Dilmun: At Sea or Not at Sea? A Review Article." *Journal of Cuneiform Studies* 39, no. 1 (Spring 1987): 54–117.

Human Rights Watch. "The Bedoons of Kuwait." August 1995. https://www .hrw.org/reports/1995/Kuwait.htm.

Hvidt, Martin. "The Dubai Model: An Outline of Key Development-Process Elements in Dubai." *International Journal of Middle East Studies* 41, no. 3 (2009): 397–418.

———. "The Emergence and Spread of the 'Dubai Model' in the GCC Countries." In *Routledge Handbook of Persian Gulf Politics,* edited by Mehran Kamrava, ch. 16. New York: Routledge, 2020.

Ibn al-Balkhi. *Description of the Province of Fars in Persia*. Translated by G. Le Strange. London: Royal Asiatic Society, 1912.

Ibn al-Kalbi, Hisham. *The Book of Idols*. Edited and translated by Nabih A. Faris. Princeton, NJ: Princeton University Press, 1952.

Ibn al-Mujawir. *A Traveller in Thirteenth-Century Arabia: Ibn al-Mujāwir's Tārīkh al-Mustabṣi*. Edited and translated by G. Rex Smith. London: Hakluyt Society, 2008.

Ibn Battuta. *Ibn Battuta: Travels in Asia and Africa*. Translated by H. A. R. Gibb. London: Routledge, 1953.

Ibn Khaldun. *Livre des exemples*. Translated by A. Cheddadi. Paris: Gallimard, 2002.

———. *The Muqaddimah*. Abridged by N. J. Dawood. Translated by F. Rosenthal. Princeton, NJ: Princeton University Press, 1967.

Ibn Khurdadhbih. *Le livre des routes et des provinces*. Edited and translated by C. Barbier de Meynard. Paris: Imprimerie impériale, 1865.

Ibn Majid, Ahmad. *Arab Navigation in the Indian Ocean before the Coming of the Portuguese*. Translated by G. R. Tibbetts. London: Royal Asiatic Society, 1981.

Ibn Shahriyar, Buzurg. *The Book of the Wonders of India*. Edited and translated by G. S. P. Freeman-Greenville. London: East-West, 1981.

Indicopleustes, Cosmas. *The Christian Topography of Cosmas, an Egyptian Monk*. Translated by J. W. McKrindle. London: Hakluyt Society, 1897.

Insoll, Timothy. "Changing Identities in the Arabian Gulf." In *The Archaeology of Plural and Changing Identities*, edited by C. Casella and C. Fowler, 191–209. New York: Plenum, 2005.

———. *The Land of Enki in the Islamic Era*. London: Kegan Paul, 2005.

Irfan, Habib. "Merchant Communities in Pre-colonial India." In *The Rise of Merchant Empires: Long-Distance Trade in the Early Modern World*, 1350–1750, edited by James Tracy, 371–98. Cambridge: Cambridge University Press, 1990.

Isidore of Charax. *Parthian Stations*. Translated by Wilfred Schoff. Transcription of the 1914 London edition. https://www.parthia.com/doc/parthian_stations.htm.

Jackson, Ashley. *Persian Gulf Command: A History of the Second World War in Iran and Iraq*. New Haven, CT: Yale University Press, 2018.

al-Jahiz. *Al-bayan wa al-tabyin*. Edited by Abd al-Salam Muhammad. Cairo: Maktaba al Khaniji, 1998.

———. *The Book of the Glory of the Black Race*. Translated by Vincent Cornell. Los Angeles: Preston, 1981.

———. *Kitab al-taj*. Edited by Ahmed Zaki Pacha. Cairo: Renaissance des lettres arabes, 1914.

Jash, Amrita. "Saudi-Iran Deal: A Test Case of China's Role as an International Mediator." *Georgetown Journal of International Affairs*, June 23, 2023. https://gjia.georgetown.edu/2023/06/23/saudi-iran-deal-a-test-case-of-chinas-role-as-an-international-mediator/.

Al Jazeera. "Saudi Arabia Plans $1 Trillion Mirrored Skyscraper in Neom." July 25, 2022. https://www.aljazeera.com/news/2022/7/25/saudi-arabia-to-build-1tr-mirrored-skyscraper-in-neom.

Kanna, Ahmed. *Dubai: The City as Corporation*. Minneapolis: University of Minnesota Press, 2011.

Kauz, Ralph, and Roderich Ptak. "Hormuz in Yuan and Ming Sources." *Bulletin de l'École française d'Extrême-Orient* 88 (2001): 27–75.

Kelly, J. B. *Britain and the Persian Gulf, 1795–1880*. Oxford: Oxford University Press, 1968.

Kennedy, Hugh. "The Desert and the Sown in Eastern Arabian History." In *Arabia and the Gulf: From Traditional Society to Modern States*, edited by Ian Netton, 18–27. London: Croom Helm, 1986.

———. *The Prophet and the Age of the Caliphates: The Islamic Near East from the 6th to the 11th Century*. Harlow, UK: Pearson Education, 2004.

Kennett, Douglas, and James Kennett. "Early State Formation in Southern Mesopotamia: Sea Levels, Shorelines and Climate Change." *Journal of Island and Coastal Archaeology* 1 (2006): 67–99.

Kenoyer, J. M., and Kimberly Heuston. *The Ancient South Asian World*. Oxford: Oxford University Press, 2005.

Khachikian, Lvon. "The Ledger of the Merchant Hovannes Joughayetsi."
    Journal of the Asiatic Society (Calcutta) 8 (1966): 153–86.
Khusraw, Nasir-i. *Nasir-i Khusraw's Book of Travels.* Edited and translated
    by W. Thackston. Costa Mesa, CA: Mazda, 2010.
King, L. W. *Chronicles Concerning Early Babylonian Kings.* Vol. 2. London:
    Luzac, 1907.
Kramer, S. N., trans. "Enki and Ninhursag: A Paradise Myth." In *Ancient Near
    Eastern Texts Relating to the Old Testament,* edited by James Pritchard, 37–41.
    Princeton, NJ: Princeton University Press, 1950.
Lancaster, William, and Fidelity Lancaster. *Honor Is in Contentment: Life before
    Oil in Ras al-Khaimah and Some Neighboring Regions.* Berlin: De Gruyter,
    2011.
Landen, Robert. *Oman since 1856.* Princeton, NJ: Princeton University Press,
    2015.
Lane, Edward William. *Arabic-English Lexicon.* London: Williams and Norgate,
    1863–93.
Langton, James. "British Diplomat Who Mapped the Borders of the Emirates
    Dies Aged 89." *The National* (United Arab Emirates), July 23, 2018. https://
    www.thenationalnews.com/uae/british-diplomat-who-mapped-the
    -borders-of-the-emirates-dies-aged-89-1.753231.
Leemans, W. F. *Foreign Trade in the Old Babylonian Period—as Revealed by the
    Texts from Southern Mesopotamia.* Brill: Leiden, 1960.
Léon, Heuzey. "Une statue complète de Goudéa." *Revue d'Assyriologie et
    d'archéologie orientale* 6 (1904): 18–22.
Le Strange, Guy. *Baghdad during the Abbasid Caliphate.* Oxford: Clarendon,
    1901.
Lewental, D. Gershon. "Qādesiya, Battle of." *Encyclopaedia Iranica Online.*
    Article published July 21, 2014. https://iranicaonline.org/articles/qadesiya
    -battle.
Lewis, Paul. "Kuwait's Market Bailout." *New York Times,* February 18, 1983.
    https://www.nytimes.com/1983/02/18/business/kuwait-s-market-bailout
    .html.
Lockhart, Laurence. "The Navy of Nadir Shah." *Proceedings of the Iran Society* 1,
    no. 1 (1936): 3–18.
Lopez, C. Todd. "'Major Non-NATO Ally' Designation Will Enhance U.S., Qatar
    Relationship." U.S. Department of Defense News, January 31, 2022. https://
    www.defense.gov/News/News-Stories/Article/Article/2917336/major
    -non-nato-ally-designation-will-enhance-us-qatar-relationship.

Louvre Museum. "Gudea." Accessed February 11, 2024, https://collections
.louvre.fr/en/ark:/53355/cl010119651.

Magee, Peter. *The Archaeology of Prehistoric Arabia.* Cambridge: Cambridge
University Press, 2014.

Magee, Peter, Cameron Petrie, Robert Knox, Farid Khan, and Ken Thomas.
"The Achaemenid Empire in South Asia and Recent Excavations in Akra
in Northwest Pakistan." *American Journal of Archaeology* 109 (2005):
711–41.

Manning, Patrick. *Migration in World History.* New York: Routledge, 2012.

Marcellinus, Ammianus. *The Roman History.* Translated by J. C. Rolfe. Loeb
Classical Library. Cambridge, MA: Harvard University Press, 1940.

Maritime Delimitation and Territorial Questions between Qatar and Bahrain
(Qatar v. Bahr.), Jurisdiction and Admissibility, 1994 I.C.J. Rep. 112 (July 1);
Jurisdiction and Admissibility, 1995 I.C.J. Rep. 6 (Feb. 15); Judgment, 2001
I.C.J. Rep. 40 (Mar. 16).

Marshall, Michael. "The Other Cradle of Humanity: How Arabia Shaped
Human Evolution." *New Scientist,* August 18, 2021. https://www
.newscientist.com/article/mg25133480-700-the-other-cradle-of-humanity
-how-arabia-shaped-human-evolution/.

Martins, Joaquim Oliveira, and Sónia Araújo. "The Great Synchronization:
Tracking the Trade Collapse with High-Frequency Data." VoxEU, Centre for
Economic Policy Research Policy Portal. November 27, 2009. https://voxeu
.org/article/great-synchronisation-tracking-trade-collapse-high-frequency
-data.

Massignon, Louis. *The Passion of al-Hallāj, Mystic and Martyr of Islam.* Translated and edited by Herbert Mason. Vol. 1. Princeton, NJ: Princeton
University Press, 1982.

al-Masʿudi, Abu al-Hasan. *Les prairies d'or.* Edited and translated by C. Barbier
de Meynard. Vol. 1. Paris: Imprimerie impériale, 1861.

Mathew, Johan. *Margins of the Market: Trafficking and Capitalism across the
Arabian Sea.* Oakland: University of California Press, 2016.

Matthiesen, Toby. *Sectarian Gulf: Bahrain, Saudi Arabia, and the Arab Spring
That Wasn't.* Stanford, CA: Stanford University Press, 2013.

McNeill, J. R., and William H. McNeill. *The Human Web: A Bird's-Eye View of
World History.* New York: Norton, 2003.

McPherson, Kenneth. *The Indian Ocean: A History of People and the Sea.* Oxford:
Oxford University Press, 1993.

Mehta, Sandhiya Rao, and James Onley. "The Hindu Community in Muscat: Creating Homes in the Diaspora." *Journal of Arabian Studies* 5, no. 2 (December 2015): 156–83.

Metropolitan Museum of Art. "Bowl Emulating Chinese Stoneware." https://www.metmuseum.org/art/collection/search/451715.

———. "Cup with a Poem on Wine." https://www.metmuseum.org/art/collection/search/451748.

———. "Vase with Overlapping Pattern and Three Bands of Palm Trees." https://www.metmuseum.org/art/collection/search/322483.

Mez, Adam. *The Renaissance of Islam*. Translated by Julia Bray. London: I. B. Tauris, 2024.

Miles, S. B. *The Countries and Tribes of the Persian Gulf*. London: Frank Cass, 1966.

Miller, Rory. *Desert Kingdoms to Global Powers: The Rise of the Arab Gulf*. New Haven, CT: Yale University Press, 2016.

Ministry of the Interior, Sultanate of Oman. *Al-murshid al-ʾam li-l-wilayat wa-l-qabaʾil fi-Saltanat ʿUman* [A general guide to the provinces and tribes in the Sultanate of Oman]. Edited by ʿAdil al-Hariri. Muscat: Ministry of the Interior, 1986.

Minoret, Pascal. *Joyriding in Riyadh*. Cambridge: Cambridge University Press, 2014.

Morier, James. *A Journey through Persia, Armenia, and Asia Minor to Constantinople in the Years 1808 and 1809*. London: Longman, 1812.

Morton, Michael Q. *Buraimi: The Struggle for Power, Influence and Oil in Arabia*. London: I. B. Tauris, 2013.

Munif, Abderahman. *Cities of Salt*. Translated by Peter Theroux. New York: Vintage, 1989.

al-Muqaddasi. *Aḥsan al-taqāsīm fī maʿrifat al-aqālīm*. Edited by M. J. de Goeje. Leyden: Brill, 1906.

Nadimi, Farzin. "Iran's Evolving Approach to Asymmetric Naval Warfare." Policy Focus 164, Washington Institute for Near East Policy, April 2020. https://www.washingtoninstitute.org/policy-analysis/irans-evolving-approach-asymmetric-naval-warfare-strategy-and-capabilities-persian.

Naji, A. J., and Y. N. Ali. "The Suqs of Basrah: Commercial Organization and Activity in a Medieval Islamic City." *Journal of the Economic and Social History of the Orient* 24, no. 3 (October 1981): 298–309.

al-Najjar, Ghanim Hamad. "Decision-Making Process in Kuwait: The Land Acquisition Policy as a Case Study." PhD diss., University of Exeter, 1984.

Al-Nakib, Farah. *Kuwait Transformed: A History of Oil and Urban Life*. Stanford, CA: Stanford University Press, 2016.

Nasr, Vali. *The Shia Revival: How Conflicts within Islam Will Shape the Future*. New York: Norton, 2007.

The National (United Arab Emirates). "Sheikh Abdullah Speaks Out against Racism amid Worldwide Black Lives Matter Protests." June 7, 2020. https://www.thenational.ae/uae/government/sheikh-abdullah-speaks-out-against-racism-amid-worldwide-black-lives-matter-protests-1.1030265.

Netton, Ian R. *Muslim Neoplatonists: An Introduction to the Thought of the Brethren of Purity*. London: Routledge, 2002.

Nicolini, Beatrice. "Little Known Aspects of the History of Muscat and Zanzibar during the First Half of the Nineteenth Century." *Proceedings of the Seminar for Arabian Studies* 27 (1997): 193–98.

Niebuhr, Carsten. *Travels through Arabia, and Other Countries in the East*. Translated by Robert Heron. Vol. 2. Edinburgh: R. Morison and Son, 1792.

Nonneman, Gerd. "Political Reform in the Gulf Monarchies." In *Reform in the Middle East Oil Monarchies*, edited by Anoushirivan Ehteshami and Steven Wright, 3–46. Reading, UK: Ithaca, 2012.

Olmstead, A.T. "Darius and His Behistun Inscription." *American Journal of Semitic Languages and Literatures* 55, no. 4 (1938): 392–416.

Onley, James. *The Arabian Frontier of the British Raj: Merchants, Rulers, and the British in the Nineteenth-Century Gulf*. Oxford: Oxford University Press, 2008.

———. "Britain's Native Agents in Arabia and Persia in the Nineteenth Century." *Comparative Studies of South Asia, Africa, and the Middle East* 24, no. 1 (November 2004): 129–37.

Ottwill-Soulsby, Sam. *The Emperor and the Elephant: Christians and Muslims in the Age of Charlemagne*. Princeton, NJ: Princeton University Press, 2023.

Palgrave, William. *Narrative of a Year's Journey through Central and Eastern Arabia (1862–63)*. Vol. 2. London: MacMillan, 1865.

Payne, Richard. *A State of Mixture: Christians, Zoroastrians, and Iranian Political Culture in Late Antiquity*. Oakland: University of California Press, 2015.

Pellat, C. "Al-Jāḥiẓ." In *'Abbasid Belles-Lettres*, edited by Julia Ashtiany, T.M. Johnstone, J.D. Latham, R.B. Serjeant, and G. Rex Smith, 78–95. Cambridge: Cambridge University Press, 1990.

———. *Le milieu baṣrien et la formation de Ǧāḥiẓ*. Paris: Maisonneuve, 1953.

The Peninsula. "QU Holds National Identity Conference." Published April 19, 2019; last updated November 2, 2021. https://thepeninsulaqatar.com/article/19/04/2019/QU-holds-National-Identity-Conference-2019.

Peszko, Magdalena. "Important Work: The British 1820 Survey That Charted the Gulf for the First Time." Qatar Digital Library, October 16, 2014. https://www.qdl.qa/en/important-work-british-1820-survey-charted-gulf-first-time.

Peterson, Andrew, and Alistair Northedge. "The Archaeology of Early Islamic Basra: Challenges and Potential." In *Basra: Its History, Culture and Heritage,* edited by Paul Collins, 53–58. Dorchester: British School of Archaeology in Iraq, 2019.

Peterson, J. E. "Britain and the Gulf: At the Periphery of Empire." In *The Persian Gulf in History,* edited by Lawrence Potter, 277–93. New York: Palgrave Macmillan, 2009.

——, ed. *The Emergence of the Gulf States.* London: Bloomsbury, 2016.

Piacentini, V. F. "Hormuz: Bandar and Mulk (Port and Dominion): Eleventh to Early Sixteenth Century C E." In *The Ports of Oman,* edited by Abdulrahman al Salimi and Eric Staples, 283–356. Hildesheim: Georg Olms, 2017.

Piacentini, V. F., and E. Maestri. "Rise and Splendour of the Sāhil ʿUmān al-Shamāl within a New Order (13th–16th Centuries A D)." In *New Perspectives on Recording UAE History,* 155–82. Abu Dhabi: National Center for Documentation and Research, 2009.

Pliny the Elder. *Natural History.* Vol. 2. Translated by H. Rackham. Loeb Classical Library. Cambridge, MA: Harvard University Press, 1961.

Pollard, Ann. "Indian Spices and Roman 'Magic' in Imperial and Late Antique Indomediterranea." *Journal of World History* 24, no. 1 (2013): 1–23.

Polo, Marco. *The Description of the World.* Translated by Sharon Kinoshita. Indianapolis: Hackett, 2016.

——. *The Travels of Marco Polo the Venetian.* Translated and edited by John Masefield. London: J. M. Dent and Sons; New York: E. P. Dutton, 1914. https://archive.org/details/marcopolooopolouoft.

Pomeranz, Kenneth. *The Great Divergence: China, Europe, and the Making of the Modern World Economy.* Princeton, NJ: Princeton University Press, 2000.

Potter, Lawrence. "Arabia and Iran." In *The Emergence of the Gulf States,* edited by J. E. Peterson, 100–125. New York: Bloomsbury, 2016.

——, ed. *The Persian Gulf in History.* New York: Palgrave Macmillan, 2009.

——, ed. *The Persian Gulf in Modern Times: People, Ports, and History.* New York: Palgrave Macmillan, 2014.

——. *Society in the Persian Gulf: Before and after Oil.* Georgetown Occasional Paper 18. Doha: Center for International and Regional Studies, Georgetown University, Qatar, 2017.

Potts, D. T. *The Arabian Gulf in Antiquity*. 2 vols. Oxford: Clarendon, 1991.

———. "The Archaeology and Early History of the Persian Gulf." In *The Persian Gulf in History*, edited by Lawrence Potter, 27–56. New York: Palgrave Macmillan, 2009.

———. "Rethinking Some Aspects of Trade in the Arabian Gulf." *World Archaeology* 24, no. 3 (February 1993): 423–40.

———. "Trends and Patterns in the Archaeology and Pre-modern History of the Gulf Region." In *The Emergence of the Gulf States*, edited by J. E. Peterson, 19–42. London: Bloomsbury, 2016.

Powers, James. *A Society Organized for War: The Iberian Municipal Militias in the Central Middle Ages*. Berkeley: University of California Press, 1988.

Prange, Sebastian R. *Monsoon Islam: Trade and Faith on the Medieval Malabar Coast*. Cambridge: Cambridge University Press, 2019.

Ptolemy. *Sixth Map of Asia: Which Includes Arabia Felix, Carmania, and the Persian Gulf*. Library of Congress. https://www.loc.gov/item/2021668406.

Qaboos, Sultan. *The Royal Speeches of His Majesty Sultan Qaboos bin Said, 1970–2010*. Muscat: Ministry of Information, 2010.

Qureshi, Sultan Ahmad. *Letters of the Holy Prophet*. Delhi: Noor, 1994.

al-Rasheed, Madawi. *A History of Saudi Arabia*. Cambridge: Cambridge University Press, 2011.

Razoux, Pierre. *The Iran-Iraq War*. Translated by Nicholas Elliott. Cambridge, MA: Harvard University Press, 2015.

Reardon-Anderson, James. *The Red Star and the Crescent*. Oxford: Oxford University Press, 2018.

Reynolds, Gabriel Said. *The Emergence of Islam*. Minneapolis: Fortress, 2012.

Risso, Patricia. *Merchants and Faith: Muslim Commerce and Culture in the Indian Ocean*. Boulder, CO: Westview, 1995.

Roberts, Edmund. *Embassy to the Eastern Courts of Cochin-China, Siam, and Muscat*. New York: Harper and Brothers, 1837.

Rodinson, Maxime. *Mohammed*. Translated by Anne Carter. New York: Pantheon, 1971.

Roller, Duane. *The World of Juba II and Kleopatra Selene*. New York: Routledge, 2003.

Rose, Jeffrey. "New Light on Human Prehistory in the Arabo-Persian Gulf Oasis." *Current Anthropology* 51, no. 6 (December 2010): 849–83.

Rosenthal, Leonard. *The Pearl Hunter: An Autobiography*. Translated by Herma Briffault. New York: Schuman, 1952.

Al-Rubaie, Azhar. "Date Growing Crisis in Iraq's 'Black Land.'" Middle East Eye, January 25, 2021. https://www.middleeasteye.net/discover/date -growing-persists-iraqs-basra-despite-war-and-environmental-crisis.

Saadi [Shirazi]. *Selections from Saadi's Gulistan.* Translated by Richard Jeffrey Newman. New York: Global Scholarly Publications, 2004.

al-Sabah, Souad. *Mubarak al-Sabah: The Foundation of Kuwait.* London: I. B. Tauris, 2014.

al-Salimi, 'Abd Allah. *Tuhfat al-a'yan bi sirat ahl 'Uman.* Vol. 1. Seeb, Oman: Maktabiyya Nur al-Din al Salimi, 2000.

al-Salimi, Abdulrahman. "The Banians of Muscat: A South Asian Merchant Community in Oman and the Gulf, c. 1500–1700." In *The Gulf in World History: Arabia at the Global Crossroads,* edited by Allen James Fromherz, 105–19. Edinburgh: Edinburgh University Press, 2018.

———. "The Wajihids of Oman." *Proceedings of the Seminar for Arabian Studies* 39 (2009): 1–10.

al-Salimi, Abdulrahman, and Michael Jansen, eds. *Portugal in the Sea of Oman, Religion and Politics: Research on Documents.* Corpus 2, pt. 2, vol. 13, *Documents from 1629–1640.* Hildesheim: Georg Olms, 2018.

Sanger, David. "Under Pressure, Dubai Company Drops Port Deal." *New York Times,* March 10, 2006. https://www.nytimes.com/2006/03/10/politics /under-pressure-dubai-company-drops-port-deal.html.

Schimmel, Annemarie. *Mystical Dimensions of Islam.* Chapel Hill: University of North Carolina Press, 2011.

The Sea of Precious Virtues. Translated and edited by Julie Scott Meisami. Provo: University of Utah Press, 1991.

Shaffer, Lynda. "Southernization." *Journal of World History* 5, no. 1 (Spring 1994): 1–21.

al-Shahrastani, Abu al-Fath ibn Abd al-Karim. *Kitab al-milal wa al-nihal: Book of Religious and Philosophical Texts.* 2 vols. Edited by William Cureton. London: Printed for the Society for the Publication of Oriental Texts, 1842–46.

———. *Muslim Sects and Divisions.* Translated by A. K. Kazi and J. G. Flynn. Abingdon, UK: Routledge, 2013.

Shani, Raya Y. "Illustrations of the Parable of the Ship of Faith in Firdausi's Prologue to the *Shahnama.*" *Pembroke Papers* 5 (2006): 1–20.

Sheriff, Abdul. *Slaves, Spices and Ivory in Zanzibar; Integration of an East African Commerical Empire into the World Economy, 1770–1873.* Athens, OH: Ohio University Press, 1987.

Silva y Figueroa, García de. *Comentarios de la empajada que de parte del rey de España Don Felipe III Hizo al Rey Xa Abas de Persia*. Vol. 1. Madrid: La Sociedad de Bibliófilos Españoles, 1903.

al-Sirafi, Abu Zayd. *Accounts of China and India*. Translated by Tim Mackintosh-Smith. New York: New York University Press, 2017.

Sirhan bin Sirhan, Sheikh. *Kashf al-ghumma*. Translated by E. C. Ross as *Annals of Oman*. Calcutta: G. H. Rouse, 1874.

Smith, Margaret. *Rabi'a the Mystic and Her Fellow-Saints in Islam*. Cambridge: Cambridge University Press, 1928.

Social and Economic Survey Research Institute, Qatar University. *Qataris' Attitudes towards Foreign Workers*. SESRI Executive Summary Report. March 2014. https://sesri.qu.edu.qa/static_file/qu/research/SESRI/documents/Publications/14/Qatari%20Attitudes%20Towards%20Foreign%20Workers.pdf.

Stark, Freya. *Baghdad Sketches*. London: I. B. Tauris, 2011.

Stavridis, James. *Sea Power: The History and Geopolitics of the World's Oceans*. New York: Penguin, 2018.

Steensgaard, Niels. *Carracks, Caravans and Companies: The Structural Crisis in the European-Asian Trade in the Early 17th Century*. Copenhagen: Studentlitteratur, 1973.

Stewart, Devin. "The Structure of the *Fihrist*: Ibn al-Nadim as Historian of Islamic Legal and Theological Schools." *International Journal of Middle East Studies* 39, no. 3 (2007): 369–87.

Strabo. *The Geography*. Translated by H. L. Jones. Loeb Classical Library. Cambridge, MA: Harvard University Press, 1932. https://penelope.uchicago.edu/Thayer/E/Roman/Texts/Strabo/.

Subrahmanyam, Sanjay. "Iranians Abroad: Inter-Asian Elite Migration and Early Modern State Formation." *Journal of Asian Studies* 51 (1992): 340–63.

Sulayman the Merchant. *Voyage du marchand arabe Sulaymân en Inde et en Chine*. Translated by G. Ferrand. Paris: Bossard, 1922.

Swan, Carolyn. "An Archaeology of Glass and International Trade in the Gulf." In *The Gulf in World History: Arabia at the Global Crossroads,* edited by Allen James Fromherz, 262–91. Edinburgh: Edinburgh University Press, 2018.

al-Tabari. *The History of al-Ṭabarī*. Vol. 36. Translated and annotated by David Waines. Albany: State University of New York Press, 1992.

Takriti, Abdel Razzaq. "The 1970 Coup in Oman Reconsidered." *Journal of Arabian Studies* 3, no. 2 (December 2013): 155–73.

Teixeira, Pedro. *The Travels of Pedro Teixeira*. Translated by William Sinclair. London: Hakluyt Society, 1902.

Thesiger, Wilfred. *Arabian Sands*. New York: Penguin, 2007.

———. *Desert, Marsh and Mountain: The World of a Nomad*. London: William Collins, 1979.

Times News Service. "Oman's New Private Museum Costs OMR300,000." *Times of Oman*, May 2, 2018. https://timesofoman.com/article/58211 -omans-new-private-museum-costs-omr300000.

Toorawa, Shawkat. *Ibn Abi Tahrir Tayfur and Arabic Writerly Culture: A Ninth Century Bookman in Baghdad*. London: Routledge, 2005.

al-Tuwaim, Saud, and Abdul Rahman Almotawa. "14 Girls Die in Makkah School Stampede." *Arab News* (Saudi Arabia), March 12, 2002. Archived November 8, 2007, at the Wayback Machine. https://web.archive.org /web/20071108221730/http://www.arabnews.com/?page=1&section =0&article=13420&d=12&m=3&y=2002.

Ulrich, Brian. *The Medieval Persian Gulf*. York: ARC Humanities, 2023.

Ulrichsen, Kristian C. *Qatar and the Gulf Crisis*. Oxford: Oxford University Press, 2020.

UNESCO. "Cultural Sites of al Ain (Hafit, Hili, Bidaa Bint Saud and Oases Areas)." https://whc.unesco.org/en/list/1343/.

———. "Dilmun Burial Mounds." https://whc.unesco.org/en/list/1542/.

United Arab Emirates' Government Portal. "Preserving the Emirati National Identity." Updated January 24, 2024. https://u.ae/en /information-and-services/social-affairs/preserving-the-emirati -national-identity.

United Arab Emirates Ministry of Culture. "Tolerance Initiatives." Updated November 23, 2023. https://u.ae/en/about-the-uae/culture/tolerance /tolerance-initiatives.

United Nations Development Programme. "Human Development Insights." Accessed February 16, 2024. https://hdr.undp.org/data-center/country -insights#/ranks.

U.S. Department of Transportation, Maritime Administration. "MSCI Advisory: 2019-012-Persian Gulf, Strait of Hormuz, Gulf of Oman, Arabian Sea, Red Sea—Threats to Commercial Vessels by Iran and Its Proxies." Effective date: August 7, 2019–February 3, 2020. https://www.maritime.dot.gov/content /2019-012-persian-gulf-strait-hormuz-gulf-oman-arabian-sea-red-sea -threats-commercial-vessels.

Valeri, Marc. "Nation-Building and Communities in Oman since 1970: The Swahili-Speaking Omani in Search of Identity." *African Affairs* 106, no. 424 (July 2007): 479–96.

———. *Oman: Politics and Society in the Qaboos State.* Oxford: Oxford University Press, 2013.

Van Seters, John. *Abraham in History and Tradition.* New Haven, CT: Yale University Press, 1975.

Varthema, Ludovico di. *The Travels of Ludovico di Varthema in Egypt, Syria, Arabia Deserta and Arabia Felix, in Persia, India, and Ethiopia,* a.d. 1503 to 1508. Translated by John Winter Jones. Edited by George Percy Badger. London: Hakluyt Society, 1863.

Vassallo e Silva, Nuno. "Diplomatic Embassies and Precious Objects in Hormuz: An Artistic Perspective." In *Revisiting Hormuz: Portuguese Interactions in the Persian Gulf Region in the Early Modern Period,* edited by D. Couto and R. M. Loureiro, 217–25. Wiesbaden: Harrassowitz, 2008.

Vora, Neha. *Impossible Citizens: Dubai's Indian Diaspora.* Durham, NC: Duke University Press, 2013.

Vosmer, Tom. "Maritime Trade in the Bronze Age." In *Oman: A Maritime History,* edited by Abdulrahman al-Salimi and Eric Staples, 31–48. Hildesheim: Georg Olms, 2017.

Wallerstein, Immanuel. *World-Systems Analysis: An Introduction.* Durham, NC: Duke University Press, 2004.

Walt, Stephen. "Wikileaks, April Glaspie, and Saddam Hussein." *Foreign Policy,* January 9, 2011. https://foreignpolicy.com/2011/01/09/wikileaks-april-glaspie-and-saddam-hussein/.

Webster, Nick. "'Seeing It Like This Makes Our History Come Alive.'" *The National* (United Arab Emirates), February 3, 2016. https://www.thenationalnews.com/uae/seeing-it-like-this-makes-our-history-come-alive-1.198272.

Whitehouse, David. *Siraf: History, Topography and Environment.* Oxford: Oxbow Books and British Institute of Persian Studies, 2009.

White House, Office of the Press Secretary. "Videotaped Remarks by the President in Celebration of Nowruz" (transcript). March 20, 2009. Archived March 28, 2009, at the Wayback Machine. https://web.archive.org/web/20090328151311/http://www.whitehouse.gov/the_press_office/VIDEOTAPED-REMARKS-BY-THE-PRESIDENT-IN-CELEBRATION-OF-NOWRUZ/.

Wicki, Ioseph, ed. *Documenta Indica.* Vol. 3. Rome: Monumenta Historica Soc. Iesu, 1954.

Wiedmann, Florian, and Ashraf Salama. *Building Migrant Communities in the Gulf.* London: Bloomsbury, 2019.

Wilkinson, John. *Ibâḍism: Origins and Early Development in Oman.* Oxford: Oxford University Press, 2010.

Williamson, Andrew. "Hormuz and the Trade of the Gulf in the 14th and 15th Centuries A.D." *Proceedings of the Seminar for Arabian Studies* 3 (September 1973): 52–68.

Wilson, Arnold. *The Persian Gulf.* London: Routledge, 2011. First published in 1928.

Wintour, Patrick. "Donald Trump Tweets Support for Blockade Imposed on Qatar." *The Guardian,* June 6, 2017. https://www.theguardian.com/world /2017/jun/06/qatar-panic-buying-as-shoppers-stockpile-food-due-to-saudi -blockade.

Woodbridge, David. "'A Cessation of Plunder and Piracy . . . for Ever': The General Treaty with the Arab Tribes of the Persian Gulf." *Asian and African Studies Blog.* British Library, December 21, 2020. https://blogs.bl.uk /asian-and-african/2020/12/a-cessation-of-plunder-and-piracy-for-ever -the-general-maritime-treaty-of-1820-and-british-imperiali.html.

Woodward, Martin. "Bahrain's Economy: Buffeted between Pearls and Oil." Qatar Digital Library, August 5, 2014. https://www.qdl.qa/en/bahrain's -economy-buffeted-between-pearls-and-oil.

Woolley, Sir Leonard. "Excavations at Ur: 1930–1." *Antiquaries Journal* 11, no. 4 (October 1931): 343–81.

———. *Ur of the Chaldees: A Record of Seven Years of Excavation.* London: Ernest Benn, 1929.

Wright, Robin. *Sacred Rage: The Wrath of Militant Islam.* New York: Simon and Schuster, 2001.

Wright, Steven. *The United States and Persian Gulf Security.* Reading, UK: Ithaca, 2007.

Zahlan, Rosemarie Said. *The Making of the Modern Gulf States.* Reading, UK: Ithaca, 1998.

Zarrinkub, A. "The Arab Conquest of Iran and Its Aftermath." In *The Cambridge History of Iran,* vol. 4, edited by R. N. Frye, 1–56. Cambridge: Cambridge University Press, 1975.

Ziaii-Bigdeli, Layah. "Medieval Globalism: Fragments of Chinese Ceramics in Nishapur, Iran." Metropolitan Museum of Art, August 31, 2017. https://www .metmuseum.org/blogs/ruminations/2017/medieval-globalism-chinese -ceramics-iran.

Index

Founded in 1893,
UNIVERSITY OF CALIFORNIA PRESS
publishes bold, progressive books and journals
on topics in the arts, humanities, social sciences,
and natural sciences—with a focus on social
justice issues—that inspire thought and action
among readers worldwide.

The UC PRESS FOUNDATION
raises funds to uphold the press's vital role
as an independent, nonprofit publisher, and
receives philanthropic support from a wide
range of individuals and institutions—and from
committed readers like you. To learn more, visit
ucpress.edu/supportus.